IN DEFENSE OF THE NATIONAL INTEREST

A Critical Examination of American Foreign Policy

Hans J. Morgenthau

With a new Introduction by
Kenneth W. Thompson

UNIVERSITY
PRESS OF
AMERICA

LANHAM • NEW YORK • LONDON

Copyright 1950, 1951 by Hans J. Morgenthau

Originally published by Alfred A. Knopf, Inc. in 1951

Copyright © 1982 by
Matthew Morgenthau and Susanna Morgenthau

University Press of America,® Inc.

4720 Boston Way
Lanham, MD 20706

3 Henrietta Street
London WC2E 8LU England

Library of Congress Cataloging in Publication Data

Morgenthau, Hans Joachim, 1904-1980.
  In defense of the national interest.

 Originally published: New York : Knopf, 1951.
  Includes index.
  1. United States—Foreign relations—1945-1953.
2. United States—History—Philosophy. I. Title.
E813.M64   1982   327.73   82-18295
ISBN 0-8191-2846-5 (pbk.)

All University Press of America books are produced on acid-free
paper which exceeds the minimum standards set by the National
Historical Publications and Records Commission.

TO MY CHILDREN

MATTHEW AND SUSANNA

INTRODUCTION

Kenneth W. Thompson

The republication of Hans J. Morgenthau's *In Defense of the National Interest* is a landmark in the study of international relations in the same way its publication in 1951 was a major chapter in his contribution to the field. Then it was a novel statement of ideas to which Americans were resistant. Now it is a reaffirmation of an outlook which has stood the test of time.

In 1951, the book was a bold response to prevailing trends of thought. It called on Americans to recognize the primacy of national interest in the formulation of foreign policy. It put forward the controversial thesis that the Founders had recognized more clearly than their heirs in the twentieth century that national interest was the mainspring of foreign policy. In full view of those who saw Americans as a chosen people above the laws of politics and the United States as a part of the community of nations advancing from success to success, Professor Morgenthau argued that, "The United States offers the singular spectacle of a commonwealth whose political wisdom has not grown solely through the accumulation and articulation of experiences. On the contrary, the full flowering of its political wisdom was coeval with its birth, indeed it owed its existence and survival as an independent nation to those extraordinary qualities of political insight, historical perspective, and common sense which the first generation of Americans applied to the affairs of state." (page 3, *In Defense*) It would be difficult to conceive of a more alarming viewpoint to address to those who lived in the city of progress. Not surprisingly, some legal and political writers denounced the author as seeking to import ideas more appropriate to European than American thought.

Such critical reaction could not have found Professor Morgenthau unprepared but neither was he ready for the full weight of its effects. He had known it before particularly in the sharp responses from fellow international lawyers and political scientists to each of his most enduring contributions to political theory and international understanding. This was true in 1946 when he published *Scientific Man vs. Power Politics*, a philosophical inquiry into the false assumptions and misleading conclusions of liberal and scientific thought. It occurred again in 1948 when he sought to redirect and reorient the dominant viewpoint of international politics. *Politics Among Nations* constituted a frontal attack on a false conception of politics and foreign policy put into practice by the western democracies which had "led inevitably to the threat and actuality of totalitarianism and war." (page xv, *Politics Among Nations*). Morgenthau's critics turned on him saying he was indifferent to the moral problem, that he had made success the standard of political action and that he believed in the permanence of the existing international system, leading him in a preface to the Second Edition written in 1954 to quote a plea Montesquieu had addressed to the readers of *The Spirit of the Laws*:

> I beg favor of my readers, which I fear will not be granted me; this is, that they will not judge by a few hours' reading of the labor of twenty years; that they will approve or condemn the book entire, and not a few particular phrases. If they would search into the design of the author, they can do it in no other way so completely as by searching into the design of the work.

It is likely that Professor Morgenthau would make a similar appeal to the readers of *In Defense of the National Interest* today. When the book appeared, its criticism of American foreign policy which provoked the sharpest reaction was its discussion of the four intellectual errors of postwar American policy: utopeanism, legalism, sentimentalism and neo-isolationism. By the 1980s, the battle against these errors had largely been won. But as he contemplated a new edition of *In Defense* never completed, Morgenthau was concerned that his views of the national interest might be interpreted too narrowly. Interest, which he saw as the controlling force of all politics, was associated in our century and in the sixteenth, seventeenth and nineteenth centuries with the nation. It was the nation that governed the actions of people for substantially all of international politics. But by the 1970s, Professor Morgenthau was conscious, as were fellow students of international politics, that certain interests within the international system transcended the nation state. These included the threat of nuclear war, the population explosion, the hazards threatening the environment and world hunger. For purposes of solving or ameliorating such problems, the nation state was no longer sufficient. From a functional standpoint, it had become obsolescent.

Morgenthau liked to point out that not only was this condition something he recognized in the 1970s but that he had discussed it in 1948 in the first edition of *Politics Among Nations*. But, then and again in the 1970s, the world confronted a profound dilemma. Although even the larger nation states, let alone the dozens of mini-states that had come into being after World War II, were incapable of resolving the nuclear or environmental crises, nothing else had come along to take their place. Neither universal nor regional international organizations had the power or the authority to solve such questions.

Therefore, the nation state remained the one available and existing political institution with sovereign authority to ameliorate world problems. Morgenthau had never underestimated the necessity that national leaders search out points of convergence between their interests and the interests of other nation states. In the twilight of his days, he understood that such a necessity had grown substantially greater and constituted a late twentieth century imperative. He spoke out with ever greater fervor against those who saw the new problems as nothing more than old problems in new guise.

Yet it was essential, as he reiterated from lecture platforms around the world, to relearn on a continuing basis the enduring principles of international politics. The foremost of these principles was the proposition that nations must seek as their guide in foreign policy the national interest defined in terms of power. He never abandoned the conviction that the national interest, expanded and redefined to make possible the mitigation and relief of novel and unprecedented threats to human survival, was fundamental. It was an enduring principle for foreign policy everywhere in the world.

It is fitting, therefore, that his classic work be republished in its original form in 1982.

Acknowledgments

This book contains an enlarged version of the lectures I gave in the spring of 1950 at the University of Chicago under the auspices of the Charles A. Walgreen Foundation. It is a pleasant duty to acknowledge with gratitude the support that I have received in the preparation of the manuscript from Professor Jerome G. Kerwin, Chairman of the Foundation.

I wish also to express my appreciation to Ronald S. Crane, Distinguished Service Professor of English at the University of Chicago, who has read critically the whole manuscript; to Theodore Silverstein, Associate Professor of English at the University of Chicago, who has made valuable suggestions; to the Very Reverend Harry C. Koenig and the Reverend Charles R. Meyer, Librarian and Assistant Librarian, respectively, of the Feehan Memorial Library of the St. Mary of the Lake Seminary, Mundelein, Ill., who have translated the editorial from the *Osservatore Romano*, reprinted in Appendix I. The main burden of typing the manuscript fell upon Robert Bower, formerly a graduate student at the University of Chicago and now with the War Department. The proofs were read during my absence abroad by Mrs. Doris Graber, instructor at the University College of the University of Chicago. Mrs. Graber and Vladimir Reisky, a graduate student at the University of Chicago, have aided me in the research for the book.

I owe a great debt of gratitude to Alfred A. Knopf for his enthusiastic support and wise counsel, and to Gerald Gottlieb, of Alfred A. Knopf, Inc., for many valuable editorial suggestions.

Acknowledgments

The following publications have given permission to use material previously published: *American Political Science Review, Bulletin of the Atomic Scientists, Nation, Parliamentary Affairs, Proceedings of the Academy of Political Science, Year Book of World Affairs.* I have drawn for a few passages upon my book *Politics Among Nations* (New York: Alfred A. Knopf; 1948).

HANS J. MORGENTHAU

February, 1951.

Contents

Contents

Contents

Contents

In Defense of

the National Interest

"I do not recollect any change in policy; but there has been a great change in circumstances."

JOHN QUINCY ADAMS

"The human race cannot make progress without idealism, but idealism at other people's expense and without regard to the consequences of ruin and slaughter which fall upon millions of humble homes cannot be considered as its highest or noblest form."

WINSTON CHURCHILL

"There is no worse mistake in public leadership than to hold out false hopes soon to be swept away."

WINSTON CHURCHILL

I

The Mainsprings of
American Foreign Policy

It is often said that the foreign policy of the United
States needs to mature and that the American people and
their government must grow up if they want to emerge
victorious from the trials of our age. It would be truer to
say that this generation of Americans must shed the illusions of its fathers and grandfathers and relearn the great
principles of statecraft which guided the republic in the
first decade and—in moralistic disguise—in the first century of its existence. The United States offers the singular
spectacle of a commonwealth whose political wisdom has
not grown slowly through the accumulation and articulation of experiences. On the contrary, the full flowering of
its political wisdom was coeval with its birth as an independent nation; indeed, it owed its existence and survival
as an independent nation to those extraordinary qualities
of political insight, historical perspective, and common
sense which the first generation of Americans applied to
the affairs of state.

This classic age of American statecraft came to an end
with the disappearance of that generation of American
statesmen. Cut off from its vital sources, the rich and varied
landscape in which they had planted all that is worth while

3

in the tradition of Western political thought was allowed to go to waste. That age and its wisdom became a faint and baffling remembrance, a symbol to be worshipped rather than a source of inspiration and a guide for action. Until very recently the American people have appeared content to live in a political desert whose intellectual barrenness and aridity was relieved only by some sparse and neglected oases of insight and wisdom. What passed for foreign policy was either improvisation or—especially in our century—the invocation of some abstract moral principle in whose image the world was to be made over. Improvisation was largely successful, for in the past the margin of American and allied power has generally exceeded the degree to which American improvidence has failed the demands of the hour. The invocation of abstract moral principles was in part hardly more than an innocuous pastime; embracing everything, it came to grips with nothing. In part, however, it was a magnificent instrument for marshaling public opinion in support of war and warlike policies—and for losing the peace. The intoxication with moral abstractions, which as a mass phenomenon started with the Spanish-American War and which in our time has become the prevailing substitute for political thought, is indeed one of the great sources of weakness and failure in American foreign policy. Much will have to be said about this later.

Still it is worthy of note that underneath this political dilettantism, which is nourished by improvidence and a sense of moral mission, there lives an almost instinctive awareness of the perennial interests of the United States, This has been especially true with regard to Europe and the Western Hemisphere, for in these regions the national interest of the United States has always been obvious and clearly defined.

1. *The National Interest of the United States*

In the Western Hemisphere we have always endeavored to preserve the unique position of the United States as a predominant power without rival. We have not been slow in recognizing that our predominance was not likely to be effectively threatened by any one American nation or combination of nations acting without support from outside the hemisphere. This peculiar situation has made it imperative for the United States to isolate the Western Hemisphere from the political and military policies of non-American nations. The interference of non-American nations in the affairs of the Western Hemisphere, especially through the acquisition of territory, was the only way in which the predominance of the United States could have been challenged from within the hemisphere itself. The Monroe Doctrine and the policies implementing it express that permanent national interest of the United States in the Western Hemisphere.

Since a threat to our national interest in the Western Hemisphere can only come from outside it—historically, from Europe—we have always striven to prevent the development of conditions in Europe which would be conducive to a European nation's interfering in the affairs of the Western Hemisphere or contemplating a direct attack upon the United States. These conditions would be most likely to arise if a European nation, its predominance unchallenged within Europe, could look across the sea for conquest without fear of being menaced at the center of its power; that is, in Europe itself.

It is for this reason that the United States has consistently —the War of 1812 is the sole major exception—pursued policies aiming at the maintenance of the balance of power in Europe. It has opposed whatever European nation—be it Great Britain, France, Germany, or Russia—was likely to gain that ascendancy over its European competitors which would have jeopardized the hemispheric predominance and eventually the very independence of the United States. Conversely, it has supported whatever European nation appeared capable of restoring the balance of power by offering successful resistance to the would-be conqueror. While it is hard to imagine a greater contrast in ways of thinking about matters political than that between Alexander Hamilton and Woodrow Wilson, in this concern for the maintenance of the balance of power in Europe—for whatever different reasons—they are one. It is with this concern that the United States has intervened in both World Wars on the side of the initially weaker coalition, and has pursued European policies so largely paralleling those of Great Britain; for from Henry VIII to this day Great Britain has had a single objective in Europe: the maintenance of the balance of power.

Asia has vitally concerned the United States only since the turn of the century, and the relation of Asia to our national interests has never been obvious or clearly defined. In consequence, our policies in Asia have never as unequivocally expressed our permanent national interest as have the hemispheric and European policies; nor have they commanded the bipartisan support the latter have largely enjoyed. In addition, they have been subjected more fully to moralistic influence than the European and hemispheric policies. Yet underlying the confusions, reversals of policy, and moralistic generalities of our Asiatic policy since McKinley, one can detect a consistency that reflects, however vaguely, the permanent interest of the United States in Asia. And this interest is again the maintenance of the balance of power. The principle of the "open door" in China expresses this interest. Originally its meaning was purely commercial, but when other nations, especially Japan, threatened to close the door to China not only commercially but also militarily and politically, the "open door" was interpreted to cover the territorial integrity and political independence of China for not commercial but political reasons. However unsure the United States has been in its Asiatic policy, it has always assumed that the domination of China by another nation would lead to so great an accumulation of power as to threaten the security of the United States.

2. *The American Experience in Foreign Affairs*

Wherever American foreign policy has operated, political thought has been divorced from political action. Even where our long-range policies reflect faithfully, as they do in the Americas and in Europe, the true interests of the United States, we think about them in terms that have at best but a tenuous connection with the actual character of the policies pursued. We have acted on the international scene, as all nations must, in power-political terms; but we have tended to conceive of our actions in non-political, moralistic terms. This aversion to seeing problems of international politics as they are, and the inclination to view them in non-political and moralistic terms, can be attributed both to certain misunderstood peculiarities of the American experience in foreign affairs and to the general climate of opinion in the Western world during the better part of the nineteenth and the first decades of the twentieth centuries. Three of these peculiarities of the American experience stand out: the uniqueness of the American experiment; the actual isolation, during the nineteenth century, of the United States from the centers of world conflict; and the humanitarian pacifism and anti-imperialism of American ideology.

7

The uniqueness of the American experiment in foreign policy resides in two elements: the negative one of distinctness from the traditional power-political quarrels of Europe, and the positive one of a continental expansion that created the freest and richest nation on earth, apparently without conquest or subjugation of others.

When the founders of the republic broke our constitutional ties with Britain, they were convinced that this meant the beginning of an American foreign policy distinct from that of Europe. As Washington's Farewell Address put it: "Europe has a set of primary interests, which to us have none, or a very remote relation. Hence she must be engaged in frequent controversies, the causes of which are essentially foreign to our concerns. Hence, therefore, it must be unwise in us to implicate ourselves, by artificial ties, in the ordinary vicissitudes of her politics, or the ordinary combinations and collisions of her friendships or enmities." In 1796, European politics and power politics were identical; there were no other power politics but those engaged in by the princes of Europe. "The toils of European ambition, rivalship, interest, humor or caprice" were all that the American eye could discern of the international struggle for power. The retreat from European politics, as proclaimed by Washington, could therefore be taken to mean retreat from power politics as such.

The expansion of the United States up to the Spanish-American War seemed to provide conclusive proof of both the distinctness and the moral superiority of American foreign policy. The settlement of the better part of a continent by the thirteen original states—an act of civilizing rather than of conquering—appeared essentially different from, and morally superior to, the imperialistic ventures, wars of conquest, and colonial acquisitions with which the history of other nations was replete. Yet what permitted this uniqueness in American expansion was not so much

8

political virtue as the contiguity of the sparsely settled object of conquest with the original territory of departure.
As was the case with Russia's simultaneous eastward expansion toward the Pacific, the United States, in order to
expand, did not need to cross the oceans and fight wars of
conquest in strange lands, in the manner of the other great
colonizing nations. Furthermore, the utter political, military, and numerical inferiority of the Indian opponent
tended to obscure the element of power, which was no less
real though less obtrusive in our continental expansion
than in the expansionist movements of other nations. Thus
what actually was the fortuitous conjunction of two potent
historic accidents could take on in the popular imagination
the aspects of an inevitable natural development, a "manifest destiny," confirming the uniqueness of American foreign policy in its freedom from those power-political blem-
ishes that degrade the foreign policies of other nations.

Yet American isolation from the European tradition of
power politics was more than a political program or a
moralistic illusion. In the matter of involvement in the
political conflicts centering in Europe, and the commitments and risks implied in such involvement, American
isolation was an established political fact until the end of
the nineteenth century. This actuality was a result of deliberate choice as well as of the objective conditions of
geography. Popular writers might see in the uniqueness of
America's geographic position the hand of God unalterably
prescribing the course of American expansion as well as
isolation, but more responsible observers, from Washington on, were careful to emphasize the conjunction of geographic conditions and of a foreign policy choosing its ends
in the light of geography and using geographic conditions
to attain those ends. Washington referred to "our detached
and distant situation" and asked: "Why forego the advantages of so peculiar a situation?" When this period of

American foreign policy drew to a close, John Bright wrote to Alfred Love: "On your continent we may hope your growing millions may henceforth know nothing of war. None can assail you; and you are anxious to abstain from mingling with the quarrels of other nations."

From the shores of the North American continent, the citizens of the new world watched the strange spectacle of the struggle for power unfolding in distant Europe, Africa, and Asia. Since for the better part of the nineteenth century their foreign policy enabled them to keep the roles of spectators, what was actually the result of a passing historic configuration appeared to Americans as a permanent condition, self-chosen as well as naturally ordained. At worst they would continue to watch the game of power politics played by others. At best the time was near when, with democracy established everywhere, the final curtain would fall and the game of power politics would no longer be played.

Aiding in the achievement of this goal was conceived to be part of America's mission. Throughout our history, the national destiny of the United States has been understood in anti-militaristic, libertarian terms. Whenever that national mission finds a non-aggressive, abstentionist formulation, as in the political philosophy of John C. Calhoun, it is conceived as the promotion of domestic liberty. Thus we may "do more to extend liberty by our example over this continent and the world generally, than would be done by a thousand victories." When the United States, in the wake of the Spanish-American War, seemed to desert this anti-imperialist and democratic ideal, William Graham Sumner restated its essence: "Expansion and imperialism are a grand onslaught on democracy . . . expansion and imperialism are at war with the best traditions, principles, and interests of the American people." Comparing the tendencies of European power politics with the ideals of the American tradition, Sumner thought with Washington that they were incompatible. Yet, as a prophet, he saw that with the conclusion of the Spanish-American War America was irrevocably committed to the course that was engulfing Europe in revolution and war.

To understand the American mission in such selfless, humanitarian terms was all the easier because the United States, in contrast to the other great powers, was generally not interested—at least outside the Western Hemisphere— in particular advantages definable in terms of power or of territorial gain. Its national interest was exhausted by the preservation of its predominance in the Western Hemisphere and the balance of power in Europe and Asia. And even this interest in general stability rather than special advantage was, as we know, not always clearly recognized.

Yet while the foreign policy of the United States was forced, by circumstance if not by choice, to employ the methods, shoulder the commitments, seek the objectives, and run the risks, from which it had thought itself permanently exempt, American political thought continued to uphold that exemption at least as an ideal. And that ideal was supposed to be only temporarily beyond the reach of the American people, because of the wickedness and stupidity of either American or, preferably, foreign statesmen. In one sense, this ideal of a free, peaceful, and prosperous world, from which popular government had forever banished power politics, was a natural outgrowth of the American experience. In another sense, this ideal expressed in a particularly eloquent and consistent fashion the general philosophy that dominated the Western world during the better part of the nineteenth century. This philosophy rests on two basic propositions: that the struggle for power on the international scene is a mere accident of history, naturally associated with non-democratic government and therefore destined to disappear with the triumph of de-

11

mocracy throughout the world; and that, in consequence, conflicts between democratic and non-democratic nations must be primarily conceived not as struggles for mutual advantage in terms of power but as fights between good and evil, which can only end with the complete triumph of good, and with evil wiped off the face of the earth.

The nineteenth century developed this philosophy of international relations from its experience of domestic politics. The distinctive characteristic of this experience was the domination of the middle classes by the aristocracy. The political philosophy of the nineteenth century identified this aristocratic domination with political domination of any kind, and concluded that by ending aristocratic domination one could abolish all political domination. After the defeat of aristocratic government, the middle classes developed a system of indirect domination. They replaced the traditional division into the governing and governed classes and the military method of open violence, characteristic of aristocratic rule, with the invisible chains of economic dependence. This economic system operated through a network of seemingly equalitarian legal rules which concealed the very existence of power relations. The nineteenth century was unable to see the political nature of these legalized relations, considering them to be essentially different from what had gone, so far, under the name of politics. Therefore, politics in its aristocratic—that is, open and violent—form was identified with politics as such. The struggle, then, for political power, in domestic as well as in international affairs, appeared to be only a historic accident, coincident with autocratic government and bound to disappear with the disappearance of such government.

It is easy to see how this general climate of opinion in the Western world nourished similar tendencies that the specific experiences of American history had planted in the

American mind. Thus it is not an accident that nowhere in the Western world was there greater conviction and tenacity in support of the belief that involvement in power politics is not inevitable but only accidental, and that nations have a choice between power politics and another kind of foreign policy conforming to moral principles and not tainted by the desire for power. Nor is it by accident that this philosophy of foreign policy found its most dedicated and eloquent spokesman in an American President, Woodrow Wilson.

3. *The Three Periods of American Foreign Policy*

THE REALISTIC PERIOD

The illusion that a nation can escape, if it wants to, from power politics into a realm where action is guided by moral principles rather than by considerations of power is deeply rooted in the American mind. Yet it took more than a century for that illusion to crowd out the older notion that international politics is an unending struggle for power in which the interests of individual nations must necessarily be defined in terms of power. Out of the struggle between these two opposing conceptions, three types of American foreign policy have emerged: the realistic—thinking and acting in terms of power—represented by Alexander Hamilton; the ideological—thinking in terms of moral principles but acting in terms of power—represented by Thomas Jefferson and John Quincy Adams; and the moralistic—thinking and acting in terms of moral principles—represented by Woodrow Wilson. To these three types, three periods of American foreign policy roughly correspond, the first covering the first decade of the history of the United States as an independent nation, the second covering the nineteenth century to the Spanish-American War, and the third covering the half century after that war. This division of the history of American foreign policy—as will become obvious in our discussion—refers only to prevailing tendencies, without precluding the operation side by side of different tendencies in the same period.

It illustrates both the depth of the moralistic illusion and the original strength of the opposition to it that the issue between these two opposing conceptions of foreign policy was joined at the very beginning of the history of the United States, was decided in favor of the realistic position, and was formulated with unsurpassed simplicity and penetration by Alexander Hamilton. The memorable occasion was Washington's proclamation of neutrality in the War of the First Coalition against revolutionary France.

In 1792, the War of the First Coalition had ranged Austria, Prussia, Sardinia, Great Britain, and the United Netherlands against revolutionary France, which was tied to the United States by a treaty of alliance. On April 22, 1793, Washington issued a proclamation of neutrality, and it was in defense of that proclamation that Hamilton wrote the "Pacificus" and "Americanus" articles. Among the arguments directed against the proclamation were three derived from moral principles. Faithfulness to treaty obligations, gratitude toward a country that had lent its assistance to the colonies in their struggle for independence, and the affinity of republican institutions, were cited to prove that the United States must side with France. Against these moral principles, Hamilton invoked the national interest of the United States:

There would be no proportion between the mischiefs and perils to which the United States would expose themselves, by embarking in the war, and the

14

benefit which the nature of their stipulation aims at securing to France, or that which it would be in their power actually to render her by becoming a party.

This disproportion would be a valid reason for not executing the guaranty. All contracts are to receive a reasonable construction. Self-preservation is the first duty of a nation; and though in the performance of stipulations relating to war, good faith requires that its ordinary hazards should be fairly met, because they are directly contemplated by such stipulations, yet it does not require that extraordinary and extreme hazards should be run. . . .

The basis of gratitude is a benefit received or intended which there was no right to claim, originating in a regard to the interest or advantage of the party on whom the benefit is, or is meant to be, conferred. If a service is rendered from views relative to the immediate interest of the party who performs it, and is productive of reciprocal advantages, there seems scarcely, in such a case, to be an adequate basis for a sentiment like that of gratitude. . . . It may be affirmed as a general principle, that the predominant motive of good offices from one nation to another, is the interest or advantage of the nation which performs them.

Indeed, the rule of morality in this respect is not precisely the same between nations as between individuals. The duty of making its own welfare the guide of its actions, is much stronger upon the former than upon the latter; in proportion to the greater magnitude and importance of national compared with individual happiness, and to the greater permanency of the effects of national than of individual conduct. Existing millions, and for the most part future generations, are concerned in the present measures of a govern-

15

ment; while the consequences of the private actions of an individual ordinarily terminate with himself, or are circumscribed within a narrow compass.

Whence it follows that an individual may, on numerous occasions, meritoriously indulge the emotions of generosity and benevolence, not only without an eye to, but even at the expense of, his own interest. But a government can rarely, if at all, be justifiable in pursuing a similar course; and, if it does so, ought to confine itself within much stricter bounds. . . . Good offices which are indifferent to the interest of a nation performing them, or which are compensated by the existence or expectation of some reasonable equivalent, or which produce an essential good to the nation to which they are rendered, without real detriment to the affairs of the benefactors, prescribe perhaps the limits of national generosity or benevolence. . . .

But we are sometimes told, by way of answer, that the cause of France is the cause of liberty; and that we are bound to assist the nation on the score of their being engaged in the defence of that cause. . . .

The obligation to assist the cause of liberty must be deduced from the merits of that cause and from the interest we have in its support.

. . . .

An examination into the question how far *regard to the cause of Liberty* ought to induce the United States to take part with France in the present war, is rendered necessary by the efforts which are making to establish an opinion, that it ought to have that effect. In order to a right judgment on the point, it is requisite to consider the question under two aspects.

I. Whether the cause of France be truly the cause of Liberty, pursued with justice and humanity, and in a manner likely to crown it with honorable success.

II. Whether the degree of service we could render, by participating in the conflict, was likely to compensate, by its utility to the cause, the evils which would probably flow from it to ourselves.

If either of these questions can be answered in the negative, it will result, that the consideration which has been stated ought not to embark us in the war. . . .

The certain evils of our joining France in the war, are sufficient dissuasives from so intemperate a measure. The possible ones are of a nature to call for all our caution, all our prudence.

To defend its own rights, to vindicate its own honor, there are occasions when a nation ought to hazard even its existence. Should such an occasion occur, I trust those who are most averse to commit the peace of the country, will not be the last to face the danger, nor the first to turn their backs upon it.

But let us at least have the consolation of not having rashly courted misfortune. Let us have to act under the animating reflection of being engaged in repelling wrongs, which we neither sought nor merited; in vindicating our rights, invaded without provocation; in defending our honor, violated without cause. Let us not have to reproach ourselves with having voluntarily bartered blessings for calamities.

But we are told that our own liberty is at stake upon the event of the war against France—that if she falls, we shall be the next victim. The combined powers, it is said, will never forgive in us the origination of those principles which were the germs of the French revolution. They will endeavor to eradicate them from the world.

If this suggestion were ever so well founded, it would perhaps be a sufficient answer to it to say, that our interference is not likely to alter the case; that it would only serve prematurely to exhaust our strength.

But other answers more conclusive present themselves. . . .

It is therefore matter of real regret, that there should be an effort on our part to level the distinctions which discriminate our case from that of France, to confound the two cases in the view of foreign powers, and to pervert or hazard our own principles by persuading ourselves of a similitude which does not exist. . . .

But let us not corrupt ourselves by false comparisons or glosses, nor shut our eyes to the true nature of transactions which ought to grieve and warn us, nor rashly mingle our destiny in the consequences of the errors and extravagancies of another nation.

Must a nation subordinate its security, its happiness, nay, its very existence to the respect for treaty obligations, to the sentiment of gratitude, to sympathy with a kindred political system? This was the question Hamilton proposed to answer, and his answer was an unequivocal "no." To the issues raised by the opposition to Washington's proclamation of neutrality Hamilton unswervingly applied one standard: the national interest of the United States. He put the legalistic and moralistic arguments of the opposition, represented by Madison under the pseudonym "Helvidius," into the context of the concrete power-situation in which the United States found itself on the international scene, and asked: If the United States were to join France against virtually all of Europe, what risks would the United States run, what advantages could it expect, what good could it do to its ally?

THE IDEOLOGICAL PERIOD

Considerations such as these, recognized for what they were, guided American foreign policy for but a short period; that is, as long as the Federalists were in power. *The Federalist* and Washington's Farewell Address are their classic expression. Yet we have seen that these considerations, not recognized for what they were or even rejected, have determined the great objectives of American foreign policy to this day. During the century following their brief flowering, their influence has persisted, under the cover of those moral principles with which from Jefferson onward American statesmen have liked to justify their moves on the international scene. Thus this second period witnessed a discrepancy between political thought and political action, yet a coincidence in the intended results of both. What was said of Gladstone could also have been said of Jefferson, John Quincy Adams, Grover Cleveland, Theodore Roosevelt, the war policies of Wilson and of Franklin D. Roosevelt: what the moral law demanded was by a felicitous coincidence always identical with what the national interest seemed to require. Political thought and political action moved on different planes, which, however, inclined to merge in the end.

John Quincy Adams is the classic example of the political moralist in thought and word, who cannot help being a political realist in action. Yet even in Jefferson, whose dedication to abstract morality was much stronger and whose realist touch in foreign affairs was much less sure, the moral pretense yielded often, especially in private utterance, to the impact of the national interest upon native good sense.

Thus during the concluding decade of the Napoleonic Wars Jefferson's thought on international affairs was a reflection of the ever changing distribution of power in the

19

world rather than of immutable moral principles. In 1806, he favored "an English ascendancy on the ocean" as being "safer for us than that of France." In 1807, he was by the logic of events forced to admit:

> I never expected to be under the necessity of wishing success to Buonaparte. But the English being equally tyrannical at sea as he is on land, & that tyranny bearing on us in every point of either honor or interest, I say "down with England" and as for what Buonaparte is then to do to us, let us trust to the chapter of accidents, I cannot, with the Anglomen, prefer a certain present evil to a future hypothetical one.

However, in 1812, when Napoleon was at the pinnacle of his power, Jefferson hoped for the restoration of the balance. Speaking of England, he said:

> it is for the general interest that she should be a sensible and independent weight in the scale of nations, and be able to contribute, when a favorable moment presents itself, to reduce under the same order, her great rival in flagitiousness. We especially ought to pray that the powers of Europe may be so poised and counterpoised among themselves, that their own security may require the presence of all their forces at home, leaving the other quarters of the globe in undisturbed tranquility.

In 1814, again compelled by the logic of events, he came clearly out against Napoleon and in favor of a balance of power which would leave the power of Napoleon and of England limited, but intact.

> Surely none of us wish to see Bonaparte conquer Russia, and lay thus at his feet the whole continent of Europe. This done, England would be but a breakfast;

and, although I am free from the visionary fears which the votaries of England have effected to entertain, because I believe he cannot effect the conquest of Europe; yet put all Europe into his hands, and he might spare such a force to be sent in British ships, as I would as leave not have to encounter, when I see how much trouble a handful of British soldiers in Canada has given us. No. It cannot be to our interest that all Europe should be reduced to a single monarchy. The true line of interest for us, is, that Bonaparte should be able to effect the complete exclusion of England from the whole continent of Europe, in order, as the same letter said, "by this peaceable engine of constraint, to make her renounce her views of dominion over the ocean, of permitting no other nation to navigate it but with her license, and on tribute to her, and her aggressions on the persons of our citizens who may choose to exercise their right of passing over that element." And this would be effected by Bonaparte's succeeding so far as to close the Baltic against her. This success I wished him the last year, this I wish him this year; but were he again advanced to Moscow, I should again wish him such disasters as would prevent his reaching Petersburg. And were the consequences even to be the longer continuance of our war, I would rather meet them than see the whole force of Europe wielded by a single hand.

Similarly, in 1815, Jefferson wrote:

For my part, I wish that all nations may recover and retain their independence; that those which are overgrown may not advance beyond safe measures of power, that a salutary balance may be ever maintained among nations, and that our peace, commerce, and friendship, may be sought and cultivated by all.

21

It was only when, after 1815, the danger to the balance of power seemed to have passed that Jefferson allowed himself again to indulge in the cultivation of moral principles divorced from political exigencies.

From this tendency, to which Jefferson only too readily yielded, John Quincy Adams was well-nigh immune. We are here in the presence of a statesman who had been reared in the realist tradition of the first period of American foreign policy, who had done the better part of his work of statecraft in an atmosphere saturated with Jeffersonian principles, and who had achieved the merger of these two elements of his experience into a harmonious whole. Between John Quincy Adams's moral principles and the traditional interest of the United States there was hardly ever a conflict. The moral principles were nothing but the political interests formulated in moral terms, and vice versa. They fit the interests as a glove fits the hand. Adams's great contributions to the tradition of American foreign policy—freedom of the seas, the Monroe Doctrine, and Manifest Destiny—are witness to this achievement.

In the hands of Adams, the legal and moral principle of the freedom of the seas was a weapon, as it had been two centuries earlier when Grotius wielded it on behalf of the Low Countries, through which an inferior naval power endeavored to safeguard its independence against Great Britain, the mistress of the seas. The Monroe Doctrine's moral postulates of anti-imperialism and mutual non-intervention were the negative conditions for the safety and enduring greatness of the United States. Their fulfillment secured the isolation of the United States from the power struggles of Europe and, through it, the continuing predominance of the United States in the Western Hemisphere. Manifest Destiny was the moral justification as well as the moral incentive for the westward expansion of the United States, the peculiar American way—foreordained by the objective conditions of American existence—of founding an empire, the "American Empire," as one of the contemporary opponents of Adams's policies put it.

THE UTOPIAN PERIOD

Jefferson and John Quincy Adams stand at the beginning of the second period of American thought on foreign policy, both its most eminent representatives and the heirs of a realist tradition that continued to mold political action, while it had largely ceased to influence political thought. At the beginning of the third period, McKinley leads the United States as a great world power beyond the confines of the Western Hemisphere, ignorant of the bearing of this step upon the national interest, and guided by moral principles completely divorced from the national interest. When at the end of the Spanish-American War the status of the Philippines had to be determined, McKinley expected and found no guidance in the traditional national interests of the United States. According to his own testimony, he knelt beside his bed in prayer, and in the wee hours of the morning he heard the voice of God telling him—as was to be expected—to annex the Philippines.

This period initiated by McKinley, in which moral principles no longer justify the enduring national interest as in the second, but replace it as a guide for action, finds its fulfillment in the political thought of Woodrow Wilson. Wilson's thought not only disregards the national interest, but is explicitly opposed to it on moral grounds. "It is a very perilous thing," he said in his address at Mobile on October 27, 1913,

> to determine the foreign policy of a nation in the terms
> of material interest. It not only is unfair to those with
> whom you are dealing, but it is degrading as regards

23

your own actions. . . . We dare not turn from the principle that morality and not expediency is the thing that must guide us, and that we will never condone iniquity because it is most convenient to do so.

Wilson's wartime speeches are but an elaboration of this philosophy. An excerpt from his address of September 27, 1918, opening the campaign for the Fourth Liberty Loan, will suffice to show the continuance of that philosophy.

It is of capital importance that we should also be explicitly agreed that no peace shall be obtained by any kind of compromise or abatement of the principles we have avowed as the principles for which we are fighting. . . .

First, the impartial justice meted out must involve no discrimination between those to whom we wish to be just and those to whom we do not wish to be just. It must be a justice that plays no favorites and knows no standard but the equal rights of the several peoples concerned;

Second, no special or separate interest of any single nation or any group of nations can be made the basis of any part of the settlement which is not consistent with the common interest of all;

Third, there can be no leagues or alliances or special covenants and understandings within the general and common family of the League of Nations.

Fourth, and more specifically, there can be no special, selfish economic combinations within the League and no employment of any form of economic boycott or exclusion except as the power of economic penalty by exclusion from the markets of the world may be vested in the League of Nations itself as a means of discipline and control.

Fifth, all international agreements and treaties of

every kind must be made known in their entirety to the rest of the world.

Special alliances and economic rivalries and hostilities have been the prolific source in the modern world of the plans and passions that produce war. It would be an insincere as well as insecure peace that did not exclude them in definite and binding terms. . . .

National purposes have fallen more and more into the background and the common purpose of enlightened mankind has taken their place. The counsels of plain men have become on all hands more simple and straightforward and more unified than the counsels of sophisticated men of affairs, who still retain the impression that they are playing a game of power and playing for high stakes. That is why I have said that this is a peoples' war, not a statesmen's. Statesmen must follow the clarified common thought or be broken.

Yet in his political actions, especially under the pressure of the First World War, Wilson could not discount completely the national interest of the United States, any more than could Jefferson before him. Wilson's case, however, was different from Jefferson's in two respects. For one thing, Wilson was never able, even when the national interest of the United States was directly menaced, to conceive of the danger in other than moral terms. It was only the objective force of the national interest, which no rational man could escape, that imposed the source of America's mortal danger upon him as the object of his moral indignation. Thus Wilson in 1917 led the United States into war against Germany for the same reasons, only half-known to himself, for which Jefferson had wished and worked alternately for the victory of England and France. Germany threatened the balance of power in Europe, and it was in order to remove that threat—and not to make the world safe for democracy—that the United States put its weight into the Allies' scale. Wilson pursued the right policy, but he pursued it for the wrong reasons.

Not only, however, did Wilson's crusading fervor obliterate awareness of the traditional interest of the United States in maintaining the European balance of power, to be accomplished through the defeat of Germany; it also had politically disastrous effects, for which there is no precedent in the history of the United States. Wilson's moral objective required the destruction of the Kaiser's autocracy, and this happened also to be required by the political interests of the United States. The political interests of the United States required, beyond this immediate objective of total victory, the restoration of the European balance of power, traditional guarantor of American security. Yet it was in indignation at the moral deficiencies of that very balance of power, "forever discredited," as he thought, that Wilson had asked the American people to take up arms against the Central Powers! Once military victory had put an end to the immediate threat to American security, the very logic of his moral position—let us remember that consistency is the moralist's supreme virtue—drove him toward substituting for· the concrete national interest of the United States the general postulate of a brave new world where the national interest of the United States, as that of all other nations, would disappear in a community of interests comprising mankind.

Consequently, Wilson considered it to be the purpose of victory not to restore a new, viable balance of power, but to put an end to the balance of power once and forever. "You know," he told the English people at Manchester on December 30, 1918,

that the United States has always felt from the very beginning of her history that she must keep herself separate from any kind of connection with European politics, and I want to say very frankly to you that she is not now interested in European politics. But she is interested in the partnership of right between America and Europe. If the future had nothing for us but a new attempt to keep the world at a right poise by a balance of power, the United States would take no interest, because she will join no combination of power which is not the combination of all of us. She is not interested merely in the peace of Europe, but in the peace of the world.

Faced with the national interests of the great Allied powers, Wilson had nothing to oppose or support them with but his moral principles, with the result that the neglect of the American national interest was not compensated for by the triumph of political morality. In the end Wilson had to consent to a series of uneasy compromises, which were a betrayal of his moral principles—for principles can, by their very nature, not be made the object of compromise—and which satisfied nobody's national aspirations. These compromises had no relation at all to the traditional American national interest in a viable European balance of power. Thus Wilson returned from Versailles a compromised idealist, an empty-handed statesman, a discredited ally. In that triple failure lies the tragedy not only of Wilson, a great yet misguided man, but of Wilsonianism as a political doctrine.

Yet Wilson returned unaware of his failure. He offered the American people what he had offered the Allied nations at Paris: moral principles divorced from political reality. "The day we have left behind us," he proclaimed at Los Angeles on September 20, 1919,

> was a day of balances of power. It was a day of "every nation take care of itself or make a partnership with

27

some other nation or group of nations to hold the peace of the world steady or to dominate the weaker portions of the world." Those were the days of alliances. This project of the League of Nations is a great process of disentanglement.

4. Wilsonianism, Isolationism, Internationalism—Three Forms of Utopianism

Whereas before Paris and Versailles these moral principles rang true with the promise of a new and better world, afterwards they must have sounded rather hollow and platitudinous to many. Yet what is significant for the course American foreign policy was to take in the interwar years is not so much that the American people rejected Wilsonianism, but that they rejected it by ratifying the denial of the American tradition of foreign policy which was implicit in the political thought of Wilson. We are here indeed dealing with a tragedy not of one man, but of a political doctrine and, as far as the United States is concerned, of a political tradition. The isolationism of the interwar period could delude itself into believing that it was but the restorer of the early realistic tradition of American foreign policy. Did it not, like that tradition, proclaim the self-sufficiency of the United States within the Western Hemisphere? Did it not, like that tradition, refuse to become involved in the rivalries of European nations? The isolationists of the twenties and thirties did not see—and this was the very essence of the policies of the Founding Fathers—that both the isolated and the preponderant position of the United States in the Western Hemisphere was not a fact of nature, and that the freedom from entanglements in European conflicts was not the result of mere abstention on the part of the United States. Both benefits were the result of political conditions outside the Western Hemisphere and of policies carefully contrived and purposefully executed in their support. For the realists of the first period, isolation was an objective of policy, and had to be striven for to be attained. For the isolationists of the interwar period, isolation was a natural state, and only needed to be left undisturbed in order to continue forever. Conceived in such terms, it was the very negation of foreign policy.

Isolationism, then, is in its way as oblivious to political reality as is Wilsonianism—the internationalist challenge, to which it thought to have found the American answer. In consequence, they are both strangers not only to the first, realistic phase of American foreign policy, but to its whole tradition. Both refused to face political reality either in realistic or ideological terms. They refused to face it at all. Thus isolationism and Wilsonianism have more in common than their historic enmity would lead one to suspect. In a profound sense they are brothers under the skin. Both are one in maintaining that the United States has no interest in any particular political and military configuration outside the Western Hemisphere. While isolationism stops here, Wilsonianism asserts that the American national interest is not somewhere in particular, but everywhere, being identical with the interests of mankind itself. Both refuse to concern themselves with the concrete issues upon which the national interest must be asserted. Isolationism stops short of them, Wilsonianism soars beyond them. Both have but a negative relation to the national interest of the United States outside the Western Hemisphere. They are unaware of its very existence. This being so, both substitute abstract moral principles for the guidance of the national interest, derived from the actual conditions of American existence. Wilsonianism applies the illusory expectations of liberal reform to the whole world, isolationism empties of all concrete political content the realistic political principle of isolation and transforms it into the unattainable parochial ideal of automatic separation.

In view of this inner affinity between isolationism and Wilsonianism, it is not surprising that the great debate of the twenties and thirties between internationalism and isolationism was carried on primarily in moral terms. Was there a moral obligation for the United States to make its contribution to world peace by joining the League of Nations and the World Court? Was it morally incumbent upon the United States, as a democracy, to oppose Fascism in Europe and to uphold international law in Asia? Such were the questions raised in that debate, and the answers depended upon the moral position taken. The question central to the national interest of the United States, that of the balance of power in Europe and Asia, was hardly ever faced squarely, and when it was faced it was dismissed on moral grounds. Mr. Cordell Hull, Secretary of State of the United States from 1933 to 1944, and one of the most respected spokesmen of internationalism, summarizes in his *Memoirs* his attitude toward this central problem of American foreign policy:

> I was not, and am not, a believer in the idea of balance of power or spheres of influence as a means of keeping the peace. During the First World War I had made an intensive study of the system of spheres of influence and balance of power, and I was grounded to the taproots in their iniquitous consequences. The conclusions I then formed in total opposition to this system stayed with me.

When internationalism triumphed in the late thirties, it did so in the moral terms of Wilsonianism. That in this instance the moral postulates inspiring the administration of Franklin D. Roosevelt happened to coincide with the exigencies of the American national interest was again, as in the case of Jefferson and of the Wilson of 1917, due to the impact of a national emergency upon innate common sense, and to the strength of a national tradition that holds in its spell the actions of even those who deny its validity in words. However, as soon as the minds of the American leaders, freed from these inescapable pressures of a primarily military nature, turned toward the political problems of the Second World War and its aftermath, they thought and acted again as Wilson had acted under similar circumstances. That is to say, they thought and acted in moral terms, divorced from the political conditions of America's existence.

The practical results of this philosophy of international affairs, as applied to the political problems of the war and postwar period, were therefore bound to be quite similar to those which had made the Allied victory in the First World War politically meaningless. Conceived as it was as a "crusade"—to borrow from the title of General Eisenhower's book—against the evil incarnate in the Axis powers, the purpose of the Second World War could only be the destruction of that evil, brought about through the instrumentality of "unconditional surrender." Since the threat to the Western world emanating from the Axis was conceived primarily in moral terms, it was easy to imagine that all conceivable danger was concentrated in that historic constellation of hostile powers and that with its destruction political evil itself would disappear from the world. Beyond "unconditional surrender" there was to be, then, a brave new world after the model of Wilson's, which would liquidate the heritage of the defeated nations—evil and not "peace-loving"—and establish an order of things where war, aggressiveness, and the struggle for power itself would be no more. Thus Mr. Cordell Hull could declare on his return in 1943 from the Moscow conference that the new international organization would mean the end of power politics and usher in a new era of international collaboration. Three years later, Mr. Philip Noel-Baker, then British Minister of State, echoed Mr. Hull by stating in the House of Commons that the British government was "determined to use the institutions of the United Nations to kill power politics, in order that by the methods of democracy, the will of the people shall prevail."

With this philosophy dominant in the West—Mr. Churchill provides almost the sole, however ineffective, exception—the strategy of the war and of the peace to follow could not help being oblivious to those considerations of the national interest which the great statesmen of the West, from Hamilton through Castlereagh, Canning, and John Quincy Adams, to Disraeli and Salisbury, had brought to bear upon the international problems of their day. War was no longer regarded as a means to a political end. The only end the war was to serve was total victory, which is another way of saying that the war became an end in itself. Hence, it became irrelevant how the war was won politically, as long as it was won speedily, cheaply, and totally. The thought that the war might be waged in view of a new balance of power to be established after the war, occurred in the West only to Winston Churchill—and, of course, it occurred to Joseph Stalin. The national interest of the Western nations was, then, satisfied in so far as it required the destruction of the threat to the balance of power emanating from Germany and Japan; for to that extent the moral purposes of the war happened to coincide with the national interest. However, the national interest of the Western nations was jeopardized in so far as their security required the creation of a new viable balance of power after the war.

How could statesmen who boasted that they were not

"believers in the idea of balance of power"—like a scientist not believing in the law of gravity—and who were out "to kill power politics," understand the very idea of the national interest which demanded, above all, protection from the power of others? Thus it was with deep and sincere moral indignation that the Western world, expecting a utopia without power politics, found itself confronted with a new and more formidable threat to its security as soon as the old one had been subdued. There was good reason for moral indignation, however misdirected it was. That a new balance of power will rise out of the ruins of an old balance and that nations with political sense will avail themselves of the opportunity to improve their position within it, is a law of politics for whose validity nobody is to blame. Yet they are indeed blameworthy who in their moralistic disdain for the laws of politics endanger the interests of the nations in their care.

5. *The Moral Dignity of the National Interest*

The fundamental error that has thwarted American foreign policy in thought and action is the antithesis of national interest and moral principles. The equation of political moralizing with morality and of political realism with immorality is itself untenable. The choice is not between moral principles and the national interest, devoid of moral dignity, but between one set of moral principles divorced from political reality, and another set of moral principles derived from political reality.

The moralistic detractors of the national interest are guilty of both intellectual error and moral perversion. The nature of the intellectual error must be obvious from what has been said thus far, as it is from the record of history: a foreign policy guided by moral abstractions, without consideration of the national interest, is bound to fail; for it accepts a standard of action alien to the nature of the action itself. All the successful statesmen of modern times from Richelieu to Churchill have made the national interest the ultimate standard of their policies, and none of the great moralists in international affairs has attained his goals.

The perversion of the moralizing approach to foreign policy is threefold. That approach operates with a false concept of morality, developed by national societies but unsuited to the conditions of international society. In the process of its realization, it is bound to destroy the very moral values it sets out to promote. Finally, it is derived from a false antithesis between morality and power politics, thus arrogating to itself all moral values and placing the stigma of immorality upon the theory and practice of power politics.

There is a profound and neglected truth hidden in Hobbes's extreme dictum that the state creates morality as well as law and that there is neither morality nor law outside the state. Universal moral principles, such as justice or equality, are capable of guiding political action only to the extent that they have been given concrete content and have been related to political situations by society. What justice means in the United States can within wide limits be objectively ascertained; for interests and convictions, experiences of life and institutionalized traditions have in large measure created a consensus concerning what justice means under the conditions of American society. No such consensus exists in the relations between nations. For above the national societies there exists no international society so integrated as to be able to define for them the concrete meaning of justice or equality, as national societies do for their individual members. In consequence, the appeal to moral principles by the representative of a nation vis-à-vis another nation signifies something fundamentally different from a verbally identical appeal made by an individual in his relations to another individual member of the same national society. The appeal to moral principles in the international sphere has no concrete universal meaning. It is either so vague as to have no concrete meaning that could provide rational guidance for political action, or it will be nothing but the reflection of the moral preconceptions of a particular nation and will by that same token be unable to gain the universal recognition it pretends to deserve.

Whenever the appeal to moral principles provides guidance for political action in international affairs, it destroys the very moral principles it intends to realize. It can do so in three different ways. Universal moral principles can serve as a mere pretext for the pursuit of national policies. In other words, they fulfill the functions of those ideological rationalizations and justifications to which we have referred before. They are mere means to the ends of national policies, bestowing upon the national interest the false dignity of universal moral principles. The performance of such a function is hypocrisy and abuse and carries a negative moral connotation.

The appeal to moral principles may also guide political action to that political failure which we have mentioned above. The extreme instance of political failure on the international plane is national suicide. It may well be said that a foreign policy guided by universal moral principles, by definition relegating the national interest to the background, is under contemporary conditions of foreign policy and warfare a policy of national suicide, actual or potential. Within a national society the individual can at times afford, and may even be required, to subordinate his interests and even to sacrifice his very existence to a supraindividual moral principle—for in national societies such principles exist, capable of providing concrete standards for individual action. What is more important still, national societies take it upon themselves within certain limits to protect and promote the interests of the individual and, in particular, to guard his existence against violent attack. National societies of this kind can exist and fulfill their functions only if their individual members are willing to subordinate their individual interests in a certain measure to the common good of society. Altruism and self-sacrifice are in that measure morally required.

The mutual relations of national societies are fundamentally different. These relations are not controlled by universal moral principles concrete enough to guide the political actions of individual nations. What again is more important, no agency is able to promote and protect the interests of individual nations and to guard their existence —and that is emphatically true of the great powers—but the individual nations themselves. To ask, then, a nation to embark upon altruistic policies oblivious of the national interest is really to ask something immoral. For such disregard of the individual interest, on the part of nations as of individuals, can be morally justified only by the existence of social institutions, the embodiment of concrete moral principles, which are able to do what otherwise the individual would have to do. In the absence of such institutions it would be both foolish and morally wrong to ask a nation to forego its national interests not for the good of a society with a superior moral claim but for a chimera. Morally speaking, national egotism is not the same as individual egotism because the functions of the international society are not identical with those of a national society.

The immorality of a politically effective appeal to moral abstractions in foreign policy is consummated in the contemporary phenomenon of the moral crusade. The crusading moralist, unable in the absence of an integrated national society to transcend the limits of national moral values and political interests, identifies the national interest with the manifestation of moral principles, which is, as we have seen, the typical function of ideology. Yet the crusader goes one step farther. He projects the national moral standards onto the international scene not only with the legitimate claim of reflecting the national interest, but with the politically and morally unfounded claim of providing moral standards for all mankind to conform to in concrete political action. Through the intermediary of the universal moral appeal the national and the universal interest become one and the same thing. What is good for the crusading country is by definition good for all mankind, and if the rest of mankind refuses to accept such claims to universal recognition, it must be converted with fire and sword.

There is already an inkling of this ultimate degeneration of international moralism in Wilson's crusade to make the world safe for democracy. We see it in full bloom in the universal aspirations of Bolshevism. Yet to the extent that the West, too, is persuaded that it has a holy mission, in the name of whatever moral principle, first to save the world and then to remake it, it has itself fallen victim to the moral disease of the crusading spirit in politics. If that disease should become general, as well it might, the age of political moralizing would issue in one or a series of religious world wars. The fanaticism of political religions would, then, justify all those abominations unknown to less moralistic but more politically-minded ages and for which in times past the fanaticism of other-worldly religions provided a convenient cloak.

In order to understand fully what these intellectual and moral aberrations of a moralizing in foreign policy imply, and how the moral and political problems to which that philosophy has given rise can be solved, we must recall that from the day of Machiavelli onward the controversy has been fought on the assumption that there was morality on one side and immorality on the other. Yet the antithesis that equates political moralizing with morality and political realism with immorality is erroneous.

We have already pointed out that it is a political necessity for the individual members of the international society to take care of their own national interests, and that there can be no moral duty to neglect them. Self-preservation both for the individual and for societies is, however, not only a biological and psychological necessity but, in the absence of an overriding moral obligation, a moral duty as well. In the absence of an integrated international society, the attainment of a modicum of order and the realization of a minimum of moral values are predicated upon the existence of national communities capable of preserving order and realizing moral values within the limits of their power.

It is obvious that such a state of affairs falls far short of that order and realized morality to which we are accustomed in national societies. The only relevant question is, however, what the practical alternative is to these imperfections of an international society that is based upon the national interests of its component parts. The attainable alternative is not a higher morality realized through the application of universal moral principles, but moral deterioration through either political failure or the fanaticism of political crusades. The juxtaposition of the morality of political moralism and the immorality of the national interest is mistaken. It presents a false concept of morality, developed by national societies but unsuited to the conditions of international society. It is bound to destroy the very moral values it aims to foster. Hence, the antithesis between moral principles and the national interest is not only intellectually mistaken but also morally pernicious. A foreign policy derived from the national interest is in fact morally superior to a foreign policy inspired by universal moral principles. Albert Sorel, the Anglophobe historian of the French Revolution, summarized well the real antithesis when he said in grudging admiration of Castlereagh:

> He piqued himself on principles to which he held with an unshakable constancy, which in actual affairs could not be distinguished from obstinacy; but these principles were in no degree abstract or speculative, but were all embraced in one alone, the supremacy of English interests; they all proceeded from this high reason of state.

In our time the United States is groping toward a reason of state of its own—one that expresses our national interest. The history of American foreign policy since the end of the Second World War is the story of the encounter of the American mind with a new political world. That mind was weakened in its understanding of foreign policy by half a century of ever more complete intoxication with moral abstractions. Even a mind less weakened would have found it hard to face with adequate understanding and successful action the unprecedented novelty and magnitude of the new political world. American foreign policy in that period presents itself as a slow, painful, and incomplete process of emancipation from deeply ingrained error, and of rediscovery of long-forgotten truths.

What are the characteristics of the new political world which affect the United States in its foreign relations, and how have they affected it?

II

The Three Revolutions
of Our Age

Since the Renaissance and Reformation, the two great revolutions of the sixteenth century, the Western world has almost continuously lived in fear or expectation of some kind of revolution. Since the French Revolution of 1789, this state of mind has become endemic in the Western world, and since the end of the First World War it has become a commonplace to say that we live in a revolutionary age. However, the three great revolutions confronting the United States in the aftermath of the Second World War are different not only in magnitude but also in kind from those that preceded them. They mark the definite and radical end of the political, technological, and moral conditions under which the Western world lived for centuries. It is not too much to say that our age has broken with the traditions in these areas of life which have dominated the West for at least four hundred years. The revolutions of that break have been long in the making, yet only the cataclysm of the Second World War has made their destructive effects fully plain.

1. *The Political Revolution*

The political revolution signifies the end of the state system which has existed since the sixteenth century in the Western world. This state system was characterized by continuous conflicts among a multiplicity of nations of approximately equal strength, all located in Europe. They protected and promoted their national interests and, more particularly, safeguarded their independence by joining together in alliances and counteralliances in an unending succession of attempts to equalize and, if possible, to surpass the strength of their enemies. This system was called the balance of power.

Within this system Great Britain played a unique and vital part. It so happened that for four centuries Great Britain was both powerful enough in comparison with the other European nations and detached enough from the power struggles of the continent to be able to play the role of the stabilizer or, in technical parlance, the "holder" of the balance, the "balancer" of the Western state system. While other European nations strove for the succession to a throne, the acquisition of a strategic frontier, the annexation of a town or province, Great Britain had only one interest on the continent of Europe: that no nation or combination of nations gain such a preponderance of power as to be able to dominate the whole of the continent. In other words, the only interest Great Britain pursued consistently in Europe throughout the centuries was the maintenance of the balance of power itself.

The relationship of the non-European world to this European state system was one of isolation or subordination. That is to say, to the extent to which non-European nations came in contact with European ones, they were dominated by them. The non-European possessions were for the European nations a source of power and wealth and, hence, became a source of rivalry among them. Yet it must be borne in mind that the colonial rivalries of European nations were but the reflection and extension in space of those power relations, centered in Europe, which we call the balance of power.

THE FIVE TRANSFORMATIONS OF THE STATE SYSTEM

Of this state system, nothing is left today. Five radical transformations signify its end. First of all, the European state system has been transformed into a worldwide system. This development started when the American colonies declared their independence from the British Crown and President Monroe proclaimed the mutual political independence of Europe and the Western Hemisphere as a principle of American foreign policy. Thus the world, whose one political center until then had been in Europe, was divided into two political systems and the groundwork laid for the subsequent transformation of the European into a worldwide balance-of-power system. This transformation was accomplished when the United States, through the Spanish-American War, and Japan, through the Russo-Japanese War of 1904–5, became active participants in the worldwide struggle for power. The consummation of this development became obvious in the First World War—the very designation of that war as a "World War" is significant in this respect—in which virtually all nations of the world participated actively on one or the other side. The aftermath of the Second World War has seen an accentuation of this development in the emancipation of most of the former Asiatic colonies of European nations and their entrance as independent factors into the arena of world politics. The colonial pawns of Asia not only became independent of their European masters, as did the American colonies in the eighteenth and nineteenth centuries, but with their independence they also immediately assumed an active role in the affairs of the world.

More important for American foreign policy than this quantitative expansion of the European state system is its qualitative transformation. Europe has lost its political predominance in the world, and the center of political gravity has shifted since the beginning of the century—first imperceptibly, then with ever greater momentum—away from Europe into either completely or predominantly non-European areas. This development began with the First World War and was consummated with the Second. The issues of the First World War were still exclusively confined to Europe, and it was only the temporary intervention of a non-European power, the United States, which decided the issues. The issues of the Second World War were no longer confined to Europe, but were shared by Asia, and it was the intervention of two completely or predominantly non-European powers, the United States and the Soviet Union, which decided them.

Since the end of the Second World War, the relation between the European and the non-European world has been reversed. Europe has become the object of the power struggle of non-European forces, upon whose outcome its fate depends. For not only have the centers of power shifted from London, Paris, Berlin, and Rome to Washington and Moscow; the power concentrated in the latter capitals is also so superior to that of any other nation or possible combination of nations as to reduce the former great powers of Europe to the rank of second or third rate powers. The third aspect of the revolutionary transformation of the Western state system, then, consists in the substitution of a bipolar political world for a system composed of a multiplicity of states of approximately equal strength. In the various periods of modern history preceding the Second World War the political world consisted of six or eight or ten power centers, as the case might be, which would deal with each other on an equal footing and around which second- or third-rate powers would group themselves. To-day only two power centers of first-rate magnitude remain, drawing the other nations of the world into their orbits.

The fourth aspect of the political revolution of our time is the inevitable by-product of the preceding one. It is the decline of British power in comparison with that of the United States and the Soviet Union and, as a result, Britain's inability to continue to play the decisive role with respect to the balance of power which it played for four centuries. The key position of Britain was founded upon its naval supremacy and its virtual immunity from foreign attack. Today, the United States has far surpassed Great Britain in naval strength, and the modern technology of war has deprived navies of uncontested mastery of the seas. Modern instruments of warfare have not only put an end to the invulnerability of the British Isles, but have also transformed from an advantage into a liability the concentration of population and industries on a relatively small territory in close proximity to a continent.

What in the long run is even more important than this decline of British power is the inability of any other nation to take over the heritage of Great Britain in this respect. There is much talk of the neutrality of Europe in the struggle between East and West and of the establishment of a third force either in Europe or in Asia. This is no more than talk, for there is no power center, besides Washington and Moscow, that could even approximate the ability to perform that vital and decisive function which Great Britain has performed for so long. Thus it is not so much that the power of the traditional occupant of that key position has declined, incapacitating it for its traditional role, as that the position itself no longer exists. With two giants strong enough to determine the position of the scales with their own weight alone, there can be no chance for a third power to exert a decisive influence. Thus it is not only the decline of British power but the disappearance of the function itself, performed by Great Britain, which constitutes the fourth revolutionary change in the modern state system.

Finally, the decline of Europe as the power center of the world has brought in its wake a fundamental change in the relations between the white and the colored races. The political pre-eminence of Europe throughout modern times was primarily the result of its predominance over the colored races. It was the cultural, technological, and political differential between the white man of Europe and the colored man of Africa and Asia which allowed Europe to acquire and keep its dominion over the world. At least in so far as Asia is concerned, this dominion has come to an end. With it has dried up the main source of strength—military, economic, political—upon which the European nations could draw in order to make up for their inferiority in numbers, space, and natural resources. Furthermore, with the disappearance of the colonial frontier, the European nations have lost the opportunity for relatively effortless and profitable expansion without necessarily interfering with each other's interests. This holds true for the United States and the Soviet Union as well, in view of the consummation of their transcontinental expansion.

THE BIPOLARITY OF POWER

Much that is new and disturbing in the present world situation is the result of these political changes. They all have brought about an unprecedented concentration of power in two governments in whose hands lies truly the fate of the world. Because of the enormous disparity of power which now exists between the two super-powers and even their closest competitors, the flexibility that characterized the old state system, with its ever changing alignments and alliances, has given place to the rigidity of a two-bloc system, divided by an iron curtain that prevents a crossing of the dividing line either way. Thus the United States and the Soviet Union enjoy a freedom from restraint by other nations which no nation in modern times has enjoyed for any length of time.

During those centuries when there existed a multiplicity of nations of approximately equal strength, no player in the game of power politics could go very far in his aspirations for power without being sure of the support of at least one or the other of his co-players, and nobody could generally be too sure of that support. There was virtually no nation in the eighteenth and nineteenth centuries which was not compelled to retreat from an advanced position and retrace its steps because it did not receive the diplomatic or military support from other nations upon which it had counted.

The greater the number of active players, the greater the number of possible combinations and the greater also the uncertainty as to the combinations that would actually oppose each other and as to the roles the individual players would actually perform. Both Wilhelm II in 1914 and Hitler in 1939 refused to believe that Great Britain, and ultimately the United States, too, would join the ranks of their enemies, and both discounted the effect of American intervention. It is obvious that these miscalculations as to who would fight whom meant for Germany the difference between victory and defeat. Whenever coalitions of nations comparable in power confront each other, calculations of this kind will of necessity be close, since the defection of one prospective member or the addition of an unexpected one cannot fail to affect the balance of power considerably, if not decisively. Consequently, the extreme flexibility of the balance of power resulting from the utter unreliability of alliances made it imperative for all players to be cautious in their moves on the international chessboard and, since risks were hard to calculate, to take as small risks as possible.

In the Second World War, the decisions of such countries as Italy, Spain, or Turkey, or even France, to join or not to join one or the other side were mere episodes, welcomed or feared, to be sure, by the belligerents, but in no way even remotely capable of transforming victory into defeat, or vice versa. The disparity in the power of nations of the first rank, such as the United States, the Soviet Union, Great Britain, Japan, and Germany on the one hand, and all the remaining nations on the other, was then already so great that the defection of one, or the addition of another ally could no longer overturn the balance of power and thus materially affect the outcome of the struggle. Under the influence of changes in alignments one scale might rise somewhat and the other sink still more under a heavier weight, yet these changes could not reverse the relation of the scales, which was determined by the preponderant weight of the first-rate powers. It was only the position of the major countries—the United States, the Soviet Union, and Great Britain on the one hand, Germany and Japan on the other—that really mattered. This situation, first noticeable in the Second World War, is now accentuated in the polarity between the United States and the Soviet Union and has become the paramount feature of international politics. The power of the United States and of the Soviet Union in comparison with the power of their actual or prospective allies has become so overwhelming that through their own preponderant weight they determine the balance of power between them. That balance cannot be decisively affected by changes in the alignments of their allies, at least in the foreseeable future.

As a result, both the flexibility of the balance of power and its restraining influence upon the power aspirations of the main protagonists on the international scene have disappeared. Two great powers, each incomparably stronger than any other power or possible combination of other powers, oppose each other. Neither of them need fear surprises from actual or prospective allies. The disparity of strength between major and minor powers is so great that the minor powers have not only lost their ability to tip the scales, they have also lost that freedom of movement which in former times enabled them to play so important and often decisive a role in the balance of power. What was formerly true of a relatively small number of nations, such as certain Latin-American countries in their relations with the United States, and Portugal in its relations with Great Britain, is true now of most of them: they are in the orbit of one or the other of the two giants whose political, military, and economic preponderance can hold them there even against their will. If France, for instance, does not like American policy with regard to Germany, there is little it can do about it. In times past, if France did not find what it wanted with one alliance it would simply cross over to the other side and make a pact with another nation or group of nations. Today this has become impossible. France has no place to go. It can protest; it can try to retard the inevitable or to modify it in some minor particulars. But it has lost effective control over the matters that concern its vital interest. More particularly, it has lost that freedom of maneuver which was one of the main characteristics of the state system now at an end. It has lost the ability to change sides. What is true of France is true of all nations with the exception of the two super-powers. The

Iron Curtain is not only a dividing line in the military and ideological sense; it is also a dividing line in the political sense. It denotes a rigid, inflexible line of separation which resembles two opposing battle lines rather than the traditional diplomatic constellation with its ever changing alignments.

The apparent recent changing of sides by Yugoslavia bears this analysis out rather than contradicts it. It was not of its own volition that Yugoslavia left the Russian camp; it did not go voluntarily over to the other side of the Iron Curtain. Yugoslavia was, as it were, thrown over the Iron Curtain by the Soviet Union because it refused to subordinate its national interests and those of its ruling group to the interests of the Soviet Union. Its crime in the eyes of the Soviet Union was the refusal to accept that satellite status which conquest by the Red Army had imposed upon the other nations of eastern Europe. Thus, whether it wanted it or not, Yugoslavia found itself on the other side of the Iron Curtain. Even if it wanted to go back to the Russian side, it could not do so short of giving up its very independence as a nation. Appearances to the contrary, it, too, has lost its freedom of movement.

The disappearance of Great Britain's key position as the "holder" of the balance is but a special—and the most important—case of the loss of that flexibility and restraint which were the characteristics of the state system for four centuries. In that period of history, Great Britain was able to play the controlling and restraining role of the balancer because it was strong enough in comparison with the contenders and their allies to make likely the victory of whichever side it joined. No nation would knowingly dare to oppose Great Britain, and all nations would compete for its support. Thus Great Britain could always say: "If you want to have our support, you can go thus far but no farther." Today Great Britain's friendship is no longer of decisive importance. Its role as the "holder" of the balance has come to an end, leaving the modern state system without the benefits of restraint and pacification which it bestowed upon that system in former times. Even as late as the Second World War, the neutrality of Great Britain or its alignment with Germany and Japan instead of with the United Nations might easily have meant for the latter the difference between victory and defeat. Now, in view of the probable trends in the technology of warfare and the distribution of power between the United States and the Soviet Union, it may well be that the attitude of Great Britain in an armed conflict between these two powers would not decisively affect the outcome. Let us assume rather crudely that, while in the Russian scale there is a weight of seventy, the weight of the American scale amounts to a hundred, of which seventy is the United States' own strength, ten that of Great Britain, and the remainder that of the other actual or prospective allies. Thus, even if the British weight were removed from the American scale and placed in the Russian scale, the heavier weight would still be in the American scale.

These two super-powers and their allies and satellites face each other like two fighters in a short and narrow lane. They can advance and meet in what is likely to be combat, or they can retreat and allow the other side to advance into what to them is precious ground. Those manifold and variegated maneuvers through which the masters of the balance of power tried to either stave off armed conflicts altogether or at least make them brief and decisive, yet limited in scope—the alliances and counteralliances, the shifting of alliances according to whence the greater threat or the better opportunity might come, the sidestepping and postponement of issues, the deflection of rivalries from the exposed frontyard into the colonial backyard—these are things of the past. Into oblivion with them have gone the peculiar finesse and subtlety of mind, the calculating and versatile intelligence and bold yet circumspect decisions which were required of the players in that game. And with those modes of action and intellectual attitudes there has disappeared that self-regulating flexibility, that automatic tendency of disturbed power relations either to revert to their old equilibrium or to establish a new one.

Today there stands nothing in the way of either the Russian or American governments attempting to reach their aims with any means at hand except the self-restraint they might be able to exert upon themselves (a very weak type of restraint indeed) or the fear with which either side watches the power of the other (a much more potent restraint). For the two giants that today determine the course of world affairs only one policy seems to be left, that is, to increase their own strength and that of their satellites. All the players that count have taken sides, and in the foreseeable future no switch from one side to the other is likely to take place, nor, if it were to take place, would it be very likely to upset the existing balance. Since the issues everywhere boil down to retreat from, or advance into, areas that both sides regard as of vital interest to themselves, positions must be held, and the give and take of compromise becomes a weakness neither side is able to afford.

While formerly war was regarded, according to the classic definition of Clausewitz, as the continuation of diplomacy by other means, the art of diplomacy is now transformed into a variety of the art of warfare. That is to say, we live in the period of "cold war," where the aims of warfare are being pursued, for the time being, with other than violent means. In such a situation the peculiar qualities of the diplomatic mind are useless, for it has nothing to operate with and is consequently superseded by military thinking. The balance of power, once disturbed, can be restored only, if at all, by an increase in the weaker side's military strength. Yet, since there are no important variables in the picture aside from the inherent strength of the two giants themselves, either side must fear that the temporarily stronger contestant will use its superiority to eliminate the threat from the other side by shattering military and economic pressure or by a war of annihilation.

Thus the international situation is reduced to the primitive spectacle of two giants eying each other with watchful suspicion. They bend every effort to increase their military potential to the utmost, since this is all they have to count on. Both prepare to strike the first decisive blow, for if one does not strike it the other might. Thus, to contain or be contained, to conquer or be conquered, to destroy or be destroyed, become the watch words of the new diplomacy. Total victory, total defeat, total destruction seem to be the alternatives before the two great powers of the world.

2. *The Technological Revolution*

The tendencies toward unrestrained and destructive policies, following in the wake of the political revolution, are powerfully supported and aggravated by the revolution in the field of technology. The technological progress achieved during the first half of the twentieth century surpasses that of all previous history. While this progress gains its revolutionary momentum in the twentieth century, its beginnings date from the middle of the nineteenth. Three facets of that technological revolution bear upon foreign affairs: transportation, communications, and warfare.

Nowhere has mechanical progress in the last decades been more staggering than with regard to the ease and speed of transportation and communications. It has been remarked that the thirteen days that it took Sir Robert Peel in 1834 to hurry from Rome to London in order to be present at a cabinet meeting were exactly identical with the travel time allowed to a Roman official for the same journey seventeen centuries earlier. The best travel speed on land and sea throughout recorded history until close to the middle of the nineteenth century was ten miles an hour, a speed rarely attained on land. In 1790, it took four days in the best season to go from Boston to New York, a distance somewhat exceeding two hundred miles. Today the same time is sufficient for circling the globe, regardless of season. In terms of travel speed, Moscow is today as close to New York as Philadelphia was a century and a half ago, and the whole earth is considerably smaller than were the combined territories of the thirteen states that founded the United States of America.

The corresponding development is, however, incomparably more rapid in the field of oral and written communications. Here mechanical progress has far outstripped progress in transportation. Before the invention in the nineteenth century of the telegraph, the telephone, and the undersea cable, the speed of the transmission of oral or written communications was identical with the speed of travel. That is to say, the only way to transmit such communications, aside from visible signals, was by the usual means of transportation. These inventions reduced the speed needed for the transmission of such communications from what had been formerly days and weeks to hours. Radio and television have made the transmission instantaneous with the utterance.

A NEW CONCEPT OF WAR

We are all aware of the extent to which modern technology has increased the destructiveness of warfare. This increase is so great as to make the wars of our time different from the wars in times past not only in quantity of destruction but in kind. What was called war in the eighteenth and nineteenth centuries was something essentially different, in its destructiveness and in its effects upon society, from what goes by the name of war today. War was then indeed the continuation of diplomacy by other means. If a government could not achieve its objectives through diplomatic bargaining or pressure it would send out its soldiers—who were frequently professionals, that is, mercenaries collected from all over the world—to enter into a contest with another team of soldiers. These contests proceeded generally according to strict rules, lasted a few months out of a year, and were frequently no more bloody, in proportion to the time consumed and the men engaged, than our football matches. Machiavelli reports of a battle of the late fifteenth century, which had considerable influence upon the course of events, that in it one man lost his life, and he, Machiavelli adds, fell from his horse. In the eighteenth century, it was an accepted principle of warfare that for a military leader to avoid battle was a more convincing demonstration of military ability than to be drawn into one and win it. Only an incompetent general would allow himself to be forced into bloody combat. The clever general would avoid taking and losing lives and would, like a chess player, gain his objective by apt maneuvering. In the Spanish-American War, certainly an event of considerable importance in the history of the United States and of the world, the United States lost fewer soldiers through enemy action (it lost some thousands through disease) than die from accidents during a holiday weekend today.

Warfare today, owing to revolutionary changes in its technology, bears little resemblance to the kind of warfare of which the history books tell. The common denominator of these changes is mechanization. Its revolutionary impact on warfare is twofold: the ability to eliminate an unprecedented number of enemies through one single operation or the accelerated multiple operation of a weapon, and the ability to do so over long distances.

How great was the progress made in this respect between 1850 and 1913, and how overwhelming between 1913 and 1938, becomes apparent from a comparison with the slow progress made between 1550 and 1850. In the mid-sixteenth century, the range of the hand cannon was about one hundred yards, and one round in two minutes was about the best rate of fire attainable. While in the First World War the maximum range of heavy artillery—with great inaccuracy in aim and excessive wear on the gun, which was worn out after a maximum of thirty rounds—did not exceed seventy-six miles (attained only by the German 8.4-inch guns), at the moment of this writing guided missiles—that is, containers of explosives traveling under their own power—are available with an effective range of two hundred and fifty miles. The tactical radius of a bomber, capable of returning to its base after the execution of its mission, was in excess of fifteen hundred miles at the end of the Second World War and has since been increased to exceed seven thousand miles. Thus, while at the turn of the century the maximum distance within which a nation could attack a point in enemy territory was a few miles, it had increased in the First World War to seventy-six miles for artillery and a few hundred miles for —ineffective and lightly loaded—aircraft, in the Second World War to more than fifteen hundred miles, and it stands now at somewhat more than seven thousand.

Yet if one considers the range of aircraft not in terms of ability to return to the point of departure, but in absolute terms, the range of aircraft as a weapon has already for all practical purposes become limitless. There is obviously no place on earth which cannot be reached by air from any other place, provided the airplane is not expected to return to its base. More particularly, the distance between New York and Moscow over the great circle route is only forty-eight hundred miles, and the distance between any major city either in the United States or the Soviet Union and the other country's territory hardly exceeds six thousand miles. Consequently, an American or Russian airplane, even operating under less than optimum conditions and carrying a substantial load of bombs, is able to drop its load over any major city of the other country or, for that matter, of any country. Warfare in the mid-twentieth century, then, has become total in that virtually the whole earth is apt to be made the theater of operations by any country fully equipped with the technological instruments of the age.

This extension of the range of weapons affects modern war and its bearing upon world politics according to whether the increase in the destructiveness of war has kept pace with the increase in the range of its weapons. Through the enormous increase in destructiveness which has actually occurred during this century—more particularly in its fifth decade—modern war has transformed the potentialities of its weapons into the actuality of total war.

Until the invention of artillery and aside from naval warfare, one military operation by one single man was as a matter of principle capable of eliminating no more than one single enemy. One strike with a sword, one thrust with a spear or a pike, one shot from a musket would at best yield one disabled enemy.

This situation changed on a large scale only with the invention of the improved machine-gun in the later part of the nineteenth century. With this weapon one man in one operation could fire hundreds of rounds with the optimum effect of eliminating in one operation nearly as many enemies as there were shots fired. The radical improvement of artillery, starting in about the same period, and succeeding developments in the fields of air and gas warfare brought about a considerable increase in the number of enemies capable of being eliminated in one operation by one or very few men. The number was certainly still to be counted by the hundreds in the First World War, whose staggering losses are in the main accounted for by the machine-gun mowing down charging infantry. Even during virtually the whole of the Second World War the number of victims of one direct hit by a block-buster could hardly have exceeded the thousand mark.

Atomic warfare and, as a potentiality, bacteriological warfare, have wrought in this respect a revolution similar to, yet far exceeding in magnitude, the one brought about by the machine-gun a few decades earlier. A few men dropping one atomic bomb at the end of the Second World War disabled well over a hundred thousand of the enemy. With atomic bombs increasing in potency and the defense remaining as powerless as it is now, the number of the prospective victims of one atomic bomb, dropped over a densely populated region, will be counted in the millions. The potentialities for mass destruction inherent in bacteriological warfare exceed even those of an improved atomic bomb, in that one or a few strategically placed units of bacteriological material can easily create epidemics affecting an unlimited number of people.

THE IRRATIONALITY OF MODERN WAR

The enormous increase in the destructiveness of the weapons of warfare has fundamentally altered the political function of war. War is no longer the continuation of diplomacy by other means, an instrument of foreign policy to be used or not used as expediency advises. In centuries past, resort to war could be defended as a means to an end. The goal sought by war, such as national independence, security, power, or glory, could justify the evils war entailed. Comparing the value of the end with the repulsiveness of the means, people could rationally find that the stakes of independence, security, power, and glory were worth the price of a limited war, fought predominantly by mercenaries against mercenaries.

The total war of our age has fundamentally altered this traditional relationship between political ends and military means. War in the atomic age, fought by both sides with all the instruments of modern technology, has become the *reductio ad absurdum* of policy itself. Today war has become an instrument of universal destruction, an instrument that destroys the victor with the vanquished. None of the traditional objectives of foreign policy can justify war any more except national self-preservation itself; and even then, the nature of modern war being apt to defeat the end of self-preservation for which the war is being waged, the choice is really between two kinds of national destruction. If a great nation does not go to war in the face of a challenge to its national existence, it will lose it through the creeping dissolution of appeasement and subversion. If it goes to war in the face of such a challenge, it may at best preserve its freedom from foreign domination, but is likely to lose the substance of what made its national life worth living. At worst, victor and loser would be undistinguishable under the leveling impact of such a catastrophe, and Western civilization itself would cease to exist. At best, the destruction on one side would not be quite as great as on the other; the victor would be somewhat better off than the loser and would establish, with the aid of modern technology, his dominion over the world. For modern technology has not only fundamentally changed the nature of warfare, it has also transformed the nature of government.

It is not by accident that the age of the technological revolutions is also the age of totalitarian governments. Nor is it by accident that no popular revolution has succeeded since 1917. The technological revolutions in the fields of transportation, communications, and warfare have placed in the hands of government such powers of control over thought and action as to make totalitarian government possible. Conversely, the discrepancy between what a government can do to its citizens and what the citizens can do to their government has become so enormous as to make popular revolution impossible. As long as a totalitarian government can be certain of the loyalty of its bureaucratic and military apparatus, it matters little that the people are opposed to it. Only foreign conquest can dislodge such a government, or a *coup d'état* from within its own ranks, or both. These are indeed the ways in which the totalitarian governments of Germany and Italy have disappeared. It is this new distribution of power between government and people which explains also the longevity of the Bolshevist regime in Russia.

This concentration of overwhelming power in the hands of government through the means of modern technology has important consequences for world politics. The combination of the modern technologies of transportation, communication, and warfare, marshaled by the government of one super-power against the rest of the world, has for the first time in history made the conquest of the world possible. And what is more important still, it has made it possible for such a government, once it has conquered the world, to keep it conquered. The would-be world conquerors of the past, such as Alexander or Napoleon, were never able to achieve this; they were lacking those instruments of permanent control which are at the disposal of a world conqueror today. The results of the technological revolution, then, point in the direction we found the political revolution to be moving: the conquest of the world as an alternative to, or in combination with, universal destruction.

3. *The Moral Revolution*

The moral revolution as the third of the great revolutions of our time runs parallel with the political and technological ones, supporting and strengthening them. Throughout modern history, if not since the end of the ancient world, there has existed in the Western world a community of moral principles and of moral conduct, a community of fundamental religious beliefs, a common way of life—in one word, a common civilization. There have been temporary exceptions, such as the religious wars at the end of the sixteenth and the beginning of the seventeenth centuries and the Napoleonic Wars at the turn of the nineteenth century. But by and large that unity of the Western world has prevailed throughout the ages. It is now possible for us to refer to the Western world as not merely a geographic unit but a cultural and moral entity.

The political writers of the eighteenth and nineteenth centuries had this entity in mind when they spoke of "the family of nations." There were quarrels within that family of nations, as there are quarrels in all kinds of families. Yet there was something stronger than all those conflicts, something that kept the ambitions and rivalries of nations within certain bounds, and that was the consciousness of a unity, overriding all disruptive tendencies: the unity of Western civilization itself. All the members of that "family of nations" took the continuing existence of that common framework of values and conduct for granted. Their aspirations and policies with regard to each other would only go as far as was compatible with the continuing existence of that common framework. Foreign policy was a limited means to a limited end. Thus the restraining influence of the moral climate coincided with, and strengthened, the restraining influences of the political structure of the state system and of a stationary technology. When this civilization was about to receive its first great shock through the French Revolution, ushering in the period of its disintegration, Gibbon could propose

> to consider Europe as one great republic, whose various inhabitants have attained almost the same level of politeness and cultivation. The balance of power will continue to fluctuate, and the prosperity of our own or the neighboring kingdoms may be alternately exalted or depressed; but these events cannot essentially injure our general state of happiness, the system of arts, and laws, and manners, which so advantageously distinguish, above the rest of mankind, the Europeans and their colonies. . . . The abuses of tyranny are restrained by the mutual influence of fear and shame; republics have acquired order and stability; monarchies have imbibed the principles of freedom, or, at least, of moderation; and some sense of honour and justice is introduced into the most defective constitutions by the general manners of the times. In peace, the progress of knowledge and industry is accelerated by the emulation of so many active rivals: in war, the European forces are exercised by temperate and undecisive contests.

Of this political and moral system little is left today. Throughout most of its history, the Western world was indeed one world. The moral revolution of our age has split it into two. The influence of that revolution upon international affairs is twofold: through the rise of political religions that tend to transform fundamentally the foreign policies of the great powers, and through the revolt of Asia against the West, carried forward in the name of those very moral principles that the West had brought to the peoples of the East.

THE RISE OF POLITICAL RELIGIONS

The breakup of the one world of Western civilization into two is a moral as well as a political fact. Washington and Moscow are not only the main centers of power, they are also the seats of hostile and competing political philosophies. The two super-powers fight for political and military advantage with potential world dominion as the ultimate prize, but parallel to this political and military contest there runs a conflict between two kinds of moral principles, two types of moral conduct, two ways of life. There is, of course, nothing new in either the political conflict between two great powers or the ideological conflict between two philosophies and ways of life. What is new, the exceptions mentioned notwithstanding, is the identification of one with the other. The power conflicts of times past, as we have seen, did not try to impose the political philosophy and way of life of one nation upon another nation, let alone upon all mankind; for both political and ideological conflicts operated within the framework of one moral standard and one way of life, the one shared and taken for granted by all.

Today the very political values and the very way of life of all the nations identified with Western civilization are challenged from two quarters. One is Bolshevism, which not only asserts its superiority to the values and ways of the West, but also claims the historic—not to say sacred—mission of saving the world by making it over in its own image, and which, furthermore, professes the inevitability of this mission's success. It is this Bolshevist message of inevitable universal salvation, of which the Soviet government makes itself not only the spokesman, but also the executor, which marks the difference between Bolshevism and political philosophies of a traditional character. Bolshevism, by its own claim, is not a political philosophy among others, but a political religion.

In this tendency toward worldwide salvation, Bolshevism is being met by Western democracy at least halfway. The Napoleonic Wars gave the Western world the first taste of foreign policies pursued, and wars fought, not for limited advantage but as political crusades to insure the defense and the universal triumph of one set of moral principles, one political philosophy, and one way of life. We have seen to what extent the two world wars of the twentieth century were fought as crusades to stamp out evil political principles and institutions and make good ones prevail. And the conflict between East and West today is largely conceived by the West in similar terms, as a struggle between Bolshevism and democracy, two hostile and incompatible systems of morality, politics, and society, both claiming a monopoly of virtue, universal validity, and universal dominion, the one being bound to destroy the other. Thus the super-power of the East, armed with the instruments of modern technology, is also a religious order whose historic mission it is to remake the world in the image of the "people's democracy." The super-power of the West, similarly armed, is not unwilling to heed the noble words of Jefferson, Wilson, and Franklin D. Roosevelt, and to set out on a crusade to make the world safe for true democracy.

THE REVOLT OF ASIA

It is the echo of those postulates of freedom and justice which challenges the West from another quarter: Asia. This challenge, the other manifestation of the moral revolution of the age, is in the long run perhaps more significant for the Western world than any other. The moral challenge emanating from Asia is in its essence a triumph of the moral ideas of the West. It is carried forward under the banner of two moral principles: national self-determination and social justice. These are the ideas that for more than a century have in the West either guided policies, domestic and international, or have at least been appealed to as justifications for political action. In the wake of its conquests, the West brought to Asia not only its technology and political institutions, but also its principles of political morality. The nations of the West taught the peoples of Asia by their own example that the full development of the individual's faculties depends upon the ability of the nation to which he belongs to determine of its own free will its political and cultural destinies and that this national freedom is a good to fight for; and the peoples of Asia learned that lesson. The West taught the peoples of Asia also that poverty and misery are not God-given curses that man must passively accept, but that they are largely man-made and can be remedied by man; and the peoples of Asia learned that lesson too. It is these principles of national self-determination and social justice which Asia today hurls against the West, condemning and revolting against Western political and economic policies in the name of the West's own moral standards.

The revolution of Asia means, as we have seen, first of all the end of colonialism, the crumbling of those positions of power which Western nations had conquered in

Asia, and in consequence the disintegration of one of the foundation stones upon which the predominance of Europe in the world had rested. To the extent to which Western nations have tried to stem by force of arms the tide of this Asiatic revolution, they have either failed, as the Netherlands have in Indonesia, or, as in the case of France in Indochina, the effort has been a drain on their resources out of all proportion to the objective to be gained, and regardless of the outcome has weakened rather than strengthened the over-all position of the countries concerned.

Aside from these immediate political and military consequences, the revolution of Asia has fundamentally altered the moral relationship of Asia with the West. The particular mission that the white man thought he had to perform has been accomplished: what seemed to be exportable in Western civilization Asia has been given the opportunity to see, to judge, to accept or reject. Whatever its benefits have been for either side, Asia is resolved to be done with that mission. As British rule over hundreds of millions of Indians, maintained as it was by a few thousand officials, was primarily due to British prestige, so was the breakdown of that rule the result of the moral revolution that destroyed the faith, shared by master and subject alike, in the natural superiority of the white man. Only in some obsolescent intellects lingers the idea of the "oriental mind" needing the strong guidance of his big white brother. The contradiction between the Western ideals of national self-determination and social justice, turned by Asia against the interests and actions of the West, has engendered an acute and sometimes paralyzing moral malaise in the West, of which Britain's retreat from India and the hesitations and contradictions of the Asiatic policies of the United States are telling examples. The "oriental mind," having appropriated from the West what it deemed worthy of appropriation, turns with various degrees of enthusiasm and irrevocability toward the new creed of Moscow, which promises deliverance from the evils Asia has fallen heir to.

The three great revolutions of our age, then, have this in common: that they support and strengthen each other and move in the same direction of a bipolar political and moral world, which is one only in the sense of technological potentialities. Their coincidence in time and their parallel development aggravate the threat to the survival of Western civilization which each of them carries independently. The concatenation of these revolutions has had three important results: the permanent decline of Europe as the center of the political world, the rise of two super-powers to unchallengeable prominence, and the emergence of Asia as an independent political and moral factor. Just as the political emancipation of Asia from Europe coincides with its assumption of moral opposition to the West, so does the rise of Washington and Moscow as political centers of the world coincide with their transformation into the seats of universal political religions. The decline of Europe as the political, moral, and technological center of the world is a mere by-product of the destruction of the delicate social mechanism of the modern state system through its worldwide expansion, of the spread of modern technology from Europe to the four corners of the earth, of the triumph of Europe's moral ideas in Asia. Europe has given to the world its political, technological, and moral achievements, and the world has used them to put an end to the pre-eminence of Europe.

In the long run, the impact of these revolutions upon Asia may well carry the gravest implications for the rest of the world. It is here that space, natural resources, great masses of men aspiring to the satisfaction of elemental needs, are just beginning to use political power, modern technology, and modern moral ideas for their ends. More than a billion people—who thus far have been the objects of the policies of others—have now entered world politics as active participants. One may well anticipate that these awakening masses, animated by a spirit of independence and social justice, will sooner or later come into full possession of those modern technological instruments of control and destruction which until recently have been a virtual monopoly of the West. Such a development —such a shift in the distribution of power—would, in its importance for the history of the world, transcend all other factors. It might well mean the end of the bipolarity centered in Washington and Moscow which now puts its imprint upon world politics. After all, while the Soviet Union is still the political, technological, and moral leader of the Communist world, in terms of numbers China, and not the Soviet Union, is today the leading Communist country in the world.

But today the three great revolutions of our age are epitomized in the rise of the Soviet Union to the position of the other leading world power. It is through the breakdown of the modern state system that the Soviet Union stands virtually unchallenged today in the heart of Europe. The political revolution that has emancipated the peoples of Asia from European domination has wiped out the balance of power in Asia, symbolized for the United States in the principle of the "open door" in China; the door of China is today closed to the West and wide open to the Soviet Union. This political rise of the Soviet Union is primarily the result of Lenin's and Stalin's equation of Bolshevization with industrialization. Communism in Russia has meant first of all the transformation of society by means of the technological revolution. It was Lenin who said that "Bolshevism means electrification," and it is Stalin who has subordinated all other considerations to the introduction of modern technology into Russian industry and agriculture. Finally, the threat to the Western world emanating from the Soviet Union, and the attraction of the Soviet system for millions of people outside its borders, must also be understood in the light of the revolutionary force that from Moscow promises salvation for all the world.

Wherever American power is challenged today, the challenge can be traced to Moscow. Wherever the moral ideals of America are doubted, the Soviet creed justifies the doubt. What, then, are the issues at stake between the United States and the Soviet Union, with which the foreign policy of the United States can and must deal?

III

The Real Issue between the United States and the Soviet Union

1. *The Three Choices*

Three answers are logically possible to the question of what the issues are between the United States and the Soviet Union. One can answer that there is no real issue of a political nature separating the United States and the Soviet Union, and if only suspicion and false propaganda were eliminated, nothing would stand in the way of normal, peaceful relations. Or one can answer that the issue between the United States and the Soviet Union is that of world revolution, an objective to which the Soviet government is irrevocably committed. Or, finally, one can answer that what concerns the United States in its relations with the Soviet Union is Russian imperialism, which uses for its purposes the instrument of world revolution.

These distinctions are not mere hair-splitting. For the choice of one alternative instead of another will of necessity determine our moral and intellectual attitude toward the Soviet Union, and it is obvious that the choice of the policies to be pursued by the United States with regard to the Soviet Union must depend upon which of these three answers is chosen. If one believes that there is no real political issue, policy must concentrate either upon propaganda penetrating the Iron Curtain or upon economic aid to the countries behind it. This aid will narrow the gap in well-being between East and West, and it is this gap which is presumed to create misunderstanding and suspicion. If one believes that what confronts us as long as the Soviet government reigns in Moscow is the threat of world revolution, then there is only one way to meet that threat: extirpate the evil at its roots. If Russian imperialism is assumed to be the problem, the traditional methods of military and political policies can be employed to meet it. In the first alternative, peace can be brought to the world on the strengthened waves of the Voice of America, or can be bought by ten or twenty billion dollars. In the second alternative, the problem is not how to preserve peace but when to go to war, and the idea of a preventive war is a legitimate one. In the third alternative, military preparations must join hands with an accommodating diplomacy, and preparing for the worst while working for a peaceful settlement becomes the order of the day.

THE PRECEDENT OF REVOLUTIONARY FRANCE

The dilemma of these alternatives confronting the United States today is not a new one in the history of the Western world. It arose in the minds of British statesmen in the last decade of the eighteenth century on the occasion of the expansionist policies of revolutionary France. The three-cornered contest among three of the greatest political minds Great Britain or any other country has produced—Edmund Burke, Charles James Fox, and William Pitt—provides us with the most lucid and penetrating exposition of the problem: the expansionism of a great power which is also the seat of a universal political religion. To grasp the contemporary relevance of that debate one needs only to substitute for France, the Soviet Union; for Jacobinism, Communism; for England, the United States; for Napoleon, Stalin.

The concrete issue of that debate was the participation of Great Britain in the war that the European monarchies were waging against revolutionary France. Fox, the leader of one faction of the Whigs, believed that Great Britain was not at all threatened by France or, for that matter, by the principles of the French Revolution, which were a mere domestic concern of France, and that therefore there was no reason for Great Britain to join the coalition against France. While he detested the terror of the Jacobins, he was not willing to support a war for the purpose of eliminating Jacobinism. " He should now show," he said in the House of Commons on February 1, 1793,

> that all the topics to which he had adverted were introduced into the debate to blind the judgment, by arousing the passions, and were none of them the just grounds of war. . . . What, then, remained but the internal government of France, always disavowed, but ever kept in mind, and constantly mentioned? The destruction of that government was the avowed object of the combined powers whom it was hoped we were to join. . . . He thought the present state of government in France any thing rather than an object of imitation; but he maintained as a principle inviolable, that the government of every independent state was to be settled by those who were to live under it, and not by foreign force.

Fox summarizes his position with a statement that has in more than one respect a contemporary ring:

71

He knew that he himself should now be represented the partizan of France, as he had been formerly represented the partizan of America. He was no
stranger to the industry with which these and other
calumnies were circulated against him, and therefore
he was not surprised; but he really was surprised to
find that he could not walk the streets without hear-
ing whispers that he and some of his friends had been
engaged in improper correspondence with persons in
France. If there were any foundation for such a
charge, the source of the information could be mentioned. If it were true, it was capable of proof. If any
man believed this, he called upon him to state the reasons of his belief. If any man had proofs, he challenged him to produce them. But, to what was this
owing? The people had been told by their representatives in parliament that they were surrounded with
dangers, and had been shown none. They were, therefore, full of suspicion and prompt of belief. All this
had a material tendency to impede freedom of discussion, for men would speak with reserve, or not speak
at all, under the terror of calumny. But he found by a
letter in a newspaper, from Mr. Law, that he lived in
a town where a set of men associated, and calling
themselves gentlemen . . . not only received anonymous letters reflecting on individuals, but corre-
sponded with the writers of such letters, and even
sometimes transmitted their slanders to the secretary
of state. He could not be much surprised at any asper-
sion on his character, knowing this; and therefore he
hoped the House would give him the credit of being
innocent till an open charge was made; and that if
any man heard improper correspondence imputed to
him in private, he would believe that he heard a false-

hood, which he who circulated it in secret durst not
utter in public.

In contrast to this position, Burke, the leader of another faction of the Whigs, finds the issue in the principles
of the French Revolution. He looks on the war as a contest between two moral principles, as

the cause of humanity itself. . . . I do not exclude
from amongst the just objects of such a confederacy
as the present, the ordinary securities which nations
must take against their mutual ambition, let their internal constitutions be of what nature they will. But
the present evil of our time, though in a great measure an evil of ambition, is not one of common political ambition, but in many respects entirely different.
It is not the cause of nation as against nation; but, as
you will observe, the cause of mankind against those
who have projected the subversion of that order of
things, under which our part of the world has so long
flourished, and indeed, been in a progressive state of
improvement; the limits of which, if it had not been
thus rudely stopped, it would not have been easy for
the imagination to fix. If I conceive rightly of the
spirit of the present combination, it is not at war with
France, but with Jacobinism. They cannot think it
right, that a second kingdom should be struck out of
the system of Europe, either by destroying its independence, or by suffering it to have such a *form* in its
independence, as to keep it, as a perpetual fund of revolutions, in the very centre of Europe, in that region
which alone touches almost every other, and must influence, even where she does not come in contact. As
long as Jacobinism subsists there, in any form, or un-

der any modification, it is not, in my opinion, the gaining a fortified place or two, more or less, or the annexing to the dominion of the allied powers this or that territorial district, that can save Europe, or any of its members. We are at war with a *principle,* and with an example, which there is no shutting out by fortresses, or excluding by territorial limits. No lines of demarcation can bound the Jacobin empire. It must be extirpated in the place of its origin, or it will not be confined to that place. In the whole circle of military arrangements and of political expedients, I fear that there cannot be found any sort of *merely defensive plan* of the least force, against the effect of the *example* which has been given in France. That *example* has shown, for the first time in the history of the world, that it is very possible to subvert the whole frame and order of the best constructed states, by corrupting the common people with the spoil of the superior classes. It is by that instrument that the French orators have accomplished their purpose, to the ruin of France; and it is by that instrument that, if they can establish themselves in France (however broken or curtailed by themselves or others) , sooner or later, they will subvert every government in Europe. The effect of *erroneous doctrines* may be soon done away; but the example of *successful pillage* is of a nature more permanent, more applicable to use, and a thing which speaks more forcibly to the interests and passions of the corrupt and unthinking part of mankind, than a thousand theories. Nothing can weaken the lesson contained in that example, but to make as strong an example on the other side. The leaders in France must be made to feel, in order that all the rest there, and in other countries, may be made to see that such spoil is no sure possession.

When the war against France had been in progress for seven years, a supporter of Fox asked Pitt, the Prime Minister and leader of the Tories in the House of Commons, what the war was all about. Was Jacobinism not dead, and was Napoleon not indifferent to the principles of the French Revolution? What, then, was Britain fighting for? Here is Pitt's reply, representing the third answer which can be given to our question.

> The hon. gentleman defies me to state, in one sentence, what is the object of the war. In one word, I tell him that it is security;—security against a danger, the greatest that ever threatened the world—security against a danger which never existed in any past period of society. This country alone, of all the nations of Europe, presented barriers the best fitted to resist its progress. We alone recognized the necessity of open war, as well with the principles, as the practice of the French revolution. We saw that it was to be resisted no less by arms abroad, than by precaution at home; that we were to look for protection no less to the courage of our forces than to the wisdom of our councils; no less to military effort than to legislative enactment. At the moment when those, who now admit the dangers of Jacobinism while they contend that it is extinct, used to palliate this atrocity, this House wisely saw that it was necessary to erect a double safeguard against a danger that wrought no less by undisguised hostility than by secret machination.

2. *The American Choice*

The United States has taken all these three positions toward the Soviet Union, either simultaneously or successively. From 1917 to the entrance of the Soviet Union into the Second World War in 1941, the United States looked at the Soviet Union primarily with the eyes of Burke. It saw in it and its adherents in foreign countries a threat to the established moral and social order of the West. What the United States feared and opposed during that period of history was the Soviet Union, the instigator and master-mind of world revolution, not Russia, the great power; for as a great power Russia did not exist during that period, and its potentialities as a great power were hardly recognized by the United States.

From June 1941 to the breakdown of the Yalta and Potsdam agreements in 1946, the Soviet Union appeared to the United States as revolutionary France had appeared to Fox. The Soviet Union was considered to be no threat to the United States either as the fountainhead of world revolution or as a great imperialistic power. There was a widespread tendency to look upon the Soviet leaders as democrats at heart, somewhat ill-mannered democrats, to be sure, but democrats nevertheless, whom circumstances had thus far prevented from living up to their democratic convictions and with whom, therefore, it was possible "to get along." The Soviet Union was supposed to have lost its revolutionary fervor, and as a great power it was believed to possess enough territory to keep it satisfied, and in any case to be so weakened by the devastations of war as to be unable to embark upon imperialistic ventures even if it wanted to.

Since the breakdown of the war and postwar agreements with the Soviet Union, public opinion in the United States has gone to the other extreme and reverted to the pattern established in the years following 1917. To American public opinion the conflict between the United States and the Soviet Union appears first of all as a struggle between two systems of political morality, two political philosophies, two ways of life. Good and evil are linked in mortal combat, and the struggle can only end, as it is bound to end, with the complete victory of the forces of good over the forces of evil. The policies of the Administration, after creating and supporting this popular conception of the nature of the conflict with the Soviet Union, have sporadically and sometimes half-heartedly endeavored to counteract these popular tendencies. More particularly, some of the speeches of Mr. Acheson have emphasized the primary concern with Russian imperialism, of which Communist world revolution is a mere instrument. His speeches before the National Press Club on January 12, 1950,[1] and at Freedom House on October 8, 1950,[2] suggest the attitude of Pitt rather than of Fox or Burke.

A simple test will show which of these three conceptions of the East-West conflict are mistaken and which is correct. Let us suppose for a moment that Lenin and Trotsky had died in exile, the unknown members of a Marxist sect, and that the Czar were still reigning over a Russia politically and technologically situated as it is today. Does anybody believe that it would be a matter of indifference for the United States to see the Russian armies hardly mo: e than a hundred miles from the Rhine, in the Balkans, with Russian influence holding sway over China and threatening to engulf the rest of Asia? Is anybody bold enough to assert that it would make all the difference in the world for the United States if Russian imperialism marched forward as it did in the eighteenth and nineteenth centuries, under the ideological banner and with the support of Christianity rather than of Bolshevism?

One can turn that same question around and ask whether anybody in the United States would need to be concerned about the American Communist Party if it were not a tool in the hands of the Kremlin and, hence, the vanguard of Russian imperialism. If the American Communist

---

[1] See Appendix III.   [2] See Appendix IV.

Party were an independent revolutionary organization, such as the anarchists were at one time and the Trotskyites are now, one could dismiss them as a coterie of crackpots and misfits, not to be taken seriously. It is the power of Russia that gives the American Communists an importance they would not have otherwise, and their importance is that of treason, not of revolution. If American Communism disappeared tomorrow without a trace, Russian imperialism would be deprived of one of its minor weapons in the struggle with the United States, but the issue facing the United States would not have been altered in the least.

FOUR SOURCES OF CONFUSION

The confusion between the issue of Russian imperialism and that of Communism feeds on four sources. First, the public at large tends to view politics, domestic and international, in the simple contrast of black and white, defined in moral terms. Thus the public is always prone to transform an election contest or an international conflict into a moral crusade carried on in the name of virtue by one's own party or one's own nation against the other party or the other nation, which stands for all that is evil in the world. Secondly, this genuine and typical confusion is aggravated by Russian propaganda, which justifies and rationalizes its imperialistic moves and objectives in the universal terms of Marxist dogma. The Western counter-crusade, taking the revolutionary stereotypes of Russian propaganda at their face value, thus becomes a mere counterpoise of that propaganda, its victim, unwittingly taking for the real issue what is but a tactical instrument of imperialistic policies.

The understanding of the real issue between the United

States and the Soviet Union is still further obscured by the ambiguity of the terms "Communism" and "Communist Revolution" themselves. If those who proclaim Communism as the real issue have primarily Europe in mind, they have at least a part of the truth; for in no country of Europe outside the Soviet Union has Communism succeeded in taking over the government except as a by-product of conquest by the Red Army and as an instrument for perpetuating Russian power. What has been true in the past in eastern and central Europe is likely to be true for the future in all of the Western world. If the Soviet Union pursues the goal of world revolution, it can attain that goal only by conquering the Western world first and making it Communistic afterwards. In other words, Communist revolution can come to the Western world only in the aftermath of the victory of the Red Army. In the West, then, the opposition to Communism is an integral part of resistance to Russian imperialism, and to oppose Russian imperialism is tantamount to opposing Communist revolution as well.

If those who refer to Communism as the real issue have primarily the revolutions in Asia in mind, they speak of something fundamentally different. While the Communist revolution could not have succeeded and will not succeed in any European country without the intervention of the Red Army, the revolutionary situation in Asia has developed independently of Russian Communism, and would exist in some form, owing to the triumph of Western moral ideas and the decline of Western power, even if Bolshevism had never been heard of. The revolutions in Europe are phony revolutions, the revolutions in Asia are genuine ones. While opposition to revolution in Europe is a particular aspect of the defense of the West against Russian imperialism, opposition to revolution in Asia is counter-revolution in Metternich's sense, resistance to change on behalf of an obsolescent status quo, doomed to failure from the outset. The issue of revolution in Asia is fundamentally different from that in Europe; it is not to oppose revolution as a creature and instrument of Russian imperialism but to support its national and social objectives while at the same time and by that very support preventing it from becoming an instrument of Russian imperialism. The clamor for consistency in dealing with the different revolutions sailing under the flag of Communism is the result of that confusion which does not see that the real issue is Russian imperialism, and Communist revolution only in so far as it is an instrument of that imperialism.

Finally, this confusion is nourished—and here lies its greatest danger for the political well-being of the United States—by a widespread fear not of revolution but of change. The forces that in the interwar period erected the specter of Communist revolution into a symbol of all social reform and social change itself are at work again, unaware that intelligent social reform is the best insurance against social revolution. What these forces were afraid of in the interwar period was not a threat—actually non-existent—to the security of the United States emanating from the power of Russia, but a threat to the social status quo in the United States. That threat did not stem primarily from the Communist Party, nor did it arise from the imminence of Communist revolution, which in the United States has been at all times a virtually negligible contingency. In embarking upon a holy crusade to extirpate the evil of Bolshevism these forces embarked, as they do now, in actuality upon a campaign to outlaw morally and legally all popular movements favoring social reform and in that fashion to make the status quo impregnable to change. The symbol of the threat of a non-existent Communist revolution becomes a convenient cloak, as it was for German and Italian Fascism, behind which a confused and patriotic citizenry can be rallied to the defense of what seems to be the security of the United States, but what actually is the security of the status quo. The fact that such a movement, if it were ever able to determine the domestic and international policies of the United States, would jeopardize not only the security of the United States but also the domestic status quo, only adds the touch of tragic irony to the confusion of thought and action.

What makes the task of American foreign policy so difficult is not only the unprecedented magnitude of the three great revolutions of our age, culminating in the rise of the Soviet Union, but also the necessity for American foreign policy to deal with four fundamental factors that must be separated in thought while they are intertwined in action: Russian imperialism, revolution as an instrument of Russian imperialism, revolution as genuine popular aspiration, and the use of the international crisis for the purposes of domestic reaction.

Whenever we have fallen victim, not only in thought but also in action, to the oversimplification that reduces the variegated elements of the world conflict to the moral opposition of Bolshevism and democracy, our policy has been mistaken and has failed in its objectives, ideological and political. Whenever such oversimplification and confusion has counseled our actions, we have rendered ourselves powerless either to contain Russian imperialism or prevent the spread of Communism. Of such a dual disaster, born of the confusion as to what the real issue is, our China policy is the prime example.

THE PRECEDENT OF BRITISH POLICY
AFTER 1815

Hard as the task is of dealing adequately with the Soviet Union on the two levels of imperialism and revolution, similar tasks have faced great powers before and have been met with brilliant success. We have already mentioned the great achievement of William Pitt in understanding the nature of the relationship between the revolution of 1789 and French imperialism. When in the closing years of the Napoleonic Wars this achievement was about to bear fruit, another great British statesman, Lord Castlereagh, had occasion to show his understanding of the distinction and relationship between ideology and power politics. This time it was not France but Russia whose imperialism threatened the freedom of the nations of Europe, and it was not in the name of the ideas of the French Revolution, but in the name of Christianity and counter-revolution that Russian power threatened to engulf them. In 1815, as in 1945, the collapse of one imperialistic power called forth the rise of another. Then as now, victory was won over a common enemy by an alliance from which Russia emerged as the predominant power. Then as now, Russian imperialism established itself firmly in eastern Europe, using a device similar to that of the Yalta agreement in order to placate Western misgivings. Then as now, Russian power threatened to spread through central Europe and the Balkans, using the principles of Christianity and counter-revolutionary slogans to pave its way.

Yet while in the years after 1945 the reaction went from the utopian blindness of wishful thinking to the fanatical blindness of the crusading spirit, Castlereagh recognized the menace for what it was and counteracted it, even while the war against Napoleon was still in progress. And when the war was over, he steadfastly refused to be swayed either by the Russian invocation of the community of Christian principles or by the revolutionary appeal to the principles of liberalism. He never allowed his eyes to wander from the real issue: the threat of Russian imperialism using a counter-revolutionary ideology for its imperialistic purposes.

Castlereagh realized that, regardless of the affinity of political principles between Great Britain and Russia, Great Britain could not safely exchange the imperialism of Napoleon, claiming the heritage of the French Revolution, for the imperialism of Czar Alexander I, invoking the principles of Christianity. Thus when the power and ambitions of Russia became obvious, Great Britain turned around and opposed—continuing its opposition for almost a century—the imperialism of Russia with the same steadfastness and sober judgment with which it had opposed and defeated the imperialism of France.

Lord Salisbury, one of the great successors of Castlereagh in the guidance of British foreign policy, described in these words Castlereagh's great achievement.

> During the negotiations at Vienna, which followed the fall of Napoleon, Europe was beholden to Lord Castlereagh for the same quick judgment of character, and the same happy boldness in trusting to it. From the moment that Alexander crossed the Vistula, he had conceived the project of repaying Russia for all the efforts she was making, and all the sufferings she had undergone, by annexing the whole of Poland to his empire. Prussia he proposed to indemnify by confiscating Saxony for her benefit; and Austria, he thought, might be left to make good her own losses on the side of Italy. Such a scheme was clearly incompatible with the security of Europe. Lord Castlereagh was not wholly engrossed by the dangers and

83

the policy of the present. He saw that, in the future, the cloud of war was quite as likely to rise on the side of Russia as of France. He was utterly disinclined, therefore, to thrust Austria into her very jaws—Austria who was England's ancient and true ally, and bound to her by the only bond of union that endures, the absence of all clashing interests. But Alexander insisted. He wished to make it a preliminary to all negotiation. When the Congress assembled at Vienna, and the map of Europe lay upon the table, he laid his hand upon Poland, with the words, *C'est à moi!* He had 200,000 men in Poland, and the allies might come and turn them out if they could. His throne, he added, would not be safe, if, after all his sacrifices, he came back to Russia empty handed. It was evident that his heart was set upon the acquisition, and that if he yielded at all it would only be to force. As one of his generals observed, "Avec 600,000 hommes on ne négocie pas beaucoup." With Napoleon still at Elba, and Europe still bleeding from the wounds of twenty years of war, a more timid man than Lord Castlereagh might have hesitated before breaking up an alliance which had done such splendid deeds, and plunging upon the mere calculations of a far-sighted policy into a fresh struggle almost as formidable as that which he had just concluded. But he seems to have been thoroughly impressed with the truth, that a willingness on good cause to go to war is the best possible security for peace. . . . He did not hesitate to form a new coalition against the new enemy. By engagements which subsequently took the form of a more general treaty between England, France, and Austria, it was agreed that the demands of Russia and Prussia upon Saxony and Poland should be resisted, if necessary, by force; and the proportions in which the Allies were to contribute to the conduct of the new war were laid down. The Emperor of Russia received secret information of the preparations that were being made, and came to the conclusion that his finances were in too desperate a condition to risk the chances of another war.

It is not, however, by one or two isolated successes that Lord Castlereagh's foreign policy ought to be tried. It is best judged by its general results. During the war his aim was to overthrow Napoleon, and to reduce France within her ancient limits. After the war his aim was to uphold the balance of power, and so to secure lasting peace to Europe. When the direction of England's foreign policy passed from his hands, both objects had been attained. Not only was Napoleon overthrown, but for one generation at least the warlike passions Napoleon had evoked were stilled, and all the changes that Napoleon's genius had achieved were effaced. For forty years the peace of Europe flourished undisturbed by one single conflict between any of the five great Powers who adjusted their differences at Vienna. There have been revolutionary disturbances in sufficient abundance; and order has been frequently restored by foreign intervention upon one side or the other. But as far as international relations are concerned, there has been no rupture in Europe important enough to have been dignified by historians with the name of war. Europe has not enjoyed so long a repose from the curse of war since the fall of the Roman empire. Such an achievement is an ample justification of the acts of the Congress of Vienna and of the minister who bore so large a part in shaping its decrees.

The lesson that Castlereagh's understanding and policies carry for our day is not exhausted, however, by the sober and calculating application of the principles of the balance of power in his dealings with France and Russia. We can learn from him also the consistent refusal to be swayed by ideological preferences or animosities into embracing policies which can contribute nothing to the national interest of one's country. Thus he resisted the clamor of British public opinion to lend support to the liberal revolutions of the continent no less than he refused to be tempted by the Russian invocation of Christian principles to co-operate in suppressing them. Revolutions that adversely affected the national interest of Great Britain were to be opposed. There was neither the need to oppose all revolutions indiscriminately nor the power of doing so successfully. In the following episode reported by Sir Charles K. Webster, the historian of Castlereagh's foreign policy, Castlereagh's thinking in terms of power rather than of ideological considerations is strikingly revealed.

On October 1st [1820] the Neapolitan Government sent to the Austrian Government a protest against their equivocal attitude. Castlereagh told Lieven [Russian ambassador in London] that it was skilfully constructed, and drew once more the conclusion that the case was not one in which Britain could act. Pitt, he said had only been able to combat Jacobinism by proving it aggressive, and there was no such symptom in the Neapolitan revolution. "The system of the Emperor," he said about the same time, "did him honour as a monarch and as a man. Nothing could be more pure than the ends which he had set before himself in all his actions; but this system aims at a perfection, which we do not believe applicable to this century or to mankind. We cannot follow him along this path. It is a vain hope, a beautiful phantom, which England above all can not pursue. All speculative policy is outside her powers. It is proposed now to overcome the *revolution;* but so long as this revolution does not appear in more distinct shape, so long as this general principle is only translated into events like those of Spain, Naples and Portugal—which, strictly speaking, are only reforms, or at the most domestic upsets, and do not attack materially any other State— England is not ready to combat it. Upon any other question purely political, she would always deliberate and act in the same way as all the other Cabinets." . . . At the same time Castlereagh sent off one final warning to his brother, which was more uncompromising than anything which he had yet written. "It is not possible for the British Government, as I very early apprised you," he wrote, "to take the field in fruitlessly denouncing by a sweeping joint declaration the revolutionary dangers of the present day, to the existence of which they are, nevertheless, sufficiently alive. Nor can they venture to embody themselves *en corps* with the non-representative Governments in what would seem to constitute a scheme of systematic interference in the internal affairs of other States; besides, they do not regard mere declarations as of any real or solid value independent of some practical measure actually resolved upon; and what that measure is which can be generally and universally adopted against bad principles overturning feeble and ill-administered governments, they have never yet been able to divine.". . .

The lessons for the foreign policy of the United States ought to be clear. We are faced with four different dangers that threaten both our international security and our democratic institutions: treason and subversion, world conquest, world revolution, panic and oppression at home. Against treason and subversion allied with a foreign conqueror we must resort, in the words of Pitt, to "precaution at home" and to "legislative enactment," commensurate with the danger to be averted and the interests to be protected. For protection from the lust for power of the foreign conqueror we must look "no less to the courage of our forces than to the wisdom of our counsels." We must be strong enough to resist aggression and wise enough to accommodate foreign interests which do not impinge upon our own. Revolution which is but the spearhead and product of foreign imperialism must be dealt with as imperialism, that is, by military force. Against genuine revolution only the health of our, and our allies', social institutions can insure us.

The greatest danger that threatens us in the immediate future, aside from the military preponderance of the Soviet Union on land, is the confusion of the two great issues of our time: Russian imperialism and genuine revolution. American foreign policy ought not to have the objective of bringing the blessings of some social and political system to all the world or of protecting all the world from the evils of some other system. Its purpose—and its sole purpose—ought to be, as was England's under Pitt, the security of the nation; "security against the greatest danger that ever threatened the world." If we allow ourselves to be diverted from this objective of safeguarding our national security, and if instead we conceive of the American mission in some abstract, universal, and emotional terms, we may well be induced, against our better knowledge and intent, yet by the very logic of the task in hand, to raise the banner of universal counter-revolution abroad and of conformity in thought and action at home. In that manner we shall jeopardize our external security, promote the world revolution we are trying to suppress, and at home make ourselves distinguishable perhaps in degree, but not in kind, from those with which we are locked in ideological combat.

In these three respects, the debacle of our China policy and its consequences should be a warning. The balance of power in the Far East, which we tried to maintain, has been destroyed. The Communist revolution we tried to prevent has been successful. And as a result of these failures abroad, we hunt at home as spies and traitors innocent dissenters whom we can hold responsible for those failures, as though their roots were to be looked for anywhere but in the confusion of our own thoughts and actions. We thus silence thinking and informed counsel or force it into the mold of conformity. And if we confound the issue of world revolution with that of Russian imperialism, we disarm ourselves for intelligent thought and successful action. We ignore the real and immediate enemy or, at best, do not take him seriously enough, while we are fighting an imaginary and remote one. The weapons with which we are fighting may be useful on one level of action; they are blunt instruments of warfare on the other. Yet since we are not sure what we are fighting, we are unable to choose our weapons wisely. Thus we fight everywhere, here imperialism, there revolution, there again both at the same time. But we fight nowhere decisively, or with a clear and concrete understanding of what it is we are fighting, or of the manner in which we must fight it.

The search for a clear understanding of the real issue between the United States and the Soviet Union, then, is not a mere academic pastime. Misunderstanding and confusion over the real issue results in much that is ambiguous, fallacious, indecisive, and unsuccessful in American foreign policy; intellectual clarity in the matter is the inescapable precondition for success. It is true that intellectual clarity is not all. It makes political success possible, but does not assure it. To a clear understanding of the issues at stake must be joined the correct judgment of means and ends in terms of the power necessary and available, and the will to do what must be done.

IV

The Four Intellectual Errors
of American Postwar Policy

The United States was slow to recognize that its victory
in the Second World War, eliminating one threat to its security, opened the door for a new threat more dangerous
than the one against which the Second World War had
been fought. Now the United States, no longer in doubt
that it is threatened by something, still is not able to understand clearly what it is that threatens. Is it Russian imperialism? Is it world revolution? Or is it both at the same
time? And if the latter is the case, what is the relation between them? Since the answers to these questions are hesitant, ambiguous, and contradictory, so is the United States
in the choice of the ends and means of its foreign policy
uncertain, impractical, and inconsistent. We have already
pointed to the enormous demand upon understanding and
action which the great revolutionary changes of our time
would make of the foreign policy of any nation, however
well prepared and qualified. The main handicaps that
American foreign policy must overcome, however, are not
to be found in the challenges confronting it from the
outside. They lie in certain deeply ingrained habits of
thought, and pre-conceptions as to the nature of foreign
policy.

Most of the shortcomings of American foreign policy must be attributed not to the weakness of this or that man or this or that party, but to certain intellectual errors in which all men and all parties share to a greater or lesser degree. Four such intellectual errors stand out: utopianism, legalism, sentimentalism, neo-isolationism. While more often than not they are intertwined in practice, they must be discussed separately for purposes of understanding.

1. *Utopianism*

AFTER WAR—THE MILLENNIUM

Foreign policy, like all politics, is in its essence a struggle for power, waged by sovereign nations for national advantage. In this struggle there may be victory or defeat and, in between, longer or shorter stages of apparent inactivity and quiet. By its very nature this struggle is never ended, for the lust for power, and the fear of it, is never stilled. Thus the challenger of today may well be challenged tomorrow, and the challenge met tomorrow may well be followed by a new one the day after. The best a nation longing for tranquillity and peace can expect is to be passed by for a time by the stream of events; but it must ever be ready to man the ramparts for defense or attack. In the life of nations peace is only respite from trouble—or the permanent peace of extinction.

These stark and simple facts of the real political world have been replaced in the American mind by the picture of a political world that never existed, but whose reality, for reasons discussed before, appears only too plausible. In that fictitious world the struggle for power is not a continuum, with each solved problem giving rise to a new one in a never ending succession. It is rather a kind of criminal disturbance, like a street brawl, disrupting a normalcy that knows only peaceful competition and co-operation. Consequently, the peace-loving nations have the triple task of restoring order in the street by disarming and punishing the culprit, the "war criminal"; of reforming and bringing him to reason; and of taking measures designed to "solve" the problem of street brawls once and for all, and thus make a repetition of the disturbance impossible. Once these three tasks are performed, the peace-loving nations can, as it were, forget about power politics, imperialism, armaments, and the like and direct their energies toward undertakings more pleasant and worthwhile.

The United States flatters itself that in its dealings with other countries it seeks no selfish advantage but is inspired by universal moral principles. It is difficult for the United States to understand that other nations, in opposing American policies, may pursue their national interests, as legitimate as those which the United States denies pursuing but actually pursues just the same. The logic of the utopian image it has formed of its own position among the nations compels the United States to see the policies of other nations in the same light of utopian moralism. Since American foreign policy is by definition selfless and moral, the foreign policies of nations opposing it are by definition selfish and immoral. Since the United States is the policeman of the world seeking only peace and order and the welfare of all, only evil nations can dare oppose it. They are criminals when they act alone, conspirators when they act in unison.

The conspirational interpretation of international politics is especially plausible in a bipolar political world; for here all opposition can be traced to the other center of power, the seat of the worldwide conspiracy. Such a picture of the political world is not only satisfying to moral pride. Its simplicity is also a boon to understanding. It saves us the trouble of probing into the complexities and ambiguities of any specific adversity and opposition. What happens anywhere in the world is all of one cloth: it is all the fault of the conspiracy of the Fascists, the Communists, the British, the Central Powers. And the cure is bound to be as simple as the disease.

Against the background of such a picture of the international world—but against no other—the political policies pursued by Wilson, Roosevelt, and Truman during the two World Wars make sense. What was responsible in 1917, as in 1941, for the disturbances on the international scene, for the risks, threats, and uncertainties facing the nations of the world? The autocracies of the Central Powers, the tyranny of the Axis Powers. If such is the challenge, the remedy, in short- and long-run terms, is clear. Crush the enemy; force him into unconditional surrender; re-educate him in the ways of democratic, peace-loving nations; and with democracy established everywhere, peace and good will among nations will be assured. The organization of all democratic, peace-loving nations in a League of Nations or a United Nations provides the finishing touch for the brave new world from which war and, in the words of Mr. Cordell Hull, power politics itself will have been banished. Such an organization will be able to nip in the bud any attempt at disturbing the new normalcy of peace and order.

For a conception of international affairs which denies that the struggle for power never ends and instead asserts that it consists of an unconnected number of "criminal disturbances," the job is done with the elimination of the specific disturbance at hand and with the reduction to impotence of the particular disturber. With the "police action" against the "criminal aggressor" successfully accomplished, the peace-loving nations can lay down their arms, disband their armies, and prepare for the enjoyment of the millennium, the coming of which had been but temporarily delayed. Thus in 1945, as in 1918, the United States brought its soldiers home, sold its military equipment as surplus, and thought that with the downfall of the Axis powers, the source of the specific trouble, the source of all trouble had disappeared.

It is within the logic of the same utopian approach to international politics to expect a specific remedy for any disturbance of international normalcy. With the application of the remedy the disturbance will disappear, and one can, as it were, forget about it. The Soviet Union has replaced Germany and Japan as the threat to international peace and order. The American monopoly of the atomic bomb and, after the disappearance of the monopoly, preventive atomic war, is the remedy that will meet and eliminate the Russian threat. The monopoly of the atomic bomb was supposed, in one form or another, to last forever and to subdue Russian ambitions, if not to force an unconditional surrender. Preventive atomic war is believed capable of knocking the Soviet Union out with one blow. The elimination of the disturbance emanating from the Soviet Union will put us in the position we enjoyed in 1918 and 1945, and with all disturbances removed we will have a clear road on which to travel toward another peaceful, orderly world.

THE UTOPIA OF THE POSTWAR SETTLEMENTS

The same illusory mode of thought which disarmed the United States militarily at the end of the two World Wars made it impotent politically. Since war was considered an isolated catastrophe, an "act of aggression" brought about by an evil nation, the political—like the military—purpose of fighting was consummated with victory and the downfall of the aggressor. And since all nations allied with the United States were by definition good and peace-loving ones, there was no need to take precautions against them beyond making sure that they fought the common enemy with all their might. Much has been made of the latter consideration in order to explain the concessions that the United States made to the Soviet Union at the wartime conferences of Teheran and Yalta. In any case, nothing in the memoirs of the participants indicates that the framers of American foreign policy saw the international struggle for power as a continuum. Nor did they seem to be aware that the downfall of one ambitious nation calls forth the ambitions of another, and that the business of war does not end with military victory but only with the establishment of a viable distribution of power, the groundwork for which must be laid while the war is still in progress. Least of all did it occur to the framers of American policy that the Soviet Union might be destined to succeed Germany and Japan as a threat to the balance of power in Europe and Asia, and hence to the security of the United States. In the eyes of the American leaders the Soviet Union was not only a peace-loving nation by virtue of its opposition to the Axis powers; it had also lost its revolutionary fervor and was not supposed to be in need of additional territory, controlling as it did a land mass stretching from the Baltic to the Pacific. It did not occur to the framers of American policy that the expansionism of a great power or the lack of it does not so much depend upon a temporary configuration brought about by hostile attack or the political manners and morals of a leader or a ruling group, but upon the objective interests, traditions, and opportunities that impose themselves as necessities upon all rational framers of policy.

The nature of this utopian, non-political approach is strikingly revealed in a remark that General Deane, the chief of the United States Military Mission in Moscow during the Second World War, makes in his memoirs about the conference at Teheran:

> Stalin appeared to know exactly what he wanted at the Conference. This was also true of Churchill, but not so of Roosevelt. This is not said as a reflection on our President, but his apparent indecision was probably the direct result of our obscure foreign policy. President Roosevelt was thinking of winning the war; the others were thinking of their relative positions when the war was won. Stalin wanted the Anglo-American forces in Western, not Southern Europe; Churchill thought our postwar position would be improved and British interests best served if the Anglo-Americans as well as the Russians participated in the occupation of the Balkans.

In other words, for Churchill and Stalin the Second World War was the instrument of a foreign policy whose objectives had existed before the outbreak of hostilities, and were bound to continue to exist when the war had come to an end. For Roosevelt, as has been pointed out in another context, the war was an end in itself, its purpose exhausted with total victory and unconditional surrender. Churchill and Stalin knew that they were fighting for the perennial interests of their respective countries, for which Pitt and Castlereagh, Peter the Great and Alexander I had fought. For Roosevelt, as for Wilson before him, the war was being fought for universal humanitarian ideals, this time formulated in the Four Freedoms and the Atlantic Charter, yet, as before, unrelated to the concrete distribution of power which the United States had a vital interest in creating and maintaining after the end of hostilities.

Another wartime episode illustrates perhaps even more

sharply the contrast between a utopian, non-political conception of foreign policy, as practiced by the United States, and the realistic approach its allies take to international problems. That episode concerns a conflict over war and postwar policy between Churchill and Cordell Hull. In 1944, Churchill and Stalin, on the suggestion of the former, concluded an agreement providing for the division of the Balkans into British and Russian spheres of influence. Russian influence was to be paramount in Bulgaria, Hungary, and Rumania; British influence in Greece; Yugoslavia was to be subject to the influence of both. When the news of this agreement reached Mr. Hull, he made full use of his principal diplomatic weapon, moral indignation, which sentiment was certainly not weakened by Mr. Churchill's pointed reminder that the United States occupied in the Western Hemisphere a position hardly distinguishable from a dominant position within a sphere of influence. It was this agreement between Great Britain and the Soviet Union which moved Mr. Hull to his condemnation (which we have quoted above), on principle, of the balance of power and spheres of influence.

The reason for this condemnation must again be looked for in the utopian approach to foreign policy, an approach of which Mr. Hull was the champion and Mr. Roosevelt the hesitant and not always reliable supporter. Great Britain and the Soviet Union, fighting as they did for national advantage in terms of power, sought to strengthen their postwar power positions while the fighting was still in progress, and hence the situation was fluid. The United States, on the other hand, had only one immediate aim: the defeat of the Axis powers. Hence, political considerations ought not to be mingled with military ones, let alone supersede them. In this view, political settlements concluded by the great powers during the war would have been tantamount to a betrayal of the lofty war aims of the

United States. "It is believed," said Mr. Hull in 1942 in a memorandum to Mr. Roosevelt,

> that it would be unfortunate if, at the present time, an ally of the American Government of such standing as Great Britain, which also has thus far refused to make any commitments of a territorial nature on the European continent, should begin bargaining with the Soviet Union or any other continental country with regard to frontiers. There is little doubt that if the principle is once admitted that agreements relating to frontiers may be entered into prior to the peace conference, the association of nations opposed to the Axis, which thus far has been based upon the common aim of defeating the enemy, may be weakened by the introduction among its members of mutual suspicion and by efforts of various members to intrigue in order to obtain commitments with regard to territory at the expense of other members.

THE UNITED NATIONS—A SUBSTITUTE FOR POWER POLITICS

The long-range argument against the mingling of military with political considerations or even the subordination of the former to the latter, which counted most with the framers of American policy, was the commitment of the United States to the establishment of a postwar world in which an international organization would provide for the security of its members, who in turn would not need to seek military and political advantage through territorial bargains. To quote again Mr. Hull:

> As for our postwar policies, we pointed out that these had been outlined in the Atlantic Charter which

represented the attitude also of Great Britain and the Soviet Union. . . .

I could sympathize fully with Stalin's desire to protect his western borders from future attack. But I felt that this security could best be obtained through a strong postwar peace organization. . . .

I felt that zones of influence could not but derogate from the over-all authority of the international security organization which I expected would come into being.

For the United States the new world organization in the form of the United Nations was a substitute for power politics; it was supposed to do away with the balance of power, spheres of influence, alliances, the very policies seeking national advantage and aggrandizement. In one word, the United Nations was an end in itself, the ultimate end of American foreign policy. By Great Britain, and more particularly, the Soviet Union, on the other hand, the United Nations has always been regarded and used as an instrument of national policies. The objectives of these national policies were unalterably fixed; the political and military methods through which to obtain them had been developed in a long tradition of statecraft and war. The United Nations provides an additional instrument for the pursuit of those policies, and is to be used in conjunction with the others, but not instead of them. For those nations, membership in an international organization such as the United Nations is a means to an end, the end of national policies, and not an end in itself, defined in the utopian terms of permanent peace and non-competitive, trustful co-operation among the great powers.

The United Nations did not put an end to power politics, as Mr. Hull expected on his return from the Moscow conference of 1943. On the contrary, it has become the forum where the nations of the world fight their battles for power neither with the weapons of war nor with those of traditional diplomacy, but through the legalistic manipulation of the procedures, especially those concerning voting, of the international organization. These legalistic battles have generally been ineffectual and inconclusive. Yet they have strengthened, by giving it a new field of apparently successful operation, another erroneous tendency in American thinking on foreign affairs: the legalistic approach to foreign policy.

2. *Legalism*

The legalistic approach, by its very nature, is concerned with isolated cases. The facts of life to be dealt with by the legal decision are artificially separated from the facts that precede, accompany, and follow them and are thus transformed into a "case" of which the law disposes "on its merits." Once a legal case has been decided or otherwise disposed of, the problem is solved, until a new legal case arises to be taken care of in similar fashion.

It is easy to see to what extent this legalistic approach to foreign policy is but a logical development from the utopian, non-political conception. The legalistic approach follows logically from the assumption that international politics is not a continuous struggle for power in which all great nations are of necessity involved. International politics is rather assumed to be an undertaking by peace-loving nations, if not indifferent to, certainly not greedy for power, for the purpose of making the world safe from the power-lust of aggressor nations. There is obviously but a short step from the juxtaposition of peace-loving and aggressor nations to that of law-abiding and criminal ones. For the peace-loving nations are necessarily those who defend the

101

existing legal order against violent change and the aggressor nations are those who are oblivious of their legal obligations. The conflict between the two groups, instead of
being seen in terms of relative power, is conceived in the
absolute terms of peace, law, and order vs. aggression,
crime, and anarchy. The United Nations, then, becomes
the forum before which the peace-loving, law-abiding nations summon the criminal aggressors. The former cite
chapter and verse of the Charter against the latter and
outvote them with monotonous majorities, and the latter,
with equal monotony, veto, whenever they can, the decisions of the majority.

THE UNITED NATIONS AS LEGAL FORUM

It is unnecessary to show that these legalistic exercises
have done nothing at all to bring closer to solution the
great political issues outstanding between the contenders
on the international scene. At best, they have left the political issues where they found them; at worst, they have
embittered international relations and thus made a peaceful settlement of the great political issues more difficult.
Something needs, however, to be said about the ability of
the United Nations to contribute substantially, in contrast
to its procedural contributions, to the peaceful settlement
of conflicts among great powers. We have already said that
the United Nations is not and never could have been a
substitute for power politics. We can now go one step farther and say that by its very structure and intent the
United Nations is unable to make a substantial contribution to the peaceful settlement of conflicts among the great
powers. On the contrary, its successful operation is predicated upon the absence of serious conflict among them.
For the intention of the Charter, a kind of limited world

government by the five permanent members of the Security Council—China, France, Great Britain, the Soviet Union, the United States—was capable of realization only if the wartime unity of purpose of the great powers continued in peacetime, a unity upon which the United Nations was to be built, but which it could not itself create. The Charter provisions concerning voting procedure, especially the veto, express in procedural terms the same need for a pre-existing unity among the great powers.

By the same token the United Nations is unable to impose through collective action a settlement upon a great power. For the imposition of such a settlement always implies at least the possibility of a war between the United Nations and the great power to be coerced. Faced with the risks and sacrifices of such a war, all nations will be guided in their decisions by what they regard as their national interests rather than by legal abstractions. For this reason collective coercion of a great power is inherently impossible, save in those rare cases when the national interests of all the nations concerned happen to require such collective action.

The functions that the United Nations could have performed for the peaceful settlement of conflicts among the great powers, then, are twofold. It could have provided for the peaceful settlement of secondary conflicts in which the vital interests of the great powers were not at stake and which they, therefore, might have been willing to refer for settlement to an international organization where one or the other of them might have been outvoted. In the settlement of disputes affecting the vital interests of the great powers, the possible contribution of the United Nations lies primarily in the field of procedure.

An international organization such as the United Nations provides opportunities for the development of new techniques of diplomacy which, if used properly, can contribute much to the mitigation and the peaceful settlement of international conflicts. Especially under the conditions of the cold war, when diplomatic relations between East and West are reduced to a bare minimum, the different agencies of the United Nations make it inevitable that the representatives of the contending camps remain in constant personal contact, a circumstance that can be used unobtrusively for political purposes. The use of the United Nations for the discreet settlement of the Berlin blockade is a case in point.

Secondly, in so far as national policies are channeled through the United Nations, they need the approval of whatever majority of members the Charter stipulates, in order to enable the United Nations to take action. National policies, then, must be presented in such a way as to gain the approval of other nations having different national interests and policies. This requirement will always lead to the ideological justification and rationalization of national policies in terms of supra-national ones. Yet it will sometimes also result in the blunting of the sharp edges of a national policy, its reformulation and adaptation in the light of the point of view of the most influential members whose support is needed. This influence of an international organization upon national policies is indeed a very subtle one, its strength depending primarily upon the distribution of power between the nation seeking support for its policies and the nations whose support is sought.

These influences are different both in quality and in importance from those generally supposed to exist between international organization and foreign policy. Yet they are no less real for being less tangible and less radical. They are, however, a far cry from the substitution of a United Nations policy for national policies and from the elimination of power politics itself by the United Nations.

Legalism

In actuality, the legalistic misuse of the United Nations through the interminable repetition of futile and embittering votes has well-nigh crowded out the limited possibilities the United Nations provides for the genuine conciliation and peaceful settlement of power conflicts. The legalistic approach to foreign policy has also impeded the understanding of the roots of that great power conflict which in the postwar era has become the paramount concern of all humanity. The origins of the conflict between the United States and the Soviet Union are generally— and correctly—traced back to the violations of the Yalta agreement of February 1945 by the Soviet Union. This agreement stipulated that in the countries of eastern and southeastern Europe, which were occupied by the Red Army, democratic governments should be established on the basis of free elections through which the popular will was to be ascertained. The ink was hardly dry on the signatures to this agreement when it was methodically violated by the Soviet Union with the obvious aim of establishing in all the countries concerned governments unquestionably subservient to Moscow. The shock these violations caused in the Western world, and particularly in the United States, and the wave of indignation they called forth were commensurate with the completeness of the surprise with which those acts of bad faith hit public opinion in the West.

Public opinion, especially in the United States, had been saturated with the utopian expectation that the wartime co-operation between the Western allies and the Soviet Union, subordinating all other considerations to the common goal of victory over the Axis, was ushering in a new era of international relations where great nations would forever co-operate for the common good of humanity without a thought of selfish advantage. Like a stroke of lightning out of a clear sky, the violations of the Yalta agreement by the Soviet Union dispelled these illusions. They brought public opinion from the heights of utopian expectation down to an earth where a nation that we thought to be peace-loving and law-abiding, as we were, revealed itself to be as bad as those we had just been fighting in unison. Our dream of peace on earth became the nightmare of Bolshevist power politics where the red devil took the place "Uncle Joe" once held. The whole shock of our surprise, all our resentment against the shatterer of our dreams, mingled with a sense of humiliation at having been duped, we released against the defiler of sacred obligations, the faithless ally and deceptive friend. He was responsible for power politics still being with us, he was the new international criminal against whom law, order, and the sanctity of treaties had to be defended, as we had defended them against Wilhelm II, Hitler, and Hirohito.

Of this state of mind, approaching the international scene with a lawyer's rather than a statesman's tools, Mr. Cordell Hull is again the prime example, as he is its most revealing witness. The tendencies of the Soviet Union toward selfish national policies culminating in the wholesale violation of the Yalta agreement appeared, as was to be expected, at the very moment when victory over the Axis seemed to be assured.

"As Autumn, 1944, approached," reports Mr. Hull in his *Memoirs,*

> my associates and I began to wonder whether Marshal Stalin and his Government were commencing to veer away from the policy of cooperation to which they had agreed at the Moscow Conference, and which, with a few exceptions, they had followed since then. We were beginning to get indications that the Russians were

about to drive hard bargains in their armistice agreements with Hungary, Bulgaria, and Rumania, which
would give them something in the nature of control
over those countries. . . . Accordingly I cabled Ambassador Harriman in Moscow on September 18. . . .
I added that I had begun to wonder whether Stalin
and the Kremlin had determined to reverse their policy decided upon at Moscow and Teheran and to pursue a contrary course. I therefore asked Harriman's
estimate of the present trend of Soviet policy so that
we might decide how to meet this possible change in
Russian attitude.

I stated to Harriman that I should find particularly
helpful his views as to the causes that had brought
about this change in Soviet policy toward the United
States and hardening of attitude toward Great Britain. . . . Harriman replied the following day giving
a number of instances of Russia's unilateral actions
or apparent unwillingness to collaborate with Britain
and the United States. He said we had sufficient evidence to foresee that, if a world organization were
established requiring agreement of all permanent
members for the consideration of any dispute, regardless of whether or not one of them was involved, the
Soviet Government would ruthlessly block consideration by the Council of any question that it considered
affected its interests. The Soviet Government would
also insist that such a matter be settled by the Soviet
Union with the other country or countries involved,
particularly any disputes with her neighbors.

Harriman stated his conviction that Stalin and his
principal advisers placed the highest importance on
the association of the Soviet Union in a major way
with the three great Powers, but that they expected
their political and military strength would enable

them to dictate the conditions . . . there were powerful elements close to Stalin who were unwilling to give up the right of independent action where Russia's interests were affected or to see Russia depend for her security solely on an untried world organization with associates whom they did not fully trust. Stalin, he thought, liked to have two strings to his bow, and it did not appear inconsistent to the Marshal to pursue simultaneously these two methods to obtain security for his country and to promote its national interests as he envisaged them. . . . He said it was difficult to put one's finger on the causes for the change in the Soviet attitude toward the United States and Great Britain. He thought, however, that when the Russians saw victory in sight they began to put into practice the policies they intended to follow in peace.

This last sentence in Mr. Harriman's reply is indeed the decisive one. It not only explains the source of Russian conduct before and after Yalta, but also sheds an indirect, yet illuminating light upon the policy the United States might have pursued toward the Soviet Union before the conclusion of the Yalta agreement, upon the lack of realism of the Yalta agreement itself, and upon the error of the legalistic preoccupation with the violations of the latter.

When the Russians in the autumn of 1944 "began to put into practice the policies they intended to follow in peace," they set themselves two objectives: the domination of eastern Europe, and the advance of Russian might as far as possible into central and southeastern Europe. Both these objectives expressed the traditional national interest of Russia in Europe as clearly as opposition to both of them was required by the traditional American national interest in the maintenance of the European balance of power. As far as eastern and southeastern Europe were concerned, the time to oppose Russian objectives was before 1944, that is, before these regions were conquered by the Red Army. The Western powers were then in a political and military position which would have permitted them to conclude with the Soviet Union agreements that, because of the power relations then existing and to be prepared in the future, would at least have had a chance to last. At the time of the Yalta agreement the Western powers were faced with an accomplished military fact: the conquest of eastern and southeastern Europe by the Red Army. The stipulations of the Yalta agreement concerning democratic governments for the nations of those regions of Europe were a feeble attempt, doomed to failure from the outset, to redress the balance of power which military conquest had decisively inclined toward the Soviet Union. To invoke against the stark fact of Russian military domination the abstract principle of co-operation and the ideal of universal democracy was as noble in motivation as it was futile as a political act. There are only two answers to military power: the threat of stronger military power or the assurance of a political advantage that will outweigh the military one. In concrete terms, one could force the Red Army to retreat or one could persuade it to retreat. In the absence of either possibility, it was from the outset a forlorn hope to use multi-party governments as an entering wedge through which to exert a measure of that Western influence which Russian military conquest had eliminated from eastern and southeastern Europe. When the Soviet Union disregarded the stipulations of the Yalta agreement, it used the power that the fortunes of war and the policies of the Western allies had given it, and to counter which the Western powers had nothing but the legalistic invocation of the sanctity of treaties.

The damage to the interests of the West was done before Yalta. It was done when the framers of American political and military policies decided the military strategy of the war in terms of military efficiency only, without giving adequate consideration to the political settlement that would grow from the distribution of military power at the end of the war. The decision to invade the continent through western Europe rather than through the Balkans; the decision taken at the Teheran conference that the line of demarcation at the end of hostilities should roughly follow the lines of battle, with virtually all later deviations favoring the Russians; the decisions of the Western commanders with respect to military occupation, giving the Russians a maximum of advantage; a mode of thought, underlying all these positions, to which long-range considerations of power politics were both genuinely distasteful and alien— such was the stuff of political abnegation which the Yalta agreement did not create, but upon which it put the stamp of legal ratification.

It can, of course, be argued that the military decisions taken during the war and at the moment of its termination were the result of inescapable military necessity. If this were so, then the leaders of the United States were confronted with a dilemma between military necessity and political expediency. The political liabilities of the Yalta agreement, then, were the price we had to pay for winning the war. Yet whatever interpretations one puts on the surrender of eastern Europe and most of the Balkans to the Soviet Union, whether or not one considers it justified by military necessity, and hence unavoidable, there can be no doubt that at the time of the Yalta conference it was not possible either to force or to persuade the Red Army to retreat. Nor is it open to doubt that the stipulations of the Yalta agreement concerning free elections and democratic governments were a mere illusion if they were supposed to have any reference to the sharing of control over the countries concerned.

Legalism

The legalistic insistence upon compliance with these stipulations and the moral indignation at their violation by the Soviet Union are as misplaced as they are psychologically revealing. They are misplaced; for the real issue of control over eastern and southeastern Europe was already settled when the issue of the Yalta stipulations and their violations arose. The insistence upon fulfillment and the indignation at non-compliance were directed at the mere legal symbols of long-accomplished facts. We were beating, and we have been beating ever since, the thermometer that registers a temperature too cold for our comfort, but it was ourselves who failed to put the heat on when there was still time to do so.

We know this, or we are at least vaguely suspicious of our responsibility in the matter. Yet we are unwilling to draw the logical conclusion from what we know or suspect. For to do so would imply renouncing the utopian approach to foreign policy and starting to think about foreign policy in terms of power rather than of moral abstractions. And it is not easy, nor is it pleasant, to change deeply ingrained habits of mind and modes of thought in the light of adverse experience. Thus we must persist in our intellectual errors and try to reconcile them with our political failures. This is easier and less wounding to pride than to attribute our failures to our errors, confess our intellectual errors with our political sins, to mend our ways in thought and action.

In meeting this psychological need the legalistic insistence upon the letter of the Yalta agreement performs a useful function. No other event in the recent history of Russo-American relations has had so lasting and profound an effect upon the American mind as the violations of the Yalta agreement by the Soviet Union. These violations have become the symbol both of Russian perfidy and of American gullibility and humiliation. As such they have influenced in an important, if not decisive, fashion American policy toward the Soviet Union ever since. Yet this simple juxtaposition reflects but incompletely and with distortion the political significances of that turning-point in the relations between the United States and the Soviet Union.

The violations of the Yalta agreement by the Soviet Union showed beyond the shadow of a doubt, as the policies of Wilhelm II, of Hitler, and of Hirohito had shown before, that the millennium of a world free from power politics and animated with the spirit of selfless co-operation had not yet come. Moreover, these violations demonstrated with a poignancy wounding to pride that in politics moral right and legal title are as nothing in the face of superior power. The American people had been cheated again of the fruits of victory, defined in terms of a utopian ideal; they were impotent onlookers at its defilement. From this experience, we drew two conclusions, of which only one is sound.

We came finally to realize—in theory, it is true, rather than in practice—that in international affairs power is as indispensable to the righteous as it is to the wicked. And we resolved to put that power at the service of the ideals we thought we had always held. It was less painful and more rewarding in terms of those ideals to put the blame for the disappointment we had just sustained, and the humiliation it involved, on some easily identifiable source that could be exorcised morally and held to account legally than to search in our own processes of thought and action for the root of such recurrent failures. While we rearmed, however hesitatingly and belatedly, we never tired of pointing to the violations of the Yalta agreement as justification for what would otherwise appear to have been an unnecessary waste of effort and resources. Thus we gave moral dignity to our power, which we should never have allowed to degenerate in the first place, by making it appear a means

112

to the end of our utopian ideals. In this fashion we reconciled our involuntarily permanent involvement in power politics with the continuing possession of our utopian, nonpolitical ideals. With the legalistic insistence upon the violations of the Yalta agreement we could build a bridge between our utopian ideals and the bitter realities of power politics, without giving up the one or disregarding the other. We could move again, and with increased vigor, in a world we seemed to understand, and in which utopian expectations, power, and lawlessness had their assigned places.

3. *Sentimentalism*

Underlying the utopian as well as the legalistic thinking on foreign policy there is naturally the basic conviction, which we have encountered before, that national interests are not worthy objectives for a nation to pursue and that, on the contrary, only universal moral values can justify the means and ends of foreign policy. Gratitude, common dedication to liberty, manifest destiny, the Christian duty to civilize our Philippine brothers, support of democracy, good neighborliness, generosity—such are some of the moral principles and values that at one time or other have been invoked as the ultimate objectives and motivations of American foreign policy.

This sentimental invocation of moral principles is not identical with true morality; as we have tried to show, it serves neither the purposes of morality nor those of politics. What distinguishes this sentimental approach to foreign policy from the common and well-nigh inevitable ideological justification of political action, domestic and international, is the fact that we are here not in the presence of a mere ideology, superimposed upon the actual motives and objectives of political action, which, unaffected by it, follows its own pragmatic course. The American people have not used their moral principles as mere ideologies, that is, for the exclusive purpose of deceiving themselves and others. They have taken them seriously, devoted themselves to them, and in not a few instances have been ready to shed their blood, to spend their treasure, to jeopardize the very existence of the country, in order to make those moral principles prevail on the international scene. In one word, they have allowed them, nay, required them to influence political action itself.

Time and again in the history of American foreign policy, and in our time with increasing frequency and ever more serious consequences for the national interest of the United States, ends and means of policy have been chosen, and the national interest itself has been defined, not in terms of the power available and necessary for the attainment of a certain end, itself determined by its influence on American power, but in terms of universal moral principles bearing on the well-being of all mankind. Thus political action has been bent to conform to moral abstractions, political requirements have been subordinated to moral ones, and in the process political success has been sacrificed without appreciable gain in universal morality. Whatever the intrinsic nobility of a sentimental approach to foreign policy may be, whatever emotional attraction it may hold for many, its failings as a guide to political action are to be found in this distortion of the political process and in the jeopardy into which it puts the objective, be it moral or political, for which the political action is being undertaken. Two examples will serve to illustrate the point: the Truman Doctrine and aid to foreign countries.

THE TRUMAN DOCTRINE

What has come to be known as the Truman Doctrine was formulated by President Truman on March 12, 1947, in his message to Congress. It bears the title "Recommendations on Greece and Turkey." The President recommended the appropriation of four hundred million dollars for assistance to Greece and Turkey and the authorization to send civilian and military personnel as well as commodities, supplies, and equipment to these two countries. The immediate occasion for these requests was the inability of Great Britain to continue to perform the historic function, which she had performed for almost a century and a half, of protecting the eastern shores of the Mediterranean from Russian penetration. Since the end of the Napoleonic Wars one of the basic assumptions of British foreign policy had been that Russian control of Greece and of the Dardanelles constituted a threat to the European balance of power. Great Britain was no longer able, for reasons pointed out before, to shoulder the over-all responsibility for the maintenance of the balance of power in Europe, and she had just notified the United States that she no longer possessed the military and economic resources to defend Greece against Communist attack.

The interest of the United States in the maintenance of the European balance of power had been historically identical with that of Great Britain, and by the beginning of 1947, the United States had already become—by the logic of the distribution of power, if not by design—the successor of Great Britain as the main counterweight against a threat to the independence of the nations of Europe. It was then almost inevitable that the United States take over the particular British burden for the protection of the independence of Greece and the territorial integrity of Turkey,

115

an action justified both by the traditional interest of the United States in the European balance of power and by the particular conditions prevailing in the eastern Mediterranean at the beginning of 1947.

Such were the concrete occasion and the concrete purpose that made the requests of President Truman's message of March 12, 1947, necessary. Yet that message justified American aid to Greece and Turkey not primarily in terms of the traditional American interest in the maintenance of the European balance of power, but in terms of a universal moral principle. This principle is derived from the assumption that the issue between the United States and the Soviet Union, from which arises the necessity of assisting Greece and Turkey, must be defined in terms of "alternative ways of life"; it is to be understood as a struggle between totalitarianism and democracy. In its positive application this principle proclaims the defense of free, democratic nations everywhere in the world against "direct or indirect aggression," against "subjugation by armed minorities or by outside pressure." In its negative application it postulates the containment of the Soviet Union everywhere in the world. Thus the Truman Doctrine transformed a concrete interest of the United States in a geographically defined part of the world into a moral principle of worldwide validity, to be applied regardless of the limits of American interest and of American power. Upon what in its immediate import was a limited request for a limited purpose, the Truman Doctrine erected a message of salvation to all the world, unlimited in purpose, unlimited in commitments, and limited in its scope only by the needs of those who would benefit.

The Truman Doctrine starts with a sound realization of what the American national interest is in certain parts of the world, and it proposes policies well calculated to protect and promote those interests. Underlying it there is the sound realization that it is in the American interest to protect certain strategic key regions against direct or indirect aggression by the Soviet Union. In other words, it assumes correctly that for the sake of American security the power of the Soviet Union must at certain points be contained. In terms of policy, it understands that under certain conditions the military and economic support of the existing governments, preferably democratic ones, will best serve the purpose of containing the Soviet Union. In so far as the Truman Doctrine defines the objectives and method of American policy with respect to the concrete conditions prevailing in Greece and Turkey, it is sound doctrine upon which, as the results have shown, a successful foreign policy can be built. In so far as the Truman Doctrine defines its objectives and methods in terms of a world-embracing moral principle, it vitiates its consideration of the national interest and compels a foreign policy derived from it, as the results have shown, to be half-hearted and contradictory in operation and threatened with failure at every turn. As a guide to political action, it is the victim, as all moral principles must be, of two congenital political weaknesses: the inability to distinguish between what is desirable and what is possible, and the inability to distinguish between what is desirable and what is essential.

A foreign policy, to be successful, must be commensurate with the power available to carry it out. The number of good deeds a nation, like an individual, desires to do is infinite; yet the power at the disposal of a nation, as of an individual, to carry them through is finite. It is this contrast between what a nation wants to do and what it is capable of doing, this excess of the desirable objectives of its foreign policy over its power, which compels all nations to limit their objectives in view of the relative scarcity of available power. Unable to spend their limited resources on every desirable objective in sight, nations must draw a sharp distinction between those possible objectives which, either in terms of the national interest or of a moral principle, are merely desirable, and those which are essential in view of the national interest. There are objectives which must be pursued at all costs, for their attainment is indispensable for the national existence and welfare. There are those which might be pursued under certain favorable circumstances. There are those which, however desirable in themselves, can never be pursued because they are beyond the reach of available strength.

To establish a hierarchical order, an order of priorities, among all possible objectives of a nation's foreign policy must be the first step in framing a rational foreign policy. The second step must of necessity be the allocation of the available resources to the objectives chosen, in view of their respective importance for the national interest. For the American statesman who weighs his actions in view of their probable influence on his nation's relative power, France's or Canada's freedom from foreign control is obviously of vastly greater importance for American foreign policy than Poland's or Korea's; however much he might desire an independent and strong China, he cannot be unaware of the strict limits set by the available resources, especially in view of other more important commitments, upon American foreign policy.

This differentiating and discriminating mode of thought, peculiar to the statesman, is naturally alien to the sentimental way of thinking. In the sentimentalist's mind all action is related to the absolute moral laws with which the action if it is right conforms and from which it deviates if it is wrong. In such a view, prudence, which is the adaptation of morality to circumstances, is not a virtue. The prime virtue of the sentimentalist is consistency in conforming to a moral principle, not differentiation of individual cases in view of their bearing upon the distribution of power. Before the moral law all objectives are equal. Since aggression is morally wrong, it can make no difference to the sentimentalist whether the aggression has been committed by Bolivia, Italy, North Korea, or China. Prudential considerations of interest and power must not be allowed to blemish the purity of moral abstractions. "Aggression is aggression," to quote the title of an editorial [1] in the *New York Times,* and that is all there is to it. If the protection and promotion of democracy everywhere in the world is the moral standard by which political action is to be judged, then Korea is as important as France, China is as worthy an objective as Canada, and there is no difference between Poland and Panama.

It is obvious that no statesman could pursue indiscriminately a policy of protecting democratic governments everywhere in the world without courting certain disaster. Commitments would necessarily outrun resources, and failure would ensue. The foreign policy of the United States has clearly, then, not lived up to the message of the Truman Doctrine. Yet it is quite possible to pursue such a sentimental policy, as it were, by fits and starts, taking up the cause of democracy here half-heartedly and with insufficient means, there with all-out military commitments, there again not at all, changing from one policy to the other according to the pressure of circumstances. And this is about what the United States has been doing. In Europe, as we have seen, the defense of democracy is indeed an intricate part of the defense against Russian imperialism. Here the requirements of the Truman Doctrine and of the national interest of the United States happen to coincide. The situation in Asia is fundamentally different, and it is here that the Truman Doctrine has caused great confusion in thought and action.

The China policy of the United States has been pri-

[1] *New York Times,* January 21, 1951, p. E8.

marily criticized in terms of, and partly influenced by, the sentimental objectives of the Truman Doctrine. Taking it at its face value, there is indeed no escaping the conclusion that the China policy of the Truman administration has thrown the moral principle of the Truman Doctrine overboard. To make matters worse, from the sentimental point of view, it has maintained that same principle in Europe. Thus the charge of inconsistency is irrefutable, as long as the argument proceeds within the framework of the Truman Doctrine.

The Truman administration is caught in the pitfalls of its own sentimental philosophy. This philosophy lends itself to the purposes of domestic propaganda as long as it is not put to the test of actual policy. Once that test is made, it becomes obvious that it is incapable of guiding a nation toward successful political action. The government has, then, only two alternatives. Either it will pursue a policy that is at variance with the moral objective and exposes itself to the reproach of inconsistency, if not of moral indifference or even of treason, or the government will act, however hesitatingly and half-heartedly, in accordance with the moral principle, regardless of resources and consequences, and the inevitable failure of such a policy will again be laid at its doorstep. Of this latter alternative, the China policy of the Truman administration has provided a sample.

It is one of the historic achievements of Mr. Acheson to have cut down—at least in words—the Truman Doctrine to the size of the national interest of the United States and of the resources available to support it. His speech before the National Press Club on January 12, 1950, is in substance a reinterpretation of the Truman Doctrine, amounting virtually to a reformulation of American policy in Asia, and bearing hardly any semblance to the sweeping pronouncements of the original document. In this speech the issue between the United States and the Soviet Union is removed from the ideological plane to that of power politics. "I hear almost every day someone say," remarked Mr. Acheson, "that the real interest of the United States is to stop the spread of Communism. Nothing seems to me to put the cart before the horse more completely than that." The thing to oppose is Russian imperialism, of which Communism is but "the most subtle instrument . . . the spearhead." [2] To combat this threat, different methods must be used in different countries. Here it is military defense, there it is economic and political reform, there again it is technical assistance. Some countries must and can be defended by the military might of the United States; that is, there the Soviet Union must be contained. Other countries might be defended under certain conditions through the combined efforts of the United Nations; under other conditions, they cannot be defended. Such subtlety and discrimination is a far cry indeed from the sweeping generalizations of the Truman Doctrine. Yet nothing could illuminate more strikingly the depth of our sentimental illusions than the fact that the Secretary of State, who here so clearly understands the realistic requirements of American foreign policy, has been responsible for policies, at least in Asia, that have been marred and frustrated by those very sentimental considerations he refutes so convincingly in the speech from which we have quoted.

AID TO FOREIGN COUNTRIES

The sentimental error that has deflected the over-all foreign policy of the United States from the strict course of the national interest has also confused specific issues of American foreign policy. The outstanding example of such confusion in recent times has been the public debate on

2 See Appendix III for full text.

foreign military and economic aid, such as the Marshall Plan; the North Atlantic Defense Treaty and its implementation; aid to Germany, India, Yugoslavia, and Spain; and Point Four.

The United States emerged from the Second World War as the richest country on earth and as one of the two great world powers, and at the same time found itself involved in a struggle for power with the Soviet Union. For the United States the objective of that struggle in Europe is the restoration of a viable balance of power, to be brought about in part by making the nations of Western Europe strong enough to withstand internal subversion and external aggression. To this end the United States has given money and arms to the nations of Western Europe through the Marshall Plan and the North Atlantic Defense Treaty.

There is nothing extraordinary in the strongest ally of a coalition coming to the economic and military assistance of the weaker members. This is obviously the common-sense way in which rich and powerful nations contribute to the success of a common political and military enterprise. It is the way in which, for instance, Great Britain in the seventeenth and eighteenth centuries through the systematic use of subventions gained and strengthened allies on the continent of Europe. Yet to American public opinion the issue of military and economic assistance to Western Europe presented itself primarily not as a question of national interest, but as one of moral principle, of selfless generosity. Such aid was defended as a mandate from America's humanitarian past; it was opposed in terms of the unworthiness of the recipients and of the sacrifices it imposed upon the giver.

Thinking in such moral terms, neither friend nor foe had an adequate standard for determining the kind and amount of assistance to be given. The friends were liable to err on the side of too much and, more particularly, of too much in the way of mere technical efficiency and productivity. The foes could not help being wrong on the side of too little. For both sides looked at aid to Europe as an end in itself, to be justified or condemned in the light of a moral abstraction. Neither side had a clear understanding of the fundamental fact that aid to Europe was not of the order of aid to famine-stricken Chinese or homeless Bolivians, but an act of high policy. It was not an end in itself, but a means to a political end, to be defended or attacked in terms of national policy. As such, it was subject to only one standard of evaluation: the national interest of the United States. In practical terms, the amount and kind of aid to be given was to be determined solely in view of the contribution it was likely to make to the political ability of the nations of Western Europe to resist Communist subversion from within and to their military ability to resist Russian aggression from without. Increase in economic productivity, social and political reforms, efficiency of administration, the political philosophies and practices of the governments concerned, the sacrifices required of the United States—all these factors had *per se* no place in such determination; they were to be considered only as they bore upon the military and political objectives of the aid.

That there is no other rational approach to the problem of American assistance to foreign governments must become obvious from a cursory examination of the cases of Spain, India, Yugoslavia, and Western Germany. There are those who would give aid to Spain because her government is anti-Communist; there are those who would withhold aid from Spain because her government is Fascist. And those who favor aid to Spain for that reason would by the same token refuse it to Yugoslavia because her government is Communist, and would give it to Western Germany because her government opposes Communism. Aid to India, on the other hand, is predicated upon India's good behavior, that is, its support of our Asiatic policies.

If we assume, as the sentimentalists do, that international politics is a struggle between good and evil, virtue and vice, then it follows that we must lend our support only to those governments we have endowed with political virtue, however defined. Were we to apply this principle of selecting our friends consistently, we would probably find very soon that nobody lives up to our ideal of a virtuous nation but ourselves, and that we must avoid the moral contamination of associating with anybody else. This is indeed, as we shall see, the neo-isolationist position.

No responsible statesman could, of course, be as consistent in error as that. Here again, however, the prevailing sentimental pattern of thought imposes itself upon the better insight of the responsible statesman and leads him astray. Every consideration of the national interest should compel us to put aid to Yugoslavia in a high place on the list of priorities of our foreign policy. The great opportunity of American foreign policy may well lie in the chance, not to stop Communist revolution all over the world, but to demonstrate in practice that the Communist form of government is not necessarily identical with subservience to the objectives of Russian imperialism, that a national leader can be a good Communist ideologically and still be opposed to Russia as a great power, and hence that the lines of the political division between East and West do not of necessity follow the lines of the ideological division between Communism and democracy. In other words, there may well be Communist governments on this side of the Iron Curtain. The stabilization of the Communist regime in Yugoslavia, then, and its integration into the Western alliance is one of the foremost tasks of American diplomacy. Following this line of reasoning, we support the government of Yugoslavia. Yet following the sentimental line of reasoning, we have supported it thus far but half-heartedly, hesitatingly and, in contrast to what we have been doing for the democratic governments of Western Europe, "ungenerously," as it were.

In Asia, we have pursued the sound objective of stemming the tide of Communism. With China lost, the great prize in the struggle between East and West is India. It is here that British statesmanship has won a great victory by keeping India within the British Commonwealth. India is today the last stronghold of democratic order and individual liberty on the continent of Asia, the only great nation of Asia that shares the anti-Communist objectives of the West. Yet beneath the thin layer of constitutional order a volcano is brewing, fed by social dislocation, economic discontent, and a poverty that is worse today than it was twenty and even fifty years ago. In view of our objective of containing Communism in Asia, economic aid to India ought to have a high place among the priorities of our Asiatic policy. Yet Prime Minister Nehru had joined most of the statesmen of the world in taking a dim view of certain phases of our Asiatic policy. Mr. Nehru, then, must be punished; if that means the strengthening of the forces of Communism in India, it serves Mr. Nehru right. If India should go Communist because we are too sentimental to follow our interests rather than our emotions, we can at least console ourselves that we have sacrificed our interests to our principles. Conversely, those who advocate aid to India regardless of its government's attitude on certain issues are forced by the same climate of sentimental opinion to justify that aid in sentimental rather than political terms.

To what extent our policy toward Germany has been the victim of these contradictory modes of thought is clear for everyone to see. On the one hand, we know that the domination of all of Germany is the great prize in the struggle between East and West; for he who controls all of Germany controls all of Europe, and he who controls all of Europe is well on his way toward controlling the whole world. To tie Western Germany as closely as possible to the Western alliance is, then, an indispensable prerequisite of a successful American foreign policy. Yet, on the other hand, did we not fight Germany twice in a generation, as a moral outcast who had flouted international law and the basic rules of conduct by which civilized humanity lives? And were we satisfied with anything less than unconditional surrender, the punishment of the war criminals, and the re-education of the whole nation? Thus we have conceived of our relations with Germany primarily in sentimental terms. We have approached Germany as a virtuous nation approaches a vicious yet reformable one. It is not surprising that, forced by the logic of events to see Germany only as a potential great power devoid of moral opprobrium, we find it hard to act, as we know we must think from now on, in terms of power rather than of moral abstractions. Thus we equivocate and temporize and fall from the extreme of sentimental condemnation into the other extreme of sentimental fraternization. Caught in these emotional excesses, we lose the only sure guide of policy, the consideration of the national interest in terms of the advantages to be expected and the risks to be avoided.

We might point out in passing that concluding from the virtue of a nation its right to expect our generosity can also be turned around, with equally unhealthy political results. We supported the Soviet Union during the Second World War on a large scale, thinking ourselves to be generous. Since we could allow ourselves to be generous only toward a nation that deserved our generosity because of its virtue, the Soviet Union became by definition endowed with virtue. In truth, of course, we were not being generous when we aided the Soviet Union in her fight against Germany, nor had the Bolshevist tiger changed its spots. Both powers pursued their national interests, as they understood them. Only we deluded ourselves into believing that aid in war among allies is founded upon something different from self-interest and presupposes a certain measure of virtue in the recipient, as it requires of him a sense of gratitude after the event.

The outstanding example in our time of the obstruction of sound policy by sentimental considerations is the abortive character of the Point Four Program. In his message to Congress of June 24, 1949, President Truman recommended as a fourth point the enactment of legislation authorizing a program of technical assistance to underdeveloped areas and encouragement to the investment of private capital in these areas. The area that the President had primarily in mind was southeast Asia. The Point Four Program is motivated by our national interest, which requires the restoration of the balance of power in Asia through the limiting of Russian power and the political and economic stabilization of the new nations of southeast Asia. Why has the Congress done so little—in view of the enormity of the task, virtually nothing—to implement the President's recommendation?

The reason for the lack of interest and activity in a task so closely connected with the national interest of the United States must again be sought in the intrusion of moral abstractions into political considerations. The tendency is very strong, again on the part of both friend and foe of the measures proposed, to conceive of Point Four as a manifestation of generosity rather than as an instrument of national defense. This tendency is strengthened by the similarity and partial identity of the Point Four Program with certain programs of social and economic improvement, planned not as means to a political end but for their own sake, by some agencies of the United Nations. Yet what is a legitimate undertaking for a world organization with humanitarian purposes is hardly appropriate for an already hard-pressed single nation. As a gigantic TVA, dedicated to the welfare of backward peoples as its ultimate objective, Point Four has been easy to attack, especially by those who oppose the "welfare state" in all its manifestations. Since they do not recognize an obligation on the part of the government to aid its own "backward" citizens, how can they be expected to support a scheme that presents itself to them as a misguided and ruinous attempt to have good old Uncle Sam shoulder the burdens of hundreds of millions of backward foreigners? Here again, the sentimental presentation of what is essentially a political proposition, dictated by our national interest, has met rejection in terms of an isolationist attitude of mind which is widely believed to be extinct.

4. *Neo-isolationism*

There can, of course, be no doubt that the isolationism of the twenties and thirties is dead as a serious political movement. Yet the attitude of mind which gave rise to this isolationism is by no means dead. In the interwar period that attitude of mind expressed itself in the abstentionist terms of non-interference and non-participation in the affairs and activities of non-American nations. This negative and passive attitude toward the outside world assumed that the United States was self-sufficient as a world power, that it could live its political life and take care of its national interest without regard for other nations. Still very much alive among us, this attitude of mind expresses itself in a variety of ways, but it always turns inside out the old isolationism, and approaches the world in a spirit of active participation, provided that participation takes place on its own terms. While the old-style isolationist used to say "We want to have nothing to do with the world," the neo-isolationist says "We shall deal with the world, but only on our terms."

Two manifestations of this neo-isolationism deserve further discussion: the belief in American omnipotence, especially as expressed in the crusading spirit, and the disparagement of traditional methods of diplomacy.

AMERICAN OMNIPOTENCE AND THE CRUSADING SPIRIT

The belief in our omnipotence arises in part from a historic experience that spared us the memory of some powerful neighbor who threatened the existence of the nation. The American advanced from the Alleghenies to the Pacific not like a conqueror fighting for his life, but like a colonizer clearing forests, tilling the land, and killing a few Indians here and there. There was no threat to the vital interests or the existence of the nation, from the east or west, from the north or south. We did what we set out to do, and no human force arose to stop us. Even when we went outside the confines of the continent to fight, as in the war against Spain and in the two World Wars, we won easily. The history of the United States knows of many victories and few defeats, and of no threat to its existence which did not come from its own midst. What was true in the past might well be true in the future, and what was actually the result of a number of momentary configurations was interpreted as an endowment of nature which would last forever.

Joined with this misinterpretation of historic experience, there is a sense of moral mission, referred to before, which imposes upon the United States the duty to see to it that right prevails and good is done all over the world. As there is an inner relationship between the indiscriminate moralistic interventionism and the old-style isolationism of the interwar period, there is an intimate relationship between the extroverted isolationism of our time and the sentimental trend in our thinking on foreign affairs. A nation with so all-embracing a moral mission obviously needs enormous power. Since the accomplishment of that moral mission appears to be ordained by the moral purposes of the universe, nature must have endowed the nation with power commensurate with its mission. Wicked nations believe that might makes right; the righteous trust that right will triumph in the end. Given a righteous cause, one's ability to carry it to victory is easily assumed. We can achieve what we want, since what we want is only what is right.

This belief in American omnipotence experienced its first great and lasting shock in the aftermath of the Second World War. For the first time we came up against a wall not erected by nature and not to be scaled at will. Soviet imperialism in Europe, and the revolutions of Asia, are of a different order of magnitude and manageability from the international problems that in the past we mastered with comparative ease. Accustomed to dealing with Mexico and Spain and, at worst, with an over-extended Japan and a Germany already haunted by the specter of defeat, we transferred the successful methods of the past to the novel situations that confronted us in Europe and Asia. We had sent the marines to Mexico to deal with its revolutions, and we sent the marines to Asia to deal with the revolutions there. We had twice in the past saved Western Europe from foreign conquest by putting the economic and military potential of the United States behind the European nations who bore the brunt of battle, and we continue to think in terms of a Europe defending itself with our aid. We say that it would be a good thing if Europe were able to defend itself, and hence we act as though this were possible. We say that it would be a good thing if the Communist revolutions in Asia could be prevented or undone, and act as though we had the power to prevent or undo them.

When political failure and military defeat ought to show us the limits of our power, we still cling to the delusion of our omnipotence. The only way to explain failures and defeats when we assume ourselves to be omnipotent is to look for some devilish machinations depriving us of the successes and victories that are rightfully ours. So it becomes plausible that we are unable to stop the revolutions in Asia by military means, not because they cannot be stopped that way, but because the State Department is full of Communists. In the light of new experiences, we could revise the traditional evaluation of our power; but we prefer the comfort of our delusion to the recognition of inconvenient facts. We invent the scapegoat of collective treason, and use it to reconcile the delusion of our omnipotence with the experience of limited power.

It is but a small step from this belief in morally required omnipotence to the substitution of a crusade for a foreign policy. The political crusade is nothing but alleged omnipotence actively pursuing a universal moral goal. It is a worldwide expansion of the sense of moral mission, based on a belief in omnipotence. The political crusader has his opportunity when his country is engaged in a worldwide struggle with another great power, which lends itself to a moral interpretation. Thus the two wars with Germany and the present conflict with the Soviet Union and China have been widely understood, not in terms of competing and hostile powers or incompatible philosophies and ways of life, but in terms of a struggle between light and darkness, with light bound to drive out darkness by dint of its superiority in virtue and strength.

There is only a seeming paradox in the jocular definition of an isolationist as a man who wants to fight in Asia. In view of neo-isolationist premises there is perfect logic behind indifference to Europe and indiscriminate intervention in Asia. Abstention from European affairs, as a political principle and a tradition of foreign policy, seems to go back to Washington. To become involved in their squabbles by aiding one European state against another is but to lose one's moral purpose, since they all are tainted with the evil of power politics. The situation in Asia is different. Here the conception of our traditional role—the disinterested foe of imperialism and the providential friend of China—joins with the opposition to Communism, and the conception of American omnipotence, challenged by developments in China and throughout Asia. These factors co-operate to produce the crusading fervor that knows only its own strength, but not the strength that opposes it.

DISPARAGEMENT OF DIPLOMACY

In a political world that has seen the universal triumph of virtue over vice, carried on the wings of unchallengeable power, there is no room for the traditional methods of diplomacy. These methods presuppose a political world peopled by approximate equals, in strength and in virtue, with a consequent inability of any one nation or combination of nations to have it all their own way. These methods consist in diplomatic negotiations, bargaining, mutual concessions, compromises, with a negotiated settlement as the goal. The settlements they achieve cannot help being provisional, for they reflect the distribution of power at the moment of settlement, and that distribution of power changes. "Unconditional surrender" is not in their vocabulary; "appeasement," only as a mistake.

Neo-isolationism

The traditional methods of diplomacy, then, require a state of mind opposite to that of neo-isolationism. The neo-isolationist is perfectly logical in view of his own premises when he abhors consideration of the other side's interests and point of view, the precondition for a conciliatory and accommodating diplomacy, as akin to, if not identical with, treason. For he assumes that his country is good and strong enough to do as it pleases. To him, negotiations are tantamount to submission to evil forces, to contamination with vice, which establishes one's guilt by association; compromise is a synonym for appeasement; and agreement on spheres of influence, which by definition limits one's own dominion and recognizes the dominion of another nation, reveals both weakness and vice. The omnipotent crusader can envisage no other outcome of the conflict but unconditional surrender, and no other way of reaching it but the use of overwhelming force. For both himself and the enemy, the neo-isolationist sees only two alternatives: a fight to the finish, or unconditional surrender. Between them the middle ground of compromise and peaceful settlement is lost.

In *Speaking Frankly,* the account of his tenure as Secretary of State, James F. Byrnes reports an episode at the Paris Peace Conference in 1946 which illustrates this state of mind.

> After a heated session in Paris one afternoon, Chip Bohlen [then Advisor to the American delegation and later Counselor of the Department of State] remained behind talking to a member of the Soviet delegation. The Soviet representative said it was impossible for him to understand the Americans. They had a reputation for being good traders and yet Secretary Byrnes for two days had been making speeches about principles—talking, he said, like a professor.

"Why doesn't he stop this talk about principles, and get down to business and start trading?" the Soviet representative asked Chip in all sincerity.

Chip attempted most unsuccessfully to explain that there were some questions which, in the opinion of Americans, involved principle and could not be settled by bargaining.

It may be noted in passing that in this respect the contemporary neo-isolationist is the true heir of the isolationist of the twenties and thirties. Under Coolidge and Hoover "diplomacy by storm" became a byword for the diplomatic practices through which the United States endeavored to solve controversial issues at international conferences. These practices consisted mainly in the sudden presentation of an agreement to be accepted or rejected by the other nations as it stood. The intrinsic merits of the agreement were supposed to command approval by all right-thinking nations. These same merits excluded the possibility of its being subjected to the indignity of modification by bargaining and compromise.

The neo-isolationist approach to foreign policy is actually fused with the other three main intellectual errors of American foreign policy. It is in particular a reaction to the inevitable disappointments produced by those other errors. The neo-isolationist is often a disappointed utopian, legalist, or sentimentalist. He fought two wars to end all wars, to make the world safe for democracy, and to establish an international organization as a substitute for power politics; all to no avail. Now he is done with all this international nonsense and swindle and will rely on nothing but American right and American might. He is also done with those diplomatic practices which weak and wicked nations use to deceive good and strong ones and to rob them of their strength. Yalta and Potsdam underline the point.

Neo-isolationism

Thinking now in as non-political terms as he did before his disappointments, the neo-isolationist sees only two alternatives in dealing with another nation: either to concede everything, as we did at Yalta and Potsdam, because we trust the other side, or to concede nothing because we do not trust it. During the Second World War the Russians were thought to be so good that there was no need to bargain with them. Since the breakdown of the Yalta and Potsdam agreements the Russians have been thought to be so bad that it was impossible to bargain with them. The disenchanted sentimentalist and utopian cannot understand the elemental truth of international politics: that no nation can be so good as not to take advantage of a power vacuum, and that no nation can be so bad—although it may be so foolish —as to refuse to safeguard and promote its own interests through a negotiated settlement. At no stage in his intellectual pilgrimage does it occur to him that to negotiate or not to negotiate, to concede or not to concede might hinge not upon the moral character of the other side, but upon considerations of power and national advantage. The issue of trustworthiness will sometimes enter, but as one among many constituent factors.

For the actual conduct of foreign policy, neo-isolationism and its companions in error have three important consequences: the underestimation of the enemy, the overrating of one's own strength, the inability to preserve peace.

The consistent underestimation of Russian strength by the West in general and the United States in particular will be spoken of later. The overrating of one's own strength leads, among all kinds of political and military miscalculations, to a Maginot line psychology which relies for the perpetuation of American security upon a specific natural phenomenon, such as the barrier of the oceans, or upon certain "miracle" weapons, such as the atom bomb and special armor-piercing equipment, or upon a certain military technique, such as strategic bombing, or upon a specific economic or legal device, such as the Marshall Plan or the North Atlantic Defense Treaty, or upon the arming of others, such as the rearmament of Western Europe and Western Germany. From behind that impenetrable protective wall the crusading giant watches the international scene, a sort of policeman for the world, defending the law-abiding nations and getting tough with those who disturb law and order.

The most fateful of all the practical consequences of these intellectual errors is the implacable hostility to the idea that diplomatic negotiations are the only alternative to war. This hostility finds its main intellectual support in the equating of a negotiated settlement with the moral approval of the settlement itself, and the equating of a negotiated settlement with appeasement.

A negotiated settlement implies that the parties to the agreement recognize two factors: the interests of either side and the power at the disposal of either side to support these interests. A negotiated settlement does not imply the moral approbation of these interests. I may feel deeply—as I actually do—that many of the uses to which the Russians have put their power are obnoxious to the moral sense of mankind. Yet as a statesman I could not be oblivious of the extent to which Russian power is capable of supporting these interests. Nor could I disregard the evils—immeasurably greater than the moral wrong I oppose—which would follow a challenge to that power where it is unchallengeable. Nor could I finally be unaware of the limits of that power, and hence of the opportunity of making American interests prevail with American power. A negotiated settlement involves nothing but the recognition of the limits of the mutual interests and power. It is a pact with the inevitable, not an embrace between virtue and vice in which virtue must perish.

Appeasement is a politically unwise negotiated settlement that misjudges the interests and power involved. We speak of appeasement when a nation surrenders one of its vital interests without obtaining anything worth while in return. The surrender of Czechoslovakia to Germany by Great Britain and France at the Munich conference of 1938 opened eastern and southeastern Europe to German conquest by disarming the strongest military power in eastern Europe, and made one of the German flanks secure in case of war with the West. In return, Great Britain and France secured Hitler's assurance that he had no more territorial ambitions in Europe. This is indeed appeasement and is indefensible. But for a nation to exchange one advantage for another advantage at least as important is as far removed from appeasement as common sense is from foolishness, and statesmanship from dilettantism.

Since its first use, following the disastrous consequences of the surrender at Munich, the term "appeasement" has exercised a nefarious influence upon the policies of the West by being used to discredit all attempts at establishing peace through negotiations. Mr. Churchill sets the matter right when he said in his speech in the House of Commons on December 14, 1950:

> The declaration of the Prime Minister that there will be no appeasement also commands almost universal support. It is a good slogan for the country. It seems to me, however, that in this House it requires to be more precisely defined. What we really mean, I think, is no appeasement through weakness or fear. Appeasement in itself may be good or bad according to the circumstances. Appeasement from weakness and fear is alike futile and fatal. Appeasement from strength is magnanimous and noble and might be the surest and perhaps the only path to world peace.

Future historians will have to decide whether the Western world has suffered more from the surrender at Munich—that is, from appeasement as political practice—or from the intellectual confusion that equates a negotiated settlement with appeasement and thus discredits the sole rational alternative to war.

V

The Road to Peace

1. *The Two Alternatives: Negotiations or War*

A nation can try to obtain its international objectives in three ways: it can go to war, it can bring overwhelming power to bear upon its opponent, or it can negotiate for a settlement.

Spokesmen for our government have sometimes believed in a fourth way: the cold war, with a minimum of relations between East and West and with the issue of peace or war hanging uneasily in the balance, lasting perhaps for a generation. This possibility is so extremely unlikely as to be no real possibility at all. Even if the United States and the Soviet Union had the psychological and material resources necessary to withstand for decades the pressure of open hostility short of war, two factors would sooner or later bring the cold war to an end. One is the threat of ever more potent weapons of mass destruction, making for caution but also for desperation. The other is the extreme instability in the regions, such as Western Germany and all of southeast Asia, not firmly controlled by either side, but strongly contested. In those regions fundamental changes in the status quo, affecting the power relations between East and West, will inevitably occur. Under the conditions of the cold war only superhuman wisdom, foresight, and self-restraint would be able safely to localize revolutions, civil wars, and international wars likely to take place in those regions. As Mr. Churchill put it in his survey of the prospects of the cold war in the House of Commons on January 23, 1948: "We may be absolutely sure that the present situation cannot last." Either it will get better or it will get worse.

One of the logical alternatives to the cold war is no longer practical today: overwhelming power on the side of the United States. Overwhelming power is no longer at the disposal of the United States and probably will not be at its disposal in the future. There was a time when the United States and the Soviet Union might have been able to negotiate a settlement on the basis of the supremacy of American power. When President Truman announced on September 23, 1949, that an atomic explosion had occurred in the Soviet Union, that possibility was gone and, in view of Western weakness on land and in the air, it is gone for a long time. There remain only two choices before the American people: a negotiated settlement or war.

These alternatives are for obvious reasons highly unpopular with us and, more particularly, with our government. War is no longer, as it once was, a rational instrument of foreign policy, but has become an instrument of universal destruction. Thus war is an unacceptable alternative for us except as an extreme necessity imposed from without. Yet we are not prepared to accept a negotiated settlement as the sole alternative to war, for we have formed a distorted picture of the nature of a negotiated settlement, of what it entails, and of its prerequisites under present world conditions. So our policy has refused, until very recently, either to prepare seriously for war or to face the problem of a negotiated settlement on realistic terms. Instead, it has endeavored to transcend those two distasteful alternatives by pursuing a policy of drift, which is neither total diplomacy nor preparation for total war.

That policy derived its inspiration from a series of expectations recalling the Maginot-line psychology of the interwar period. We have already referred to the expectations, necessarily disappointed, which were placed in the atomic bomb and other super-weapons, in the Marshall Plan and the North Atlantic Pact, and in the rearmament of other nations. At the end, there was the expectation, supporting all the others, that something was bound to turn up sooner or later; perhaps Russian policy would change after Stalin's death or the Bolshevist regime would disintegrate, and without any particular effort on our part everything would turn out all right. All these futilities were able, for a time at least, to conceal the basic dilemma of our foreign policy, which wanted neither war nor a negotiated settlement and, though bound to lead to war in spite of itself, refused to initiate an all-out national effort commensurate with our global commitments, which would give us the power for equal negotiations with the Soviet Union—negotiations with a chance for success.

2. *The Conditions for a Negotiated Settlement*

An all-out national effort, then, is required for war as well as for peace. And the question of peace or war hinges upon the prospects of a negotiated settlement. Here is the crux of our foreign policy. We have proceeded on the assumption that an early negotiated settlement with the Soviet Union is impossible, and we have defended that negative attitude with four basic arguments:

1. The Russians keep agreements only so long as it is in their interest to keep them, and break them at will when they think it advantageous to do so.

2. The United States has always maintained that it will not enter into bilateral negotiations with the interests of third nations at stake.

3. In order to bargain successfully with the Russians, one has to be strong, for only the irresistible logic of "situations of fact" will make the Russians keep their bargains.

4. The objective for which the Russians are willing to negotiate; i.e., the division of the world into spheres of influence, is unacceptable to the United States.

The first of these arguments is derived from undeniable facts, but it is irrelevant to the issue. The second argument is hardly to be taken seriously. The third argument is correct as a general proposition, but debatable in its practical application to current problems. The fourth of these arguments goes to the core of the matter. The negative attitude toward negotiations with the Soviet Union stands or falls with the soundness of this argument. In the terms in which it is generally formulated, it is hard to see how its soundness can be defended.

TWO UNTENABLE ARGUMENTS—THE RUSSIAN ATTITUDE AND THE INTERESTS OF THIRD PARTIES

It is undeniable that since the end of the Second World War, and even before, the Soviet Union has violated the international agreements it thought advantageous to violate. (The number of these violations—our official count is about forty—matters little.) It is also undeniable that the Russians have engaged in treaty violations with a cynical disregard for the niceties of diplomatic intercourse, with a complete unconcern for the sensibilities of the other side

—which more subtle diplomats might well have spared without sacrificing their political objectives—and, finally, with a brutal frankness bound to come as a shock to those who like to think of the moral standards of international politics in terms of the ideals of a well-behaved, law-abiding business community.

Yet while it is true that the Russians have violated those agreements the keeping of which they did not deem to be in their interest, it is also true that they have kept those agreements which they thought it to be in their interest to keep. We have for the correctness of this statement the testimony of Mr. Churchill, who on January 23, 1948, said in the House of Commons: "It is idle to reason or argue with the Communists. It is, however, possible to deal with them on a fair, realistic basis, and, in my experience, they will keep bargains as long as it is in their interest to do so, which might, in this grave matter, be a long time, once things were settled."

If this assessment of the Russian attitude toward international agreements is correct, then this attitude differs only in manner and form, but not in substance, from the attitude all great powers have traditionally taken with regard to international agreements. The road the great powers have traveled throughout history is strewn with broken fragments of solemn promises and scraps of torn paper inscribed with treaty stipulations. "Perfidious Albion" has become a byword summarizing the experience of centuries with the fickleness of British balance-of-power policies and with British imperialism's disregard for legal scruples. The faithlessness of Italian diplomacy was proverbial from the days of the Republic of Venice to Cavour. And it was that greatest of Italian statesmen who said, looking back on his public life: "If we had done for ourselves what we have done for Italy, what scoundrels we would have been."

From that iron law of international politics, that legal obligations must yield to the national interest, no nation has ever been completely immune. The self-righteousness of a blind nationalism may at times imagine itself with such immunity, and the needs of propaganda may make it necessary to assume it. Yet in truth there are but two differences among nations concerning the respect for legal obligations, one affecting the manner of getting rid of burdensome obligations, the other affecting the need for doing so. Certain nations have a flair for throwing burdensome obligations overboard in an elegant, unobtrusive fashion, or for chiseling them away with the fine tools of legal misinterpretation; French diplomacy has developed the latter method into an art. Other nations, such as Germany and Russia, have the disconcerting habit of announcing to all the world that a certain inconvenient treaty has become "a scrap of paper," as did the German chancellor in August, 1914, when he denounced the treaty guaranteeing the neutrality of Belgium, and of throwing the scraps in the face of the world.

Concerning the need to violate treaty obligations, a distinction can be drawn between nations pursuing a policy of the status quo and those pursuing a policy of expansion. The former, primarily interested in preserving the existing distribution of power, especially with regard to territory, are most likely to formulate their policies in the legalistic terms of existing treaties that embody the territorial status quo. Thus the status quo policies of France in the interwar period were formulated in terms of respect for the provisions of the Treaty of Versailles and of the Covenant of the League of Nations. On the other hand, nations pursuing expansionist policies will disregard legal obligations that stand in the way of their expansionist aims. This is what France did under the two Napoleons.

The truth of the matter has been well summarized in a

treatise on *Sanctions and Treaty Enforcement* by Professor Payson S. Wild, former Dean of the Harvard Graduate School of Arts and Sciences and at present Vice-President and Dean of the Faculties of Northwestern University.

The more one goes into the topic of treaty sanctions at present, however, the more is he puzzled concerning their value and usefulness. It is true that treaty observance is important, but is it not also true that, in a world where nationalism is rampant, only those treaties which states consider to be to their advantage will be kept regardless of special sanctions and that where treaties stand in the way of what Professor Schuman has termed the "politics of power," no amount of implementation or coercion on paper will deter a violator? No state thinks of infringing upon the provisions of the International Postal Convention, while the whole League Covenant, the Nine Power Treaty and the Pact of Paris did not stop Japan in Manchuria. In other words, is it not the nature of the treaty rather than the nature of the sanctions which determines compliance? Such a question goes back to the international standard of justice discussed earlier as a sanction, and it seems safe to say that only insofar as all signatory states firmly believe a treaty to be a "good" one, a "just" one or a "useful" one is it really sanctioned, and that it is of small avail to attempt to pin sanctions upon treaties which are apt to run athwart the national policies of powerful states.

In sum, the real issue posed by the frequent violations of international agreements by the Soviet Union is not whether or not the Soviet government is inherently, by some kind of natural depravity, oblivious of legal obligations, but whether or not the conception of the Russian national interest which gave rise to those violations is compatible with the national interest of the United States. This is not a contest between virtue and vice, defined in the terms of a lawyer's code of conduct, but a clash between the foreign policies of two great powers pursuing apparently incompatible objectives. The test, therefore, of whether a negotiated settlement with the Soviet Union is possible is to be sought not through the lawyer's concern with legal obligations, but through the statesman's concern with the reconciliation of apparently irreconcilable national interests.

The second argument, about the interests of third parties, deserves only passing mention. This argument pretends to be oblivious of the fact that nations differ in power and, hence, also in influence and responsibility, and that by tradition and logic the great powers have settled in direct negotiations their disputes over the regions where their interests, power, and responsibility were paramount. It is hard to see how the business of statesmanship could be carried on in any other way. Or is anybody bold enough to suggest that it would have been easier for England and Russia to settle their differences in 1878 at the Congress of Berlin, enabling Disraeli to bring home "peace with honor," if aside from the great powers the Bosnians, Herzegovinians, the inhabitants of Novi Bazar, the Montenegrins, Serbians, Bulgarians, Rumanians, Greeks, Albanians, Macedonians, Cypriots, Tunisians, Armenians, had participated in the deliberations and decisions?

A VALID ARGUMENT—THE PREREQUISITES OF STRENGTH AND CONCURRING INTERESTS

It is, then, on the level of policy and not of law that the issue must be joined. What are the preconditions for a political settlement that has a chance to last? To this question Mr. Acheson, at his news conference of February 12, 1950, has given an answer, admirable for the lucidity of its presentation and for its intellectual grasp of at least one side of the problem. The core of Mr. Acheson's remarks is the distinction between paper agreements and agreements "which register the existing facts." The former are useless, for they will be broken whenever it is in the interest of one or the other of the contracting parties to do so. The latter are useful, for to observe them is in the interest of the parties concerned. In the words of Mr. Acheson, "it is not a matter of agreement but a matter of registering the existence of a situation. . . . Thus what I want to stress here is that agreements with the Soviet Union are useful when those agreements register or record an existing situation of fact, but that otherwise they are not of much use. So it has been our basic policy to build situations which will extend the area of possible agreement, that is, to create strength instead of the weakness which exists in many quarters."

This analysis is unexceptionable as far as it goes, and it need not be limited to the postwar relations between the United States and the Soviet Union. For it is a general law of international politics, applicable to all nations at all times, that only those agreements have a chance to be effective and to last which express in legal terms the identical or complementary interests of the contracting parties, and that they last only as long as their terms coincide with those interests. No period of recorded history has provided such overwhelming negative proof for the generality of that law as the interwar period. This was the period that has been appropriately called one of "pactomania," when every unsolved international problem, from war in general to the relations of two nations in particular, called for an international agreement to proclaim in legal terms the "solution" of the problem. All these agreements, from the

Briand-Kellogg Pact to the Locarno Treaties and the innumerable arbitration, friendship, and non-aggression agreements, left a problem exactly where they had found it. Yet they created, especially in the legalistically minded statesmen and masses of the West, the illusions of security and false hopes that, despite renewed disappointments, were carried from one international conference and the paper agreement concluding it to the next.

Of such international agreements, which confound a legal promise with a situation of fact, probably the most destructive for the cause of peace in our time was the Yalta agreement of 1945 with regard to eastern Europe. The military agreements between the Western allies and the Soviet Union and, more particularly, the Western strategy providing for the invasion of Europe through France rather than through the Balkans had made, as a matter of military fact, all of eastern Europe, central Europe to the Elbe, and all of the Balkans, with the exception of Greece, a Russian sphere of influence. The Western statesmen were bound to find this situation of fact as threatening to the vital interests of their countries as a similar situation had appeared to Castlereagh and Canning in the years after 1815. Yet, in contrast to the superb statesmanship of these ministers, the Western negotiators at Yalta endeavored to rectify a disagreeable and threatening situation of fact by a paper agreement in which the Soviet Union promised to give the Western allies the opportunity to exercise some influence in the countries of eastern Europe and the Balkans through the instrumentality of liberal, democratic regimes to be established in those countries. The violation of such an agreement could not have surprised those who believe in the soundness of Mr. Acheson's principle. For this is what is likely to happen whenever a situation of fact is modified by legal stipulations divorced from the existing situation of fact.

The Conditions for a Negotiated Settlement

Thus while the soundness of Mr. Acheson's principle cannot be doubted, its completeness is indeed open to doubt.

A situation of fact favorable to a negotiated settlement consists of two elements: strength and conflicting interests capable of reconciliation. Strength is an indispensable prerequisite for successful negotiation, but it is not the only one and probably not even the most important. The pacifying function of negotiated settlements consists in the reconciliation of apparently incompatible interests. "The only bond of union that endures" among nations, is in the words of Lord Salisbury, "the absence of all clashing interests." There are situations where interests inevitably clash, and which therefore cannot be settled peacefully. Between a Napoleon or a Hitler and the prospective victims of their conquests no common ground exists for a peaceful settlement except submission to the will of the conqueror. The supreme test of statesmanship is whether it is able to assess correctly the chances for peaceful settlement by ascertaining the vital interests of the opposing nations and their relation to each other. Concessions born of the false belief that conflicting interests are actually compatible is appeasement. The refusal to negotiate in the false conviction that conflicting interests are irreconcilable is to court a needless war.

The task of ascertaining what one's own nation needs and wants in order to be secure, and what the other nation needs and wants in order to be secure, and whether there is inescapable conflict or the possibility of accommodation between these needs and wants—this task is an intellectual one, the highest of those constructive tasks which the Hamiltons, the Pitts, the Cannings, the Disraelis, and the Churchills face and solve, and whose existence is ignored by the amateurs. If American foreign policy consisted of nothing but the accumulation of strength at the points of conflict with the Soviet Union, Mr. Acheson's principle would be no more than a rationalization of the cold war, of the continuation of the armaments race in the hope that time was on our side and that we would eventually be able to impose a settlement favorable to ourselves upon the Soviet Union. Such a policy would fall far short of constructive statesmanship. It could hardly be called statesmanship at all, for it would be concerned with the military and political pre-conditions of successful diplomacy rather than with diplomacy itself.

ANOTHER UNTENABLE ARGUMENT— OPPOSITION TO SPHERES OF INFLUENCE

The traditional method of settling peacefully a conflict between two nations with respect to a piece of territory which belongs to neither but in which both have an interest has been to divide the territory into spheres of influence and thus satisfy at least in part the interests of both sides. All the great peace settlements—those which lasted because they were able to create identical or complementary interests among the contracting parties—have set up spheres of influence. The Treaty of Vienna of 1815 did so for the relations between Russia and the other European nations in eastern Europe. The Congress of Berlin of 1878 did so with regard to the relations between Great Britain and Russia in the Balkans and the Near East. The same was done in the Franco-British Agreement of 1904 for Africa, and in the Russo-British Agreement of 1907 for Asia. And in 1944, Churchill and Stalin divided the Balkans into spheres of influence.

Since the breakdown of the Yalta agreement, the Soviet Union has made numerous proposals for the division of the world into two gigantic spheres of influence, one dominated by the Soviet Union with Western influence excluded, the other free from Soviet domination and under the influence of the United States. While these proposals have never been officially acknowledged by the United States, they have been occasionally referred to by reporters and columnists. Those who have mentioned them have generally assumed, Mr. Walter Lippmann being the most notable exception, that the very idea of such an agreement must *a priori* be rejected. Of all the statements thus far published, a dispatch in the *New York Times* of March 13, 1950, datelined Washington under the title "Soviet Move Seen for Deal with U.S. to Divide World," seems to come closest to reflecting the official attitude of the United States. Its opinions are attributed to "United States officials," "the best-informed officials," and "experts in official quarters," and it appears under the byline of Mr. James Reston, the most brilliant, competent, and trustworthy of diplomatic correspondents.

Mr. Reston reports that "there is no evidence that officials here are even slightly interested in such a deal." Four reasons are adduced for this lack of interest, and it must be said from the outset that the first of these reasons is irrelevant to the argument and the other three are entirely unconvincing.

A spheres-of-influence agreement, so the argument runs, "would force both Yugoslavia and China into a satellite status, and in the long run greatly strengthen the Communist world." Whether all this would come to pass obviously depends upon the terms of the agreement. If such an agreement would extend the Russian sphere of influence beyond its present state, and strengthen the Communist world while weakening the West, it should certainly not be made. This argument applies only to specific stipulations of some hypothetical agreement, and not to the mere idea of negotiation. To say that such an agreement would necessarily be to the advantage of only the Soviet Union is really tantamount to taking a desperate view of both American power and American ability to negotiate. To use one of several possible lines of demarcation between the Russian and American spheres of influence as an argument against the whole idea of spheres of influence is neither logical nor practical. It may well be that the Russian minimum conditions will be unacceptable to the United States, and it will then be necessary to reject them when they are proposed. But if the fear of such conditions were a valid argument against being even interested in negotiation, then few great nations would ever have engaged in negotiation in order to settle their differences by peaceful means.

The second reason, concerning our influence among the Russian satellites, and the third one, dealing with the problem of Stalin's succession, are contained in the following passages from Mr. Reston's dispatch:

> The best-informed officials here do not think that the Soviet Union will be able to "integrate" China and the European satellites unless we abandon those countries and force them to surrender to Moscow. They do not believe the problem of transferring power in Soviet Russia will be easy after Premier Stalin's death, especially if Yugoslavia and China are following an independent Communist policy.
>
> In fact, the speculation here is that the primary objective of Stalin's policy now is to eliminate Premier Tito and Titoism and to consolidate the Soviet postwar sphere of influence before the problem of succession arises. Nobody here seems very eager to help the Russians solve this problem at the expense of other nations' freedom.

The Conditions for a Negotiated Settlement

The United States must refuse, "washing its hand of Eastern Europe and China and forcing these peoples to make the best deal they can with Premier Stalin."

The second argument against spheres of influence is obscure, the issue confused by the lumping together of China and Yugoslavia on the one hand, and the satellite countries such as Poland, Czechoslovakia, Hungary, Rumania, and Bulgaria on the other. The case of the former is quite different from that of the latter. A spheres-of-influence agreement will of necessity take into account the extent to which China and Yugoslavia have resisted integration into the Soviet orbit. There can be no question of our washing our hands of them or bargaining their freedom away. The satellites themselves are already integrated; they have no freedom left for us to bargain away; and they slipped from our hands long ago. Their fate was sealed when we allowed the Red Army to occupy them and keep them occupied. To liberate at least some of them means to force or persuade the Red Army to retreat. To force the Red Army to retreat means a war that will destroy the satellite nations with the rest of us. To persuade the Red Army to retreat means a negotiated settlement with the Soviet Union, which would receive a *quid pro quo* for that retreat. Thus "the best-informed officials" cannot well be concerned about the freedom of the peoples of Eastern Europe and at the same time oppose a negotiated settlement with the Soviet Union, for the one cannot be obtained without the other, at least not short of war.

The third argument, dealing with the impact of Stalin's succession upon the situation of the satellites, is also obscure. Yet whatever it is intended to mean, it can be stated without equivocation that, short of the complete disintegration of Russian power, the problem of the succession can have no influence upon Russian policy in the countries bordering the Soviet Union. For approximately two centuries, all Russian governments have considered the paramount influence of Russia in those regions as a *conditio sine qua non* of Russian security. Czechoslovakia or Hungary might well be regarded by the Soviet Union as liabilities rather than assets, and this or another Russian government might accept a negotiated settlement that opened a graceful exit from those unruly and exposed regions. But no Russian government will ever fail to subscribe to Stalin's statement at Yalta that Poland is "a question . . . of life and death for the Soviet State." Nations do not make questions of life and death the objects of negotiation, and no Russian government will ever retreat from Poland unless compelled by defeat in war. If we wait for a change in the Russian government to bring about a change in the situation in the regions bordering on the Soviet Union, we might well wait forever.

The fourth argument against a spheres-of-influence agreement is generally couched in moral terms suggesting that the very idea of spheres of influence violates a fundamental principle of American policy. We have encountered it in Mr. Hull's comments on the Churchill-Stalin agreement of 1944. Here this argument is given a legalistic turn, derived from the Charter of the United Nations. "This Charter, which was signed by the Russians and the United States, was based on the idea of all nations cooperating together in all parts of the world. It did not authorize the division of the world into two spheres of influence. . . ."

In order to show how untenable this argument is, we remind the reader of our discussion of this legalistic illusion that the United Nations is a substitute for power politics rather than its reaffirmation in a new form. And it is indeed obvious from the examples given above as well as from the political history of the human race that the balance of power and concomitant spheres of influence are of the very essence of international politics. They may be disregarded at the peril of those who choose to do so, but they cannot be abolished.

THE TESTIMONY OF ARNOLD TOYNBEE AND WINSTON CHURCHILL

As Arnold Toynbee put it in a lecture given at Columbia University in 1948, applying his unequaled historic perspective to our problem:

> I suppose that when two great powers face each other one possible alternative is a partition of the world without another war. If you look at the world now, as it has been since 1945, you can imagine it, if things should go rather well, being partitioned by agreement between the United States and the Soviet Union into two spheres.
>
> You may remember that before the First World War, France and Great Britain were great rivals about local frontiers in Africa, and so forth, and Russia and Great Britain were great rivals in Asia. In 1904 France and Great Britain went into consultation, worked over the map of the world, and wherever there was friction between them they ironed it out and made a bargain on a fifty-fifty basis: "You have this, we keep that; and we will forget about that old quarrel of ours." In 1907 Great Britain and Russia did the same. This is a difficult thing to do, in view of the traditional rivalries and dislikes of nations, and we succeeded in doing it in those cases only under strong pressure; we had a common aggressive enemy of whom we were all afraid, and that was Germany. But, after all, in the

present situation America and Russia have a common enemy, too, of whom I am sure they are likewise afraid, and that is atomic energy. Though, no doubt, it needs great imagination to think of atomic energy as a common enemy whom you must not dare to let loose in the way in which Great Britain and Russia, and Great Britain and France, thought of Germany as the common enemy in the face of whom they must iron out their own former differences, perhaps it is conceivable that American and Russian statesmanship might rise to this and that there might be consultations in which they would say to each other, "You take Manchuria, and we will take the rest of China" and so forth around the globe. That would be hard on the countries that happen to be on the borderline, but it would really be much better for everybody if it could be achieved, rather than to have another war with its quite uncertain aftermath.

I think this is an important possibility to keep in mind and to work for, because if it succeeded it might give us time, and, though sometimes playing for time merely means putting off something that we ought to settle now, I do not think that in our present circumstances playing for time is a wrong or unreasonable thing for us to try to do. . . . So anything that would enable us to buy time seems worth thinking about; and therefore I suggest a provisional partition of the world into a Russian and an American sphere by agreements between the two. If this could be brought about—if things are not too far gone for that—it would be a very valuable thing for both those great powers and for the world in general. It would give us time, among other things, to try gradually to build these two spheres together and eventually to unite them in a co-operative world government.

Mr. Churchill put it even more succinctly in his speech in the House of Commons on June 5, 1946: "It is better to have a world united than a world divided; but it is also better to have a world divided, than a world destroyed. Nor does it follow that even in a world divided there should not be equilibrium from which a further advance to unity might be attempted as the years pass by. Anything is better than this ceaseless degeneration of the heart of Europe. Europe will die of that." And we may add: And the Western world with it.

It is again to the unmatched wisdom of Mr. Churchill that we owe, beyond this particular issue of spheres of influence, the most persuasive presentation of the case in favor of a negotiated settlement. In the speech to the House of Commons of January 23, 1948,[1] from which we have already quoted, he thus summarizes the case for negotiations as the sole alternative to war:

> I will only venture now to say that there seems to me to be very real danger in going on drifting too long. I believe that the best chance of preventing a war is to bring matters to a head and come to a settlement with the Soviet Government before it is too late. This would imply that the Western democracies, who should, of course, seek unity among themselves at the earliest moment, would take the initiative in asking the Soviet for a settlement.
>
> It is idle to reason or argue with the Communists. It is, however, possible to deal with them on a fair, realistic basis, and, in my experience, they will keep their bargains as long as it is in their interest to do so, which might, in this grave matter, be a long time, once things are settled. . . .
>
> There are very grave dangers—that is all I am go-

[1] See Appendix II for full text.

157

ing to say today—in letting everything run on and pile up until something happens, and it passes, all of a sudden, out of your control.

With all consideration of the facts, I believe it right to say today that the best chance of avoiding war is, in accord with the other Western democracies, to bring matters to a head with the Soviet Government, and, by formal diplomatic processes, with all their privacy and gravity, to arrive at a lasting settlement. There is certainly enough for the interests of all if such a settlement could be reached. Even this method, I must say, however, would not guarantee that war would not come. But I believe it would give the best chance of coming out of it alive.

Our conclusion, then, is that we do not know whether a settlement can be negotiated with the Russians. But neither do we know of an argument that would justify the refusal to try. For the real issue is not whether the idea of the division of the world into spheres of influence can be accepted by the United States but where the line of demarcation should run. This is a time for the dispassionate, realistic examination of the national interests of the United States and of the Soviet Union, the mutual relations of these interests, their conflicts and their coincidence, and the power available to support them.

VI

The Failure of Judgment: in Europe

The more successful is our foreign policy in Europe and Asia, the less likely is it, provided its objectives are strictly limited by the national interest, to be opposed by force of arms. Success in the protection of the vital interests of the nation will also permit American policy that flexibility and accommodation beyond its own sphere of interest upon which the preservation of peace largely depends. On the other hand, failure would not only encourage the enemies of the United States to exploit their advantage to the utmost, but also strengthen the tendency—so deeply ingrained, as we have seen, in the American mind—to be contemptuous of the traditional methods of diplomacy and to seek a substitute for them in the uncompromising stubbornness of the political crusade. Thus the failure of American foreign policy to protect the vital interests of the nation leads to policies that increase the danger of war.

The postwar foreign policy of the United States, operating with the defective intellectual equipment described in Chapter IV, could have been successful only by accident. Moreover, it has been unable to assure its supporters at home and its friends and enemies abroad of our determination to pursue certain objectives at all costs because they are vital to our national interest, and to promote certain objectives only under certain circumstances because, while they are desirable, they are not vital. A foreign policy so infused with elements alien to sound political thinking cannot help being uncertain of its objectives, their relative importance, the power necessary and available to achieve them, and the policies best calculated to that end. The failure of our political and military policies in Asia is the result of that uncertainty, which in turn grows from the intellectual errors referred to before. The success of our policy in Europe is apparent rather than real; it is the result of accidents rather than of the inherent strength and soundness of the policies we have pursued and, furthermore, its supreme test has not yet come.

To save our position in Europe before it is too late, and to retrieve what can be retrieved in Asia, it is imperative to ask again those simple, yet fundamental questions to which all the intricate and minute details of foreign policy are but fragmentary answers: What are the vital objectives of the United States in Europe and Asia? What is the power available and necessary to attain these objectives? What are the policies we must pursue in view of our vital interests and of the power available and necessary to safeguard them?

In Europe and Asia the vital objective of American foreign policy is the restoration of the balance of power by means short of war. In the words of the London *Economist* of December 2, 1950: "The object of the endeavor in which the nations of the free world are now united is to contain Russian imperialism without having to fight another world war. This is the objective—not to defeat Russia (for that could not be done without a war), and still less to defeat Communist China." Yet while our vital objective is the same in Europe as in Asia, the policies we must pursue on these two continents are bound to be fundamentally different. For the threat to the balance of power manifests

160

itself in a different way on each continent, and the kind of power we can marshal against that threat likewise varies.

1. *Threat and Deterrent*

The threat in Europe is military. It lies in the stark and simple fact of the Red Army standing in overwhelming strength somewhat more than a hundred miles from the Rhine. Western Europe has thus far been protected from Russian aggression by three factors: its own unattractiveness for conquest, the threat of atomic warfare, and the superiority of the United States in atomic weapons.

Paradoxical as it may seem, the military, political, and economic weakness of the nations of Western Europe has deprived these nations of immediate attractiveness to Russian conquest. As long as they are weak, the nations of Western Europe are no threat to the Russian position in central and Eastern Europe, let alone to the security of the Soviet Union itself. As long as the political and social disease of those countries lasts, it will strengthen native Communism and, with it, Russian influence. For defensive purposes, then, Russian conquest of Western Europe has been unnecessary; in imperialistic expansion, the Soviet Union might have gained the substance of its objective by supporting indigenous Communist movements.

Yet the absorption of the countries of Western Europe into the Soviet orbit would pose for the Soviet Union problems of enormous magnitude. The absorption of the nations of Eastern Europe has been no easy matter; the existence of a Titoist Yugoslavia shows that it was only partially successful. The nations of Western Europe have a much stronger tradition of individual freedom, national independence, and cultural achievement than those of Eastern Europe, and they can be expected to be very unruly and unreliable members of the Communist family of nations. Furthermore, the Soviet rulers cannot have forgotten the devastating effects that the first acquaintance with Western civilization had upon the morale of the Russian soldier. If the relatively low standard of living in a country such as Rumania shook his faith in the superiority of the "Fatherland of Socialism" and his loyalty to the Soviet cause, the attraction of Frankfurt, Brussels, and Paris is likely to be much more potent.

Compared with what the Soviet Union could be expected to gain by the conquest of Western Europe, the importance of what it has already gained appears all the more impressive. The Soviet Union won in the Second World War what all Russian leaders had sought for two centuries and what none of them had gained except temporarily: political and military control of eastern and much of central Europe, and military predominance on the Continent, unchallengeable from within Europe itself. This is another way of saying that the Soviet Union destroyed the balance of power in Europe and replaced it with a quasi-hegemony of its own. In view of this momentous achievement it mattered little whether the Red Army occupied another piece of real estate or gave one up, as it did in the case of the Island of Bornholm in 1946.

Furthermore, no government, especially none so coldly calculating as the Soviet government, will embark upon a war fought under the conditions of modern technology without first exhausting all rational alternatives. We have referred before to the transformation war has undergone in modern times. Formerly war was a rational alternative to diplomacy, to be made use of or not, according to considerations of expediency. Today war has become a means of universal destruction to be resorted to only as an act of desperation when all other means of protecting the national interest have failed. The consequences of full-scale modern war have become so incalculable for both the international and domestic interests of all participants, and so likely has it become that modern war will destroy not only nations but also political regimes and civilizations, that any government must hesitate before it takes a step that might lead to such a war. This is true especially of a totalitarian government, which can be removed from power neither through the normal political processes nor through popular revolution, but only as a consequence of war. For the members of a totalitarian government, loss of power is tantamount to loss of life. The restraining influence that, as we have seen, the balance of power exerted upon the policies of ambitious nations in former times is now provided by the fear of the probable consequences of modern war itself. Only that fear explains the preservation of general peace up to now in the face of incidents and provocations that in any previous period of history would have resulted in war.

For the Soviet Union, the main deterrent to war has been the power potential of the United States and, more particularly, our superiority in atomic weapons. The Russians have thus far stopped at the line they held at the end of the Second World War because the superior power potential of the United States cannot decisively be attacked without a stockpile of atomic bombs, and because the American monopoly of atomic weapons or at least our possession of a stockpile of them threatens with destruction the centers of Russian power. It is upon this American superiority in a single field that, as Mr. Churchill has pointed out so often, the peace of the world has largely depended. And it is the decisive fact in the present world situation that this superiority is rapidly decreasing and will disappear in the very near future.

Against the background of these restraining influences, which have operated in the past but will not operate to the same extent, if at all, in the future, one must consider three great misjudgments in our postwar foreign policy: the underestimation of Russian power, the misunderstanding of the nature of our own power, and the misconception of the relationship between military power and diplomatic action.

2. *The Underestimation of Russian Power*

Nations tend to underrate their enemies' power and overrate their own. These distortions are the weeds in the garden of patriotism and national pride. They may be harmful, but are not serious as long as a critical intelligence is aware of their existence and applies the corrective of objective analysis to the excesses of self-glorification and contempt for the enemy. But if these distortions persist in the face of contradicting realities, they become fatal.

Familiar in psychiatric literature is the neurotic who cannot adjust to reality his mental picture of the world about him. After a number of violent clashes between his conception of the world and the world as it actually is— clashes that have the quality of what is popularly called "hysteria"—the patient calms down, retires into himself, seems to be confident, self-reliant, at peace with the world and himself, and is "normal." But in fact he has succeeded in withdrawing completely from reality, substituting for it the "reality" created by his delusion. Now he can rest content, for his disordered mind, having created a world all its own, has made it impossible for this creation and the actual world ever to be at odds again. Yet whenever the neurotic must act in relation to the real world he fails, and his failure is complete to the degree in which he substitutes the reality of his delusion for the actual world. Frequently he ends his days in an asylum, helpless in infantile contentment.

The Underestimation of Russian Power

There is a frightening parallel between the typical neurotic reaction to a reality unpleasant and full of problems and the reaction of our public opinion to the threat of Russian power. What is so disturbing about this reaction is not that it has misjudged Russian power in isolated instances, but that it has misjudged it consistently. The Western world has insisted upon underestimating the strength of the Soviet Union, especially in its technological and military aspects, and has invariably done so to its own detriment.

The Allied intervention in the Russian civil war was based on the assumption that the weakness of the Bolshevist regime would make such intervention successful. During the twenties, a number of competent observers proved that Bolshevism could not succeed and that its disappearance was a matter of months or of a few years at worst. During the thirties, the Soviet Union figured in the calculations of the Western powers as a negligible quantity not to be taken seriously as a military factor. This attitude was generally adopted with success in the debates on the implementation of the Franco-Russian Alliance of 1935, the Russian offer of support to Czechoslovakia in 1938, and the Anglo-French military mission to Moscow in 1939. When Germany attacked the Soviet Union in 1941, the best military opinion in the West gave the Russians no more than six months until surrender. And when the Soviet Union survived, it was only logical to attribute its survival to its climate or to its wide open spaces or—preferably—to American lend-lease, but not to its own strength.

The error of all this is clearly demonstrated in a recent book,[1] one that bears a high mark of respectability. It is written by General Augustin Guillaume, commander of a Free French division in the Second World War, from 1946

[1] Augustin Guillaume: *Soviet Arms and Soviet Power* (New York: Infantry Journal; 1949).

to 1948 French Military Attaché in Moscow, and at present commander of the French Army of Occupation in Germany. In a foreword General Bedell Smith voices the conviction "that General Guillaume's reasoning and conclusions are sound and that they merit the most careful attention."

This book gives an impressive account of Russian technological achievements. Let us hear what General Guillaume has to say about the relocation of Russian industries during the war.

> The transplanted establishments resumed their activities after a short period for installation. For example, tank factory No. 183 of Kharkov, evacuated in October 1941 to the region of Sverdlovsk, furnished its first tank from the new location on December 18 and reached its prewar level of production by March, 1942. . . . Whenever it could be done, the factories themselves were moved: 75 per cent of the industrial equipment of Leningrad and the numerous factories from Moscow were transferred in this way; and the same was true of the great Putilov factories of Leningrad and the tractor plants of Stalingrad and Kharkov.

General Guillaume gives the main credit for the victory in the east to the Soviet Union:

> Nor was it Allied matériel that stopped the Germans at Leningrad, Moscow, and Stalingrad. By 1943, when the Lend-Lease matériel and tools were first flowing in quantity into the USSR, the German armies had already long been arrested or turned back on the entire front from the Black Sea to the Arctic Ocean. Like the Russian winter, the Allied matériel could only hasten the hour of victory.

166

The Russian industrial effort was part of an over-all war plan and was able quantitatively and qualitatively to hold its own against German production and even to surpass it in certain respects, such as artillery, tanks, and planes. That the over-all industrial productivity and technology of the Soviet Union is inferior to that of the United States is too apparent to need emphasis. The question, however, is whether such an over-all comparison meets the point. Over-all inferiority might well be compatible with equality, if not superiority, in particular sectors where the whole national effort is concentrated under totalitarian direction. That such might be the case in the Soviet Union is at the very least made plausible by the evidence adduced in General Guillaume's book.

The book also shows to what an extent the errors that proved to be Hitler's undoing were the errors in which the Western world has persisted to this day. As the general puts it: "To sum up: Hitler was defeated on the Eastern Front because he never realized the true import of the deep transformation that had occurred in the USSR in every field of endeavor from 1917 on." Underestimation of the Russians was the invariable source of Hitler's misjudgments. "His underestimation of the enemy strength all the way through" says General Heusinger, his chief of operations until July, 1944, "led constantly to false deductions and to errors." This holds true of the West as well.

THE CASE OF THE RUSSIAN ATOMIC EXPLOSION

It is against this background of consistent underestimation that one must consider the most recent and probably the most fateful instance of such misjudgment: the official reaction to the atomic explosion in the Soviet Union, announced by President Truman on September 23, 1949.

Ever since the end of the Second World War our leaders have been conscious of the enormous, if not decisive importance of our monopoly of the atomic bomb in the world balance of power. With that importance in mind, they tried to evaluate the Russian ability to achieve an atomic explosion within a certain time. Even the most conservative official estimates did not expect an atomic explosion in the Soviet Union earlier than 1952. To cite only one example among many: James F. Byrnes concluded in June, 1945, that "any other government would need from seven to ten years, at least, to produce a bomb." Writing from the perspective of 1947, he added: "And I think that to accomplish the task at such speed would require a quicker return to normal conditions than has taken place in any other country within the last few years." [2]

How did our leaders react when that dreaded event occurred much earlier than they had expected?

In his announcement President Truman declared: "Ever since atomic energy was first realized by man, the eventual development of this new force by other nations was to be expected. This probability has always been taken into account by us." [3]

It was this point that Secretary of State Acheson elaborated in his statement at a news conference the same day. "I want to emphasize the four basic matters which were brought out in the President's release this morning. Those are: the President has stated the fact that there has been an atomic explosion in the Soviet Union. In the second place, the President has stated that we have been fully aware that sooner or later this development would occur

[2] James F. Byrnes: *Speaking Frankly* (New York: Harper and Brothers; 1947) p. 261.

[3] *New York Times*, September 24, 1949, p. 1.

and that in our thinking it has been taken into account. That is an important fact to remember. In the third place, the President has recalled what so many people have forgotten, that in every statement made by him and by the two Prime Ministers as well as by all the commissions and bodies which have studied this matter, it has always been clearly pointed out that this situation would develop. And finally, the President has stated that this event makes no change in our policy." [4]

According to the *New York Times,* "Throughout the question-and-answer session Mr. Acheson took pains to make the point that the news from the White House was no surprise to anyone. All discussions had been conducted on the assumption that other countries would some day begin to catch up to the atomic information of the United States." [5] Mr. Hanson Baldwin stated that "Secretary of Defense Johnson refused, at first, to credit the evidence presented, and apparently still does not believe that an 'atomic explosion' necessarily means an atomic bomb." [6]

The *New York Times* reported as the reaction of "some of the most responsible members of Congress . . . that the American people could have confidence, in any possible crisis, in the military power of this country." Senator Scott Lucas, in particular, did not think "that the Soviet achievement changes the fundamental pattern of world power. The United States still has a four-year lead. . . . Our scientists and our technologists will enable us to maintain our lead. I feel sure that plans and preparations have been made by our Government for any contingency that might arise. I have the utmost confidence in the wisdom of our Secretary of Defense and our military leaders." [7] About the reactions of "high civilian and military officials," the *New York Times* reported that "In no quarter was there any hint of dismay." General Bradley stated: "We have anticipated it for four years, and it calls for no change in our basic defense plans." [8]

According to the *New York Times,* a certain official suggested "that Russia might have been getting to the point of testing a bomb that might be neither so practicable nor so effective as that [of] the United States. There was also some doubt that Russia had been able to begin stockpiling numbers of the so-called absolute weapon as the United States has been doing since the explosion over Hiroshima. . . . Guarded, carefully considered views expressed privately by high, responsible officials in the administration were to the effect that the development increased the insecurity of the United States 'by a very small degree.' . . . A military interpretation was that the explosion did not indicate a major improvement in Russian military potential. In support of this view, it was said that one experimental explosion did not mean that Russia had achieved mass production of the bomb. Also, while the United States has had a four-year headstart in atomic bomb stockpiling, Russia will be hindered by her inferiority in knowhow, raw materials, engineering facilities and electric power." [9]

The next day the *New York Times* reported "informed quarters" as saying that "This country's policy . . . is being carried forward on the assumption that Russia, as always expected, possesses the bomb although she doubtless is still far behind the United States in stockpiles and production techniques." [1]

General Eisenhower declared: "I see no reason why a development that was anticipated years ago should cause

8 Ibid., September 24, 1949, p. 2.
9 Ibid., September 24, 1949, p. 2.
1 Ibid., September 25, 1949, p. 1.

any revolutionary change in our thinking or in our actions." [2]

General Groves, wartime head of the atomic energy project, commented that

> he would not "lose any sleep over" the announcement, because this country was "certainly in the lead" in any atomic race. . . . The question was not whether Russia had built an atomic bomb "but how good that one is, and how many they have, and can they catch up with us?" . . . General Groves said he did not know whether the Russians had an atomic bomb "because I have never been in Russia—no one knows what goes on in Russia." [3]

General Bedell Smith voiced the belief "that it will take Soviet Russia at least ten years to get to the point of mass production that we have now reached." [4]

Mr. Lilienthal, then chairman of the Atomic Energy Commission, "authorized the UP to represent him as feeling now precisely as he felt before he knew Russia had the bomb," and said that "this country must do everything necessary to 'establish atomic leadership.' " [5]

Two experts of the *New York Times*, Anne O'Hare McCormick and Arthur Krock, gave an impressive summary of the official reaction. "There is no reason," said Mrs. McCormick, "why the world should be taken by surprise by the President's statement. What was bound to happen sometime happened a little ahead of schedule but not unexpectedly to scientists, soldiers, or even mere observers of the harrying pace of history." [6] And Mrs. McCormick

---

2 Ibid., September 24, 1949, p. 2.
3 Ibid., September 24, 1949, p. 2.
4 Ibid., September 28, 1949, p. 7.
5 Ibid., September 25, 1949, p. 1.
6 Ibid., September 24, 1949, p. 12.

quoted "experts" to the effect "that in the experiment the Russians destroyed the only bomb they had and probably most of the plutonium in their possession." [7]

The "sharp impact," wrote Mr. Krock, "was quickly supplanted by the philosophical reflection, 'eventually, why not now?' . . . The blend of hope in this practical acceptance of what the whole government assumed as inevitable apparently has its source in *a*) the lack of proof that what exploded was an 'atomic weapon' and *b*) in the old military theory of the balance of power." [8]

The London *Economist,* on October 8, summed up the official reaction by stating: "There has been, indeed, no glimmering of a new or original thought since the news broke; everyone is just as he was before—only more so."

It would have been more rational to admit that an error had been committed, to search for the causes of that error, and to resolve to change the attitude from which it had arisen, so that we would not commit a similar error again. But nothing of the kind happened. Even those who admitted the error refused to admit that it was of any consequence.

Q. After all, what difference does it make if what was bound to happen happens a few years earlier than expected?

A. It makes all the difference in the world, for it upsets the timetable of our foreign policy.

Q. But will we not simply put into operation now instead of later the plans we made in view of that eventuality?

A. Those plans are, of course, secret. But it is no secret that the only present defense against atomic bombs is the dispersion and the moving underground

[7] Ibid., September 28, 1949, p. 26.
[8] Ibid., September 25, 1949, p. E3.

of cities and industrial installations, and we are doing nothing like that.

Q. But is it not true that, if we just keep at it, we will always have more and better atomic bombs than the Russians?

A. Even if this were true, it would be irrelevant. "The preponderance of the United States in atomic weapons is bound to be temporary. In the not too distant future the Soviet Union will certainly have atomic weapons. If the ratio of X:O is not transformed now into O:O, it will inevitably be transformed later into X:Y. Yet, concerning atomic weapons, X=Y. In other words, once the Soviet Union has atomic weapons, it matters little that the United States will have more atomic weapons than the Soviet Union. It requires only a limited number of atomic bombs to destroy the military potential of the United States. This destruction will deprive the United States of the ability to win a war against the Soviet Union, however much damage it might be able to do by dropping a superior number of atomic bombs on Russian territory." [9]

Q. But is it possible that the Russians did not explode an atomic bomb at all, or that perhaps they used the only one they had, and perhaps consumed the bulk of their fissionable material? Or, is it not probable that it was not a particularly good bomb? Anyhow, we have nothing to worry about—let us have confidence in our leaders and forget the incident.

A. At this point the neurotic mind has withdrawn almost completely from reality and has created a world of its own in which it feels secure. Yet a collective neurosis will bring a nation not to the infantile content-

[9] Hans J. Morgenthau: *Politics Among Nations* (New York: Alfred A. Knopf, Inc.; 1948), p. 319.

ment of the asylum, but to the terror and misery of a national catastrophe, the reward of policies based upon delusions instead of facts.

The truth is that the acquisition by Russia of an atomic weapon was an event of the greatest importance. In comparison with it, all the great issues of the postwar period fade into insignificance. Certainly in the short run, and probably for the future as well, it overshadows even the passing of China into the Soviet camp. Its importance lies in the decisive change it makes in the world balance of power.

3. *The Misunderstanding of American Power*

However misguided the policy of secrecy with regard to the atomic bomb may have been in other respects, it made sense with the assumption that the monopoly of the atomic bomb was so invaluable a basis for American power that extreme measures and sacrifices were justified to prevent other nations from gaining the knowledge only we were supposed to possess. Our advantage was thought to reside in the exclusiveness of that possession. If this was correct—as we think it was—then obviously the ability of another nation to make atomic bombs was bound to destroy that advantage. Those public officials who insisted upon secrecy because of the inestimable value of the atomic monopoly, and in the fall of 1949 pretended to think nothing of its passing, could not have been right both times. Either they were wrong when they put so high a price on the monopoly, or they were wrong when they declared that the atomic bomb in Russian hands hardly impaired the power of the United States.

174

THE UNITED STATES VS. THE SOVIET UNION

Eight basic factors determine the power of a nation: geography, natural resources, industrial capacity, military preparedness, population, national character, national morale, and the quality of its diplomacy. There are some rational grounds for believing that the United States has at present an advantage in two factors: industrial capacity and national character; that the Soviet Union has an advantage in three: geography, population, and military preparedness; that with regard to two, diplomacy and natural resources, both countries are in a roughly similar position; and that one, national morale, is beyond rational calculation, for there is no way of telling in advance how a people will stand up under the conditions of modern warfare.

We have already referred to the over-all superiority of the United States over the Soviet Union in industrial capacity, a superiority that is not necessarily the same as superiority in the production of the implements of war.

We would assume that a people whose national character is marked by self-reliance, individual initiative, spontaneous manipulation of social change, and mistrust of government dictation, would possess greater intellectual and moral reserves and a greater adaptability to changing circumstances than a people who have for the whole of their history lived under authoritarian, if not totalitarian rule.

The geographic advantage of the Soviet Union over the United States consists in an extent of territory which allows an unmatched defense in depth and makes possible an equally unmatched decentralization of population and industrial centers.

Aside from this geographic advantage and from superiority in numbers of population, it is in military preparedness that the chief element of Russian strength is to be found. While certain important factors that bear upon the military power of a nation—such as quality of strategic plans, of leadership, of training, and morale—escape objective pre-determination, there are others that are susceptible of such determination. Among them two stand out: the fraction of the national effort spent for military preparedness, and the kind of weapons available.

It is obvious that a totalitarian government has a potential advantage in being able to give unified direction to the national effort and to direct as much of it as seems desirable and feasible into military channels. The Soviet government has made full use of its power and maintains an army and air force superior in numbers to any other existing army and air force or combination of them. This advantage has in the past been thought to be roughly canceled out by the absolute American superiority in one weapon: the atomic bomb. It was even widely believed that the unique destructiveness of this weapon would give the United States an edge over the Soviet Union in total military strength. It was expected that in the initial stages of a war the atomic bomb would destroy the industrial centers of the Soviet Union, and then the whole American national effort, marshaled for military purposes, would have at its command a vastly superior industrial potential.

In the near future, Russian possession of the atomic bomb will remove our counterweight—consisting in the atomic monopoly—to the superior Russian military establishment. And it will also remove the edge we possess in the balance of power. For soon the superior industrial plant of the United States will be as exposed to destruction by atomic bombs as is now the inferior Russian industrial plant.

In sum, before long a superior Russian military establishment, supported by an inferior industrial plant and armed with atomic bombs, will confront an inferior American military establishment, supported by a superior industrial plant and armed with atomic bombs. Before the initial phase of the war is over the superior American industrial plant will have been wiped out as well as the inferior Russian one. The atomic bomb is no respecter of technological achievements, and before it all industrial plants are equal. Thus the main potential source of American military superiority will have been eliminated. It is for this reason we have said that Russian possession of the atomic bomb constitutes a decisive change in the world balance of power.

It was inevitable that sooner or later the Soviet Union would be able to produce atomic bombs. What has wrought havoc with American foreign policy is the fact that the Soviet Union was able to produce one as early as it did. The postwar foreign policy of the United States had been predicated upon the assumption of the military superiority of the United States over the Soviet Union, a superiority that was supposed to last for a number of years but, as we have seen, is about to disappear long before its appointed time. In concrete terms, it was assumed that our superiority, derived mainly from the monopoly of the atomic bomb, would come to an end only after we had gained equality with the Soviet Union on land by making Western Europe strong enough to withstand a Russian attack at least during the period needed to bring American superiority in other fields into play. This assumption underlay the Truman Doctrine, the Marshall Plan, and the North Atlantic Pact.

Soviet acquisition of the atomic bomb in 1949 instead of much later has upset the timetable upon which our foreign policy was based and has seriously impaired our bargaining position. This relation between the date of the first Russian atomic explosion and the timetable of American foreign policy makes that explosion a genuine catastrophe. It also makes unworthy of serious consideration the official statements that the inevitable simply happened a little earlier than expected, and that is all there is to it. Would we find very convincing an investor who, surprised by a break in the market which he expected to occur much later, commented on his bankruptcy as our leaders commented on their failure? In truth, the first atomic explosion on Russian soil has shattered American foreign policy as it had evolved since 1945. Now we need a new foreign policy, based upon new assumptions to be formulated in the light of a new balance of power.

THE SOURCES OF WESTERN STRENGTH

The objective of American policy in Europe, the peaceful restoration of the balance of power, can be attained only if the Red Army is persuaded to retreat from central and from much of Eastern Europe. To that end the United States would have to bring overwhelming power to bear upon the Soviet Union, power so great as to make likely the defeat of the Soviet Union in war. The Soviet Union then would prefer peaceful retreat to military defeat. Four factors—one condition to be maintained, three measures to be accomplished—were to have constituted this overwhelming power: the American monopoly of the atomic bomb; American rearmament; the economic, political, and military restoration of Western Europe; the economic, political, and military integration of Western Germany into Western Europe. While the Western world proceeded with these measures toward the creation of an effective counterweight, our monopoly of the atomic bomb would contain the Soviet Union; that is, would deter it from interfering directly, especially through armed aggression.

By the late summer of 1949, none of the measures designed to restore the European balance of power had been carried out or even seriously begun. Even the Marshall Plan, though it had restored the productivity of Western Europe, had left virtually untouched the social and economic evils from which indigenous Communism, and through it Russian imperialism, continued to draw their strength. The rearmament of Western Europe consisted only in the pledges of the North Atlantic Pact and of the Brussels Treaty and of a network of overlapping, competing, and un-co-ordinated committees. Beneath them Western Europe remained as defenseless as it had been since 1945. Western Germany had regained a measure of economic health, yet its political and military problems, especially in view of the defense of the West, remained unsolved. American rearmament was a euphemism for Mr. Louis Johnson's boasts and economies.

In view of this state of affairs, the atomic explosion on Russian soil directed at the framers of our foreign policy a triple warning:

1. You have wasted four valuable years in talking big, while doing little and thinking less. The age of complacency, of big words and small deeds, must end and what should have been done long ago must be done now.

2. Action now must be taken with frantic speed, determination, and circumspection. For the Russian atomic explosion has torn a big hole in the umbrella of atomic superiority under whose protection Western rearmament was to proceed. The timetable under which you proposed to proceed at a leisurely pace has contracted enormously. Looking ahead from 1949,

179

you will enjoy the protection of atomic superiority not for the expected span of ten or eight or six years, but for a mere three or four years. For this is the time the Russians are estimated to need to acquire a stockpile of atomic bombs sufficient for a war with the United States. The rearmament you cannot accomplish within those three or four years you cannot accomplish at all and maintain peace. For once the deterrent of your atomic superiority is gone, a rearmament will likewise lose its deterrent effect and will tend, to the extent that it approaches Russian strength, to invite war rather than prevent it.

3. Since it is doubtful whether you will be able, within this short span of time, to do by way of rearmament all that you plan to do, you must establish priorities between what you must do in any case and what you might do if you had enough time.

Those statements of our leaders which have been quoted indicate in a general way their reaction to these warnings. Not all the framers of American policies could on reflection continue to think and act as complacently as they had seemed to under the immediate impact of the alarming news from Russia. Mr. Acheson, in a series of remarkable speeches calling for "total diplomacy," expressed the alarm all thinking and responsible men ought to have felt. But the policy of the United States in those three fields where decisive action was now needed on a massive scale and at an accelerated pace remained more akin to total complacency than to total diplomacy. The awakening to the preciousness of time, which finally occurred in the late autumn of 1950, was the result not of a considered evaluation of the power factors involved, but of a mere historic accident. The Korean War showed that the United States had to commit virtually all its combat-ready troops, together with a considerable portion of its virtually unopposed air force and navy, to hold its own and finally to defeat an army such as that of North Korea. The Korean War also showed that under the same conditions of superiority in the air and on the sea the United States was just capable of holding its own against a fragment of the armies of China.

The demonstration of such stupendous military weakness, so painfully at variance with the official assurances of preparedness and strength, made the active pursuit of a program of rearmament for the United States, Western Europe, and Western Germany almost inevitable. Yet when finally a start was made to take those measures which men like Bernard Baruch and James Forrestal had deemed essential long before, five valuable years had been wasted. Four of those wasted years date from before the Russian atomic explosion and may be explained by the inveterate tendency to underestimate Russian power and to lend an ear to those experts who had the "facts" to bear out their estimate of Russian weakness. No such rational explanation can be given for the fifth of those wasted years. The loss of that fifth year is due to a failure of will which must be blamed for many other weaknesses of our foreign policy.

The belated rearmament near the end of 1950 was a result of the shock of military humiliation, not a deliberate choice made in view of the over-all political and military situation. And we have thus far failed to heed the third warning carried by the atomic explosion, and to establish priorities, in view of the brief span of time available, among the three spheres of rearmament: American, Western European, and Western German.

American rearmament should have had unquestioned priority, with the rearmament of Western Europe and of Western Germany following in that order. In view of the enormous superiority of the Soviet Union on land, it has always been impossible to build "situations of strength," to use Mr. Acheson's phrase, at any particular point of friction. There has been only a single "situation of strength," the strength of the United States, and the assurance that this strength would be brought to bear against any infringement of the territorial status quo at any place in Europe. It is a profound misunderstanding of the policy of containment to think that the Soviet Union could be, or has ever been, contained by the rearmament of those countries at its periphery which seem to be threatened by Russian aggression.

There was never a possibility that we could contain the Soviet Union at all points, or for that matter at any one of them, around the enormous perimeter that stretches from Finland through central and southeast Europe and the whole length of Russia's Asiatic frontier to the Bering Straits. A potential aggressor can always shift the point of pressure from an armed to an unarmed neighbor, and thus continually frustrate efforts at local rearmament. Furthermore, it is a forlorn hope that the nations of Western Europe will ever be able, either alone or with the support of American arms and troops, to match Russian power on land. At the beginning of 1951, General Eisenhower commanded ten divisions, against approximately one hundred and seventy-five divisions at the disposal of the Soviet Union. Plans call for twenty divisions to be stationed in Western Europe by the fall of 1951. And would there be a decisive difference if there were fifty or sixty such divisions, even assuming that the Russians did not in the meantime increase theirs? But this mechanical counting of divisions can be deceptive, if not stultifying, for the strength of a nation depends not only, and not even primarily, upon the number of men it has under arms.

What has restrained the Soviet Union has not been the

power, negligible in comparison with that of the Soviet Union, which the United States could commit at any particular point around the twenty-thousand-mile perimeter of the Soviet empire. The Soviet Union was restrained, aside from the fear of modern war as such and the peculiar conditions that seemed to make the conquest of Western Europe unattractive, by one thing alone: American power actual and potential, centered in the United States itself. West Berlin, an island in a Red sea, has thus far been protected against overwhelming Russian superiority not at the border dividing East and West Berlin, but in Washington. The divisions that the United States has now or can have in Europe in time of peace are not capable of stopping the Russian armies with the physical strength at their disposal. They are only able to serve as an emphatic and unmistakable assurance in fact, underlining repeated assurances in words, that the Soviet Union cannot attack Western Europe without attacking the United States.

It has not been the presence of two American divisions in Western Germany which has prevented the Soviet Union from marching to the Rhine or to the Pyrenees or beyond; nor has it been the military aid given to Greece and Turkey which has protected those countries from Russian invasion. The real deterrent has been the certainty that any step taken by any unit of the Red Army beyond the line of demarcation of 1945 would call forth an atomic attack upon the Soviet Union, against which it was unable either to protect itself or to retaliate effectively. It is this fundamental fact which should have determined the political and military policies of the United States vis-à-vis the Soviet Union, and it was the inevitability of the disappearance of that fact in the not-too-distant future which should have determined the timetable of those policies.

More particularly, the recognition of that fact should

have protected the United States from the delusion that the dispatch of weapons or troops to a danger zone, beyond suppressing local disorders, strengthening local morale, and serving as a token of the American resolution to resist, can influence in any way the over-all distribution of power between the United States and the Soviet Union. Strangely enough, when we look across the Iron Curtain, we consider only the strength of the Soviet Union and tend to disregard the contributions Poland or Bulgaria might be able to make to Soviet strength. Yet in our calculations of Western strength, France looms large in comparison with the United States. Here again the Maginot-line psychology leads us astray. It makes us forget that we did not defend ourselves and defeat Japan by sending reinforcements to the Philippines, Guam, and Wake Island, and by dispatching arms to Singapore and the Netherlands Indies. We prevailed because we were able to bring the concentrated strength of the United States to bear upon the most vulnerable positions of the enemy. Furthermore, while we are duly impressed with the wide spaces of the Soviet Union and the resulting decentralization of its industrial and population centers, that same psychology tends to make us forget that one of our prime defenses lies in the dispersal of our industries and centers of population, thus making the United States unattractive for an atomic attack. As the Soviet Union has been deterred in the past by the power of the United States, it might well be deterred in the future by the expectation that that power is beyond the reach of effective atomic destruction. Compared with so momentous and fundamental a consideration, the increasing of some divisions here and the rearming of some divisions there takes on the aspect of a pastime ludicrous in its morbid futility.

The Western world, then, is being defended and will be defended—as it was saved twice—by the strength available within the continental limits of the United States. With that strength undeveloped or frittered away, neither Western Europe, however well armed it may be, nor the United States can be defended against the Soviet Union. That strength, developed and concentrated for the highest possible deterrent effect, will protect both the United States and Western Europe, as it has in the past. But maintaining the priority of American rearmament is not tantamount to saying that the United States ought to wash its hands of Western Europe and refrain from supporting Western Europe's efforts to rearm itself. The question is not whether we should defend Western Europe but how we ought to defend it. While it is true that the core of the world balance of power is determined by the relative power of the United States and the Soviet Union, it cannot be a matter of indifference either to the United States or to the Soviet Union whether a rich and populous territory on the western fringes of the Soviet empire lies open to virtually bloodless conquest or whether it can be conquered only at a price. In other words, it makes a difference whether the Russians will be able, as they are now, to march westward as far as they wish virtually unopposed, or whether they will meet determined opposition which they must overcome while American power comes into play. The rearmament of Western Europe, then, can only enable the nations of Western Europe to deter the Soviet Union from attacking them. It is not a matter of holding a line at the Elbe, at the Rhine, or at any other particular place.

The rearmament of the United States must have priority over the rearmament of Western Europe, because of the nature of American and Soviet power. That priority is required also as a pre-condition for the rearmament of Western Europe. It is naïve in the extreme to expect countries such as France to rearm with any degree of seriousness, let alone determination, without a reasonable assurance that their rearmament will not become the pretext for Russian aggression to be followed inevitably by Russian conquest. As the United States can safely rearm only under the protective umbrella of its atomic superiority, so the nations of Western Europe can safely rearm only under the protective umbrella of American power. The stronger the United States, the more serious will the nations of Western Europe be about rearming. Their indecision and fear are the reflection of American weakness. Their confidence and determination will increase to the degree to which American power appears to be able to deter Russian aggression. To ask a Frenchman to take up arms in defense of his country makes sense for him only if there is a chance for that defense to prove effective. Only the deterring power of the United States can provide such a chance. In the absence of such deterring power, and hence in the certainty of general war, to ask a Frenchman to take up arms is little short of absurd. The prospect before him would be annihilation either by American or by Russian atomic bombs. Faced with such a prospect, no man will fight.

The power considerations that require priority of American rearmament over that of Western Europe also apply to the rearmament of Western Germany. And, for the same psychological and military reasons that hold for Western Europe, American rearmament is a pre-condition for German rearmament. The rearmament of Germany must, however, be subordinated to the rearmament of the United States and of Western Europe by virtue of special military and political factors. These factors, if disregarded, will at the same time impede the rearmament of Western Europe and provoke the Soviet Union to go to war instead of deterring it from doing so. These consequences can be avoided only if Western Germany is fully integrated into the Atlantic community not only militarily, but also politically and economically. Here lies the great importance of the Schuman plan for the internationalization of the iron and coal industries of Western Europe. If this plan succeeds, it will make impossible the use of a Western German army for any purposes other than those of the whole Atlantic community, for the industrial potential of Western Germany will be controlled by all the nations of Western Europe.

Without such full integration into the Atlantic community, three political and military developments, destructive of the interests of the United States, would almost inevitably ensue from the rearmament of Western Germany. The re-establishment of an independent German army would be followed by the revival of an independent German foreign policy. That policy would find its minimum objective in the unification of Eastern and Western Germany and its probable objective in the rectification of the eastern frontiers of Germany at the expense of Poland and Czechoslovakia. The natural conditions of its existence would drive Germany to aspire to a dominant position on the continent of Europe. Unification without demilitarization would make it, by virtue of the quantity and quality of its population and its industrial potential, the master of all of Europe west of the Russian sphere of influence.

Neither the nations of Western Europe nor the Soviet Union and its Eastern European satellites could watch such a development with equanimity. While the nations of Western Europe could do nothing to prevent it, they would certainly not help to bring it about; they would find in the hopelessness of their power position vis-à-vis a rearmed Western Germany, moving inexorably toward unification with the Eastern half, an additional reason for passively awaiting the inevitable. The inevitable in this case would be the violent reaction of the Soviet Union.

In the Second World War Germany came close to defeating the Soviet Union, then allied with all the nations of the West. Remembering this, the Soviet Union would not allow the power of a unified and independent Germany to be added to the combined strength of the Western coalition. Yet the Soviet Union would have to intervene even against a much less extreme contingency. German rearmament even on a small scale would necessarily threaten the Western frontiers of Poland and Czechoslovakia and with them the whole power structure erected by the Soviet Union on its own western frontiers during and after the Second World War. The Soviet Union would have to defend the western frontiers of its satellites as though they were its own, or else face the likelihood of an irresistible spread of Titoism. Under such conditions the rearmament of Western Germany, far from being a deterrent, would make a Third World War almost inevitable.

The government of the United States has not faced squarely the priority of American rearmament over the rearmament of Western Europe and of Western Germany. Nor has it acted as if it were aware of the new and drastically contracted timetable created by the unexpectedly early Russian acquisition of atomic bombs. It has for the most part spoken and acted as though the three phases of strengthening the West operated on one and the same plane, as though it made little difference which one was tackled first, and as though it could accomplish all three simultaneously. The government of the United States has also spoken and acted as though that crucial moment were not fast approaching when the Russian possession of a stockpile of atomic bombs would put Western rearmament at the mercy of Russian power. (In the matter of rearmament, the American government acted at the beginning of 1951 as it might have acted in 1948 or 1949, while in those wasted years it acted with an unconcern unwarranted under any circumstances.) It has also acted as though there did not exist an intimate and necessary relationship between the priorities and the timetable of Western rearmament, on the one hand, and the chances for a negotiated settlement preventing a Third World War, on the other.

4. *Military Power and Diplomatic Action*

The primary preoccupation with restoring the productivity of Western Europe and raising a number of divisions from its manpower has made us well-nigh forget that rearmament is but a means to an end and that this end is the prevention of war. While we have been busy adding and equating divisions, we have virtually forgotten the shortness of the time left to us to make another—perhaps the last—effort to save the cause of peace. We have refused to listen to Mr. Churchill's repeated warning, so forcefully expressed—to mention but one occasion among many—in his speech to the House of Commons on March 28, 1950:

> But if there is a breathing space, if there is more time, as I feel and do not hesitate to say, it would be a grave mistake . . . perhaps a fatal mistake to suppose that, even if we have this interlude, it will last for ever, or even last more than a few years. Time and patience, those powerful though not infallible solvents of human difficulties, are not necessarily on our side. When the last Parliament met, I mentioned four years as the period before any other Power but the United States would possess the atomic bomb. That period has already gone by, and our position is definitely worse than it was in this matter both as regards our own safety and as to the conditions which are, I believe, effectively preserving the peace of the world.

. . . . .

Therefore, while I believe there is time for a further effort for a lasting and peaceful settlement, I cannot feel that it is necessarily a long time or that its passage will progressively improve our own security. Above all things, we must not fritter it away.

Yet frittered it away we have, strengthening ourselves neither for peace nor for war, expecting conditions for negotiations to materialize which we could not command, and conjuring up thereby three mortal dangers to the security of the nation: the dissipation of American power, the dissolution of the Atlantic Alliance, the specter of a Third World War.

THE DISSIPATION OF AMERICAN POWER AND THE PROBLEM OF NEGOTIATIONS

We have quoted with approval Mr. Acheson's statement of February 12, 1950, that only those agreements are useful which "record an existing situation of fact. . . . So it has been our basic policy to build situations which will extend the area of possible agreement, that is, to create strength instead of the weakness which exists in many quarters." We have said that this analysis is unexceptionable as far as it goes. But we must now disagree with the practical application to which Mr. Acheson has put his thesis. He mentions as examples the Berlin blockade, Greece, Turkey, and China. Yet the strength the United States has applied at those focal points of conflict has not served to contain and deter the Soviet Union and induce it to enter into agreements and carry them out. At best, American strength applied locally has prevented or suppressed internal subversion and civil war. Where there has been lasting agreement with the Soviet Union, as in the case of the Berlin blockade, it was the over-all power of the

United States, actual and potential, that made agreement possible and has thus far supported its execution. This is the "situation of strength" upon which the United States must rely for a peaceful settlement as well as for a successful deterrent to war. We have referred to the misjudgment of this fundamental fact in the rearmament policy of the United States. The same misjudgment has thus far thwarted the peace policy of the United States.

What makes us strong as a deterrent against war also strengthens our bargaining position for a negotiated settlement. The dispersal of American strength to local points of conflict for other than strictly local purposes is on both counts fatal for the preservation of peace. The strengthening of local bastions arbitrarily chosen around the enormous perimeter of the Eurasian land mass is futile and self-defeating in either case. Far from making the bargaining position of the United States stronger for negotiations with the Soviet Union, it amounts at best to that policy of drift against which Mr. Churchill has warned so often, a policy that refuses to act decisively in time and instead wastes its resources on hopeless little undertakings. At worst, such a policy squanders the national strength and leaves a country weakened for peace as for war. Such has indeed been the result of the policy of drift, of waiting for better bargaining conditions, of building local situations of strength.

Mr. Acheson's principle rests on the assumption that the United States has been in the past not strong enough to negotiate successfully with the Soviet Union, but that it has a good chance of becoming strong enough for that purpose in the future. In order to ascertain how sound the policy of the Administration has been in refusing to negotiate with the Soviet Union in the past, we must remember how strong the United States was in the past in comparison with the Soviet Union and how strong it is likely to be in the future. Mr. Acheson's practical conclusion that at present it is impossible to negotiate with the Russians because we are not strong enough is sound only on the assumption that in the future we will be relatively as well as absolutely stronger, and hence that the chances for a favorable settlement with the Russians will be better in the future. In other words, the problem that confronts us here is one of timing our negotiations with the Soviet Union. It is one thing to state the general conditions without which negotiations with the Soviet Union have no chance to succeed. It is quite another to assert that these conditions do not exist at present but will exist in the future.

To speak first of things that are certain because they are history, there can be no doubt that thus far the policy of waiting has not improved the bargaining position of the United States. Up to September 23, 1949, the United States, secure in the continuing monopoly of the atomic bomb, thought it should postpone negotiations with the Soviet Union until the military and economic recovery of the nations of Western Europe had restored the balance of power in Europe. But in retrospect it is obvious, in view of the disappearance of our atomic monopoly and the deteriorating situation in Asia, that our bargaining position with the Soviet Union was better a year or two years ago than it is now. As Winston Churchill put it in the House of Commons on December 19, 1948:

> Finally, I wish to say one word—and it shall be only a very brief one—about the greatest topic of all which overhangs our minds, our relations with Soviet Russia. I have frequently advised that we should endeavour to reach a settlement with Russia on fundamental, outstanding questions before they have the atomic bomb as well as the Americans. I believe that in this resides the best hope of avoiding a third world war. I wish to make it clear—and this is the principal rea-

son why I refer to this matter in the Debate—that I have never attempted to suggest the timing of such a solemn and grave negotiation. I have not the official knowledge necessary to form an opinion about that.

Our policy of waiting for a better bargaining position was certainly mistaken in the past. Is our bargaining position likely to be better a year from now, when we might well be worse off in Asia than we are now? Is it likely to be better two years from now, when the Soviet Union will have a stockpile of atomic bombs? Is it likely to be better three years from now, when the Soviet Union may well possess hydrogen bombs? All political predictions of course are risky, and timing is the most delicate of diplomatic tasks. Spectacular events, unforeseen and unforeseeable, may upset the most careful calculations of the experts—on either side. But this much can be said with certainty: It is an awful gamble to suspend the processes of diplomacy while the Western world is engaged in a race to redress the balance of power on land before the Soviet Union has acquired a stockpile of atomic bombs sufficient for a devastating attack upon the West. That gamble may succeed, but its failure will make a Third World War inevitable.

Nor are those all the risks that waiting incurs. What we have said thus far assumes that the question of peace or war, that is, of a negotiated settlement or war, will remain under the control of the two great powers who would be the main protagonists in war as they are the main opponents in peace. This, however, is not so. Here again, we can let the greatest of contemporary actors on the international scene, who is also the greatest of its observers, speak for us. To quote again from Winston Churchill's speech of January 23, 1948:

I will only venture now to say that there seems to me to be very real danger in going on drifting too long. I believe that the best chance of preventing a war is to bring matters to a head and come to a settlement with the Soviet Government before it is too late. This would imply that the Western democracies, who should, of course, seek unity among themselves at the earliest moment, would take the initiative in asking the Soviet for a settlement. . . . We may be absolutely sure that the present situation cannot last. . . . There are very grave dangers—that is all I am going to say today—in letting everything run on and pile up until something happens, and it passes, all of a sudden, out of your control.

There are so many inflamed points of contact between East and West that only an optimism uninformed by the past and oblivious to the present could expect that the flames of war might not break out at any such point at any time, with no one wanting it but with no one being able to prevent it. There are today any number of candidates for the role that Serbia played in bringing about the First World War: the match that ignites the flimsy structure of great power relations. Failure of nerve or recklessness in Berlin, at one of the borders of Yugoslavia, at the frontiers of Hong Kong, could start a chain of events that soon would pass out of the control of all concerned. And what is a threat to the peace today will be a still greater threat a year, or two years, or three years from now. Then the countries that are the prizes of the power contest between the East and the West will have grown either stronger—as, for instance, Germany—and will therefore be able to play a more active role in international affairs, or will have grown weaker—as, perhaps, the countries of southeast Asia—thus becoming more tempting objects of internal subversion and foreign conquest.

The United States has passed the pinnacle of its power

in relation to the Soviet Union and cannot hope to enjoy soon again the same freedom of action that was at its disposal in the past. The policy of "getting tough" with Russia and the policy of containment are about to become obsolete. One can afford to get tough with someone and be able to contain him if one is unquestionably his superior in strength. But toughness between equals becomes a two-way street, and containment becomes a matter of choice for the one to be contained. In other words, the unilateral application of pressure as the sole means of achieving our objectives has become impossible, which is another way of saying that the period of the cold war itself has come to an end. The atomic flash somewhere in Asiatic Russia ended that twilight state between peace and war in which we have been drifting. From now on, it will be either peace or war.

The moment before the crucial hour when American superiority in atomic weapons will have disappeared finds the United States ill prepared for peace or war. It finds our bargaining position weak in comparison with what it was at any time since we demobilized. It finds the rearmament of the Western world only beginning, and in danger of being misdirected. And it finds our deterrent power at its lowest ebb since 1945. In proportion to the decline of that deterrent power the danger of a Third World War has increased.

THE PRECARIOUS STATE OF THE ATLANTIC ALLIANCE

It is this relative disadvantage of the United States, combined with the threat of war, which puts the Atlantic Alliance to a severe test. For, as we have tried to show, the European will to fight depends upon the expectation that there will be no need to fight. As the danger of war increases with American weakness, so does the European will to fight decrease with the danger of war. Doubtful of their chances of successful resistance, the peoples of Western Europe will ask themselves if there is no other way out. This state of mind will give Russian diplomacy the opportunity of showing a way out; that is, the neutrality of the nations of Western Europe in a war between the United States and the Soviet Union. There is apparent plausibility in the proposal that the nations of Western Europe stand aside in a war which in its initial stages promises to be a long-distance intercontinental war. Aside from this promise, Soviet diplomacy has yet another asset with which to induce Western Europe to remain neutral: the support of Germany.

Here Stalin's hand contains two jokers that no other player in the game can match. Only the Soviet Union has it in its power to satisfy the irreducible minimum of German aspirations: the unification of Germany. Nobody will doubt that the Soviet Union would not hesitate to throw the Communists of Eastern Germany overboard if it could buy with so insignificant a sacrifice the neutrality, if not the support, of a unified German nation. Looking at the international scene through the distorting lenses of ideological animosity, we tend to forget that other nations are much less likely than we are to subordinate their perennial national interests to emotions, and that neither the Germans nor the Russians are likely to take the issue of Communism as seriously as we do. The mutual support of, first, Prussia, then Germany and Russia in challenging the rest of Europe is older than the issue of Communism. A tradition of two centuries testifies to its persistence. If Stalin was able to come to an understanding with Hitler— which Hitler, not Stalin destroyed, and much to Stalin's regret—he can be expected to deal with whoever may succeed Hitler as the head of a united Germany, on terms advantageous to both and surely for Germany less disadvantageous than to serve as the battleground in the initial stages of a Third World War.

Furthermore, only the Soviet Union is capable of satisfying to whatever extent it wishes a probable objective of a united Germany which ranks second only to unification itself: the rectification of Germany's eastern frontiers. The Soviet Union has championed the territorial aggrandizement of Czechoslovakia and, more particularly, of Poland at the expense of Germany for reasons of power politics. There is no stronger cement sealing the alliance between the Soviet Union and its two strongest neighbors to the west than the latters' dependence upon Russian protection for their new frontiers. What ties Czechoslovakia and Poland to the Russian chariot is not national sympathy nor is it the affinity of political ideologies. It is the overwhelming power of the Soviet Union, which in its own interest must defend the western frontiers of these two satellites against a Germany allied with the West. However, if the Soviet Union could advance the western limits of its sphere of influence from the Oder-Neisse line and the Elbe to the Rhine by winning a united Germany over to its side, what reason would there be for the Soviet Union to protect the new frontiers of Czechoslovakia and Poland against a friendly Germany, especially if the friendship of that Germany could be bought by the surrender of these frontiers? Faced with a choice between the potent enmity or sullen indifference of a resentful Germany and the hapless enmity of its abandoned satellites, Stalin would not hesitate to do what the Czars did time and again, and what he himself did once before: sacrifice the interests of Poland on the altar of Russo-German friendship.

The remilitarization of Western Germany, joined to the restoration of its political independence, will not counter these possible moves by the Soviet Union; it is rather likely to support them by giving Western Germany the power to bargain with the Russians. There is only one way to prevent the danger of the unification of a militarily and politically independent Germany under the auspices of Russia: the neutralization of a unified Germany. Germany is today both the main battleground and the main stake in the struggle between the United States and the Soviet Union. Both powers have one legitimate interest: to withhold control of all of Germany from the other. The United States must prevent Russia from adding the manpower and the industrial potential of all of Germany to its own, and the Soviet Union must deny the United States the same opportunity.

The choices before the United States are two: either military, economic, and political integration of Western Germany into Western Europe under safeguards that make impossible the resumption of an independent foreign policy by Germany, or the neutralization of a unified Germany under military and political conditions, which would make its violation by either side both difficult and hazardous. The United States has thus far refused to face these two choices with all their implications. Instead it has rejected the idea of neutralization out of hand, without embracing the idea of complete integration consistently and with determination. If neutralization is a solution to the German problem, the remilitarization of Western Germany, without the safeguards mentioned above, would contribute neither to the solution of that problem nor to the promotion of the cause of peace.

FROM DETERRENT TO PROVOCATION

Under such conditions, the temptation is acute for the United States to seek what seems to be the easy way out: to bring matters to a head with the Soviet Union and, ill prepared as it is for peace or war, to provoke the very conflict it seeks to avoid. The United States is ill prepared for war, but it is also ill prepared for peace. We are promoting rearmament measures, necessary in themselves but ill conceived in their relation to one another. This is particularly true of what we are planning for Western Europe and Western Germany. Once we do there in earnest what thus far we have only proposed to do, an odd paradox will confront us with a new dilemma. This paradox lies in the fact that too much weakness vis-à-vis the Russians is fatal, but that too much strength—especially misplaced strength—may be fatal too, fatal to the cause of peace. If we should really be able to develop the military power of Western Europe and of Western Germany to such an extent that it could threaten the status quo in Eastern Europe, we would indeed remove one of the three deterrents to war which are mentioned at the beginning of this chapter. We would make Western Europe attractive for Russian conquest and would destroy all chances for the neutralization of Germany on our terms.

Only the faint-hearted will say that a supreme effort in statecraft and military strategy could not even at this late hour succeed. Two formidable obstacles stand in the way of such a turn for the better: deeply ingrained intellectual errors, and a singular lack of courage on the part of our leaders to admit error, to tell the people the truth, and to embark upon a course of action that, however unpopular in the short run, carries the promise of "peace with honor." The strong can lead at home and compromise abroad. The weak must be stubborn at home and abroad, for they must try to save face they do not have. The proposal to drop atomic bombs whenever a problem appears incapable of solution by traditional methods of diplomacy is but the extreme manifestation of that bankruptcy of intellect and will.

In our leaders' weakness—diplomatic, military, intellectual, moral—lies the great threat to peace, in so far as peace depends at all upon what the United States does or does not do. That weakness has blinded our thought and crippled our action. It has made us incapable of recognizing, either in thought or in action, the two fundamental propositions that diplomacy without strength is futile and that strength without diplomacy can be provocative. In the past we have had neither one nor the other. Today we are trying to get one without the other. Tomorrow we must have strength and diplomacy, or we will have war. Without that supreme effort of intellect and will which is required for diplomatic action at this late hour, our military efforts to prevent a Third World War may well contribute toward that cataclysm which all must dread.

VII

The Failure of Judgment: in Asia

The vital objective of our foreign policy in Europe and Asia is the restoration of the balance of power by means short of war. Yet while our objective is the same in both Europe and Asia, the threats we face and, consequently, the measures we must take are fundamentally different. In Europe we face Russian imperialism, but in Asia we face genuine revolution. The ineffectiveness of the specific measures we have taken and the disasters that have befallen our policies in Asia can be traced to this elemental error in judgment: we have acted in Asia as though the threat that confronts us there were identical with the one we must meet in Europe.

Yet it is the measure of the improvidence and confusion of our Asiatic policies that, on the one occasion when we had to meet directly the threat of Russian imperialism in Asia, we misconceived the nature of our task. We started out by committing—to quote Mr. Truman's statement of June 27, 1950—"air and sea forces to give the Korean Government troops cover and support." On June 30, 1950, we extended our aid to "certain supporting ground units," and we ended by engaging the flower of our army in a theater that both the Joint Chiefs of Staff and General MacArthur had declared unprofitable and indefensible in case of a general war. We have continued to think of the Korean campaign in terms of a limited engagement to be terminated by some kind of legal formula establishing an independent, united Korea. We have been oblivious of the fact, which runs counter to all our preconceptions and intentions, that for centuries Korea has not been independent, but has been the object of Chinese, Russian, and Japanese imperialism. We have also been oblivious of the fact that Korea has been protected from Russian imperialism only by the permanent deployment of adequate power on the mainland of Asia, a historic function that has been performed successfully by China and Japan.

On the other hand, we have tried to stop the most dynamic of the national and social revolutions of Asia with our military power, directly or indirectly applied. The result has been failure wherever the attempt has been made. None of these failures is more momentous in its dimensions and immediate results, more pregnant with dire consequences in the long run, and more revealing of the error in judgment of all our Asiatic policies, than our failure in China.

1. *The Confusion of Our China Policy*

The real issue in China is one of genuine revolution. The domestic history of China has been for three centuries a story of civil war, of abortive or successful revolution. Most reigns during that period were established not through constitutional succession to the throne but through some form of violence. Sun Yat-sen's overthrow of the Manchu dynasty in 1911 was his eleventh attempt at revolution since 1895. Yet in 1913 Sun Yat-sen, as head of the Kuomintang or Nationalist Party, started an unsuccessful revolution against the very republic he had founded.

There is no space here to recount all the revolts, revolutions, and civil wars that have followed each other virtually without interruption since the First World War. After a long period of anarchy during which the central government was a mere shadow without effective powers, popular loyalty centered from 1927 onward in the Kuomintang under Chiang Kai-shek, on the one hand, and the Communists under Mao Tse-tung, on the other. Only Japanese imperialism, threatening Communists and Nationalists alike, brought about the temporary unification of the country under Chiang Kai-shek. It is hardly surprising that with the removal of that threat at the end of the Second World War the old cleavage should recur, with both sides trying to fill the power vacuum left by the defeated Japanese.

Faced with the inevitability of civil war between the Chinese Communists and Nationalists, the United States had to ask itself which side it wanted the victory to fall to, in view of the American national interest in seeing the balance of power in Asia maintained. Since the Communists, if they should win control of all of China, were most likely to throw the weight of China to the side of the Soviet Union, the United States was bound to wish for the triumph of the Nationalists. The next question was what we could do to insure the victory of the Nationalists.

As long as the war against Japan was in progress, we did, and perhaps could do, but little to aid effectively those whom we wanted to control China when the war was over. As elsewhere, we were only too ready to deceive ourselves about the nature of Communism and to believe that the Communists, like ourselves, had only one ultimate aim: the military defeat of the Axis powers. As elsewhere, we refused to concern ourselves with preparing a new balance of power, upon which a stable postwar world was to be built and for which the groundwork had to be laid while the war was still in progress. We wanted total victory through unconditional surrender and nothing more.

When the victory was won, we gave military support to the Kuomintang. Yet then it was too late for the kind of military support we were willing and able to give to be effective in the struggle with Communism. If the Chinese Communists had been nothing but the stooges of the Kremlin doing the bidding of their masters after the model of the Greek guerrillas or the Communists of North Korea and Eastern Europe, a large-scale police action, supported by American arms and advice, might have crushed them. But if there existed in China—as there actually did—a revolutionary situation founded on long-smoldering, widespread popular discontent and the inefficiency and corruption of the Nationalist regime, no mere aid in repression but—short of all-out intervention—only social and political reforms could forestall the overthrow of the Nationalists by the people. The Communists were able to win the politically conscious masses of the Chinese people to their side by promising, and in some measure carrying through, the social and political reforms the people demanded.

It is here that confusion over the real issue obscured the thinking and frustrated the policies of the United States. When it became obvious that the Nationalist regime was unable to cope with the revolutionary situation even if supported by American arms and advice, only two courses, which General Wedemeyer's report of 1947 clearly envisaged, were logically open to American policy. One was military intervention on such a scale as to be sufficient not only to crush the Communist armies but also to keep popular discontent permanently in check. Military intervention of this kind would have entailed military and political commitments of incalculable magnitude. This course of action was rejected by the framers of our foreign policy on the advice of, among others, Secretary of State Marshall.

The Confusion of Our China Policy

Our other course of action was predicated on the assumption, however undesirable from the point of view of American interests, that the triumph of the Communist revolution in China was inevitable. It would then have been incumbent upon American policy to reconcile itself to the inevitable—as policy, being the art of the possible, frequently must—and to exploit whatever potentialities there were for the furtherance of American interests. For while Chinese Communism is the ideological vassal of Moscow, its rise to power within China owes little to the Soviet Union, nor will it need to rely upon Russian support to maintain itself in power. This fundamental difference between Chinese Communism and the Communist parties of Eastern Europe, which would never have come to power and could not stay in power without Russian military help, allows the Communist government of China a freedom of action in international affairs which the Communist governments of Eastern Europe entirely lack. Consequently, the Communist government of China can, if it chooses, pursue a course in foreign policy which is determined not by the interests of the Soviet Union expressed in orders from Moscow but by the traditional interests of China. Those interests may or may not coincide with those of the Soviet Union, and Chinese and Russian policies may or may not run parallel. It must be remembered that the traditional objectives of Russia in the Far East have more often than not been at odds with the traditional objectives of China. The sharing of Communist ideology cannot in the long run overshadow China's traditional fear of, and enmity to, Russia. Whether there will be future coincidence or divergence of Russian and Chinese interests and policies will depend in good measure upon the policies of the non-Communist nations. Here was a chance for the United States to pursue a policy that, although difficult to explain to the general public, and necessarily devoid of spectacular short-run successes, might alone have made possible—granted the inevitability of a Communist victory—the furtherance of the traditional American interest in the maintenance of the balance of power in Asia.

The United States chose neither of the two courses logically open to it. Or rather, it chose both of them, pursuing them sometimes simultaneously, sometimes alternately, but always half-heartedly and without consistency. Thus as its harvest it reaped the worst of both worlds.

We intervened on the side of the Nationalists but limited our commitments in matériel and men so strictly as to preclude any chance for success. Simultaneously, we tried to bring about a coalition between Nationalists and Communists which, if we had succeeded, would of necessity have led to the absorption of the former by the latter. General Marshall's attempt in 1946 to end the civil war by forming a coalition government of Communists and Nationalists partook of the same underestimation of Nationalist weakness which underlay all of American policy in the immediate postwar years, and compounded it by a misunderstanding of the character of Chinese Communism. It was grounded in two false assumptions. One was that the Chinese Communists were really agrarian reformers at heart, using Marxist slogans without believing them. The other was a misplaced faith in the Nationalist regime as an efficient and reliable instrument of government. Actually it had become impossible at that stage to do business with Chiang Kai-shek with any expectation of future efficient and honest performance. And it was to misunderstand completely the nature of Communism, as it manifests itself in China as everywhere, to disregard its necessary aspirations for total power as a means through which to realize the truth of Marxism.

After the failure of these two policies we refused to have any clear-cut China policy at all. The expulsion of the

Nationalists from the Chinese mainland meant for all practical purposes that the civil war had ended in the victory of the Communists. Yet while we stopped active support, we continued to act as though something could be gained by remaining on the side of Chiang Kai-shek. The politically disastrous and militarily senseless demonstration of past American support, by means of air raids on the coastal cities of China, executed in American planes by Nationalist airmen, destroyed the last vestiges of the prestige and sympathy the United States had traditionally enjoyed in China. Conversely, we allowed our natural antipathy to Communism as a political system and our legitimate suspicions of the foreign policies of a Communist government to interfere with the pursuit of a foreign policy calculated to reap maximum advantage from a situation undesirable in itself.

Thus, in spite of the better knowledge of some of our wisest and best-informed officials, we drifted into opposing Chinese Communism as such, regardless of the benefits and disadvantages to American interests which would result from that opposition. In a word, without quite wanting or realizing it, and primarily through domestic political considerations, we drifted into a policy of counter-revolution *per se*. We deprived ourselves of the ability to separate the issue of Russian imperialism and, to the extent that it exists, of Chinese imperialism from the issue of the Communist revolution in China.

Having confused these two issues in our minds, we tended to confuse them in action. We did not ask in what measure the Chinese revolution was a mere by-product and instrument of Russian imperialism, as were the so-called revolutions in Eastern Europe, and to what extent it was the genuine result of Chinese discontent. Nor did we ask whether or not the Communist regime in China was necessarily committed to imperialistic policies that were bound to endanger our interests in the Far East. And neither did we ask whether or not the foreign policies of Communist China would irrevocably run parallel to those of the Soviet Union, supporting and strengthening Russian imperialism. Converting into a worldwide policy our domestic opposition to, and fear of, Communism as a social and political system, we were against Communism in China almost as we were against Communism in Illinois. The result has been a debacle on both counts: on that of Communism, which is triumphant in China, and on that of Russian imperialism, which has gained as an ally the most populous nation on earth, rich in untapped resources and animated with a new spirit of national pride and mission. In the short run, our failure in China constitutes one of the most resounding defeats our foreign policy has ever sustained. In the long run, it threatens to become a disaster of unprecedented magnitude for the Western world as a whole, an event from which future historians may well date the ultimate decline of the West in its relations with the colored races.

2. *The Struggle for Asia as a Struggle for the Minds of Men*

The debacle of our Asiatic policies must teach us two lessons: that the revolutions of Asia are here to stay and cannot be suppressed by military means; and that the struggle for the allegiance of Asia will be decided not by force of arms but in a contest of ideas. The question is not whether there will be revolution in Asia or whether it can be prevented or undone where it has occurred. The real question is whether the Soviet Union will capture permanently the intellectual and moral allegiance of the Asiatic revolutions or whether the West will be able to retrieve what it has lost and to defend what it still holds. Great Britain understood these alternatives when it retreated from India, thus exchanging a tenuous military and political advantage for a great moral and political triumph. The United States did not understand these alternatives when it intervened in the Chinese and Indo-Chinese civil wars, and thus gained nothing and lost almost everything.

What we require is not some tactical rearrangement here and strengthening of positions there but a complete and fundamental reorientation of our thinking about Asia. We must recognize that in Asia we are engaged in a struggle of ideas; a struggle for the minds of men. We must understand that this struggle operates by rules as precise and ineluctable as those which govern economic and military warfare.

Yet in practice the divers and ever changing psychological and political conditions prevailing at a particular time in a particular place determine the concrete ways in which these rules are to be applied. The appeal we might make successfully to certain groups in India today might well have to be different tomorrow; for the conditions that determine the receptiveness of these groups might have changed overnight. Even if these conditions were not subject to continuous change, we would have to use different approaches for different groups. The arguments that impress the industrial proletariat of Bombay might fall on deaf ears when addressed to the peasants of Hyderabad. And when we appeal not to different groups within one and the same country but to people in different countries, it must be obvious that what we want to tell an Indian might have no effect at all or even an adverse effect if we tell it to an Indonesian. Our struggle for the minds of men in Asia must take into account all this psychological and political instability and diversity. We can discuss in the following pages the basic principles that ought to guide our Asiatic policies, but only the makers of the day-by-day policies can quicken these principles with concrete detail.

TWO BASIC PRINCIPLES OF IDEOLOGICAL WARFARE

If the ideological contest between democracy and Bolshevism were to be decided by the standards of a seminar in political philosophy, we could have no doubt about the outcome. Unfortunately, what is good and true by the standards of philosophy does not of necessity win out in the political contest of the marketplace. Our weakness, in Asia as well as Europe, in the struggle for the minds of men is primarily the result of the confusion of these two standards, the philosophical and the political. Since democracy is superior to Bolshevism in the truth it contains and in the good of which it carries the promise and in part the fulfillment, we tend to believe that it must also prove itself superior to Bolshevism in the political arena.

Against this confusion in theory, and illusion in practice, two basic principles of ideological warfare must be maintained.

A political ideology, in order to be effective, must reflect the life experiences of those it endeavors to reach.

The great political ideologies of the past which captured the imagination of men and moved them to political action, such as the ideas of the American and French Revolutions and the slogans of Bolshevism and Fascism, were successful not because they were true, but because they gave the people something they were waiting for, both in terms of knowledge and in terms of action. It is important to note that while political philosophies claim the possession of truths valid everywhere at all times, men are receptive only to certain truths at particular times, according to the circumstances under which they live. These circumstances vary greatly not only in time, but also with regard to different people in one and the same period of history.

The variations in the standard of living range from mass starvation to abundance; the variations in freedom, from tyranny to democracy and from economic slavery to equality; the variations in power, from extreme inequalities and unbridled one-man rule to wide distribution of power subject to constitutional limitations. This nation enjoys freedom, yet starves; that nation is well fed, but longs for freedom; still another enjoys security of life and individual freedom, but smarts under the rule of autocratic government. While philosophically the similarities of standards are considerable throughout the world—most political philosophies agree in their valuation of the common good, of law, peace, and order, of life, liberty, and the pursuit of happiness—moral judgments and political actions diverge widely. The same moral and political concepts take on different meanings in different environments. Justice and democracy come to mean one thing here, something quite different there. A move on the international scene decried by one group as immoral and unjust is praised by another as the opposite.

Communism has been successful wherever its tenets of social, economic, and political equality have appealed to people for whom the removal of inequality has been the most urgent aspiration. Western ideology has succeeded wherever in popular aspirations political liberty has taken precedence over all other needs. Thus Communism has largely lost the struggle for the minds of men in central and western Europe, and democracy has by and large been defeated in Asia. In central and western Europe the Communist promises of equality could not prevail against the life experiences of the peoples there with the tyranny of the Red Army and the Russian secret police. In those regions Communism has succeeded only with the segments of the population in whose life experiences the longing for equality, especially in the economic sphere, has taken precedence over concern with liberty.

On the other hand, democracy has lost out in Asia because its appeal has been largely divorced from the life experiences of the peoples of Asia. What the peoples of Asia want is freedom from Western imperialism and social justice in terms of economic betterment. What chance is there for democracy to succeed in the struggle as long as democratic ideology is contradicted by the life experiences of the peoples of Asia? Upon Indians the appeal to free enterprise is lost, for it evokes the reality of profiteering, speculation, and the black market. In the minds of the people of Indochina the appeal to the blessings of democracy and the evils of Russian imperialism cannot prevail over life experiences that show the citadel of democracy allied with one of the last outposts of Western imperialism. The impotence of a political ideology divorced from the life experiences of the common man is exemplified in a report that appeared on September 30, 1950, in the *Chicago Daily News* under the byline of Fred Sparks.

> The other day I visited a small farmer near Saigon. . . .
>
> Through my interpreter I asked him to tell me what he thought of the Americans coming to Indochina. He said:
>
> "White men help white men. You give guns to help the French kill my people. We want to be rid of all foreigners and the Viet Minh . . . was slowly putting out the French."
>
> I said: "Don't you know there is a white man be-

hind the Viet Minh? Don't you know that Ho Chi Minh takes Russian orders?"

He said: "In Saigon I have seen Americans and I have seen Frenchmen. I have never heard of any white men being with the Viet Minh."

What makes this episode significant is the fact that to a large extent it is representative of Asia's reaction to Western ideologies. Nowhere has this reaction been more drastic than in China. For nowhere has the contrast between Western ideology and the life experiences of the people been more drastic. The century-old anti-imperialistic record of the United States and the good will it had created in China for the United States were wiped out in one stroke when American weapons were used to kill Chinese and when American planes dropped bombs on the coastal cities of China. As a report in the London *Economist* put it with reference to the air raids on Shanghai:

In the press these raids were represented as being quite as much the work of the "American imperialists" as that of the "reactionary, remnant lackeys" of Taiwan, and while the raids drove out any faith in Chiang which might remain amongst the less educated they no less effectively drove out any faith in America in quarters where it was still harboured.

Here again, the inherent qualities of American ideology in terms of its truth and of the good reposing in it were entirely irrelevant for success or failure in the warfare of ideas. What counted—and decided the issue—was the apparent irrelevance of democratic propaganda in the light of the experiences of the common man. The policies that we supported or seemed to support made success in the war of ideas impossible.

Ideological warfare is a mere function of political policy.

213

It can be worse than the policy it is meant to support; it can never be better.

The functions political policy must fulfill for ideological warfare are three. First, it must define clearly its objectives and the methods through which it proposes to attain them. Second, it must determine, with regard to objectives and methods, the popular aspirations of those to whom the ideological appeal is to be made. Third, it must determine to what extent political warfare is capable of supporting political policy.

Our ideological weakness in Asia results from the weakness of our political policies. Uncertain of our objectives and of the methods by which to reach them, we have been only too prone to let our ideological appeal dissolve into democratic generalities. Moreover, we are not even quite certain whether we are engaged in a holy crusade, after the models of the two World Wars, to wipe Bolshevism from the face of the earth, or whether we are waging a power struggle against the imperialism of a Soviet Union that uses the ideology of world revolution for the purpose of expanding its power. While the speeches of Mr. Acheson are emphatic in stressing the power-political aspects of the struggle with the Soviet Union, the private and official climate of opinion favors the interpretation of the East-West conflict in terms of a democratic crusade. While our Chinese policy, however awkwardly and hesitatingly, has sometimes tried to subordinate ideological considerations to those of power advantage, our over-all policy in Asia still shows strong traces of counter-revolutionary tendencies for their own sake, and accordingly our propaganda has been inclined to stress the virtues and truths of democracy and the vices and falsehoods of Bolshevism.

It is the same propensity for such moral and philosophical abstractions which has impeded the objective investigation of what other peoples want. Having provided in

214

good measure for the protection of life, and taking this biological security for granted, we concentrate our thoughts and efforts upon the preservation of liberty and the pursuit of happiness. This being natural with us, we erect our limited experience, subject to the conditions of time and space, into a universal principle that claims to be valid everywhere and at all times. Thus we assume, at least by implication, that what we are allowed to take for granted all men can take for granted, and that what we are striving for is the object of the aspirations of all mankind. Ever since Woodrow Wilson we have made the insistence upon democratic elections everywhere in the world one of the mainstays of ideological warfare.

Three basic errors lie at the root of this insistence. One is the belief, which does not need to detain us here, that democracy and peace are synonymous, and hence that to establish democracy everywhere is tantamount to making peace secure everywhere. The second error lies in the assumption that democracy is a kind of gadget capable of being installed in any political household regardless of the qualifications and preferences of the inhabitants. The historical connection between the development of democratic government and the rise of the middle classes is by implication dismissed as a coincidence that can teach us nothing about the limitations of democracy as a universal principle of government.

The final error is the conviction that the formal processes of free elections are the earmark of democratic government. Actually, these processes may mean much or little in terms of the actual choices available to the electorate and of the actual control exercised by the governed over the government. While there can be no democracy without free elections, such elections can be used for undemocratic or anti-democratic ends. In the last analysis it is the democratic ethos of a people, their philosophy of government and politics, their conception of what is right and wrong, desirable and undesirable, feasible and unfeasible, that determine the function free elections fulfill in a given society. A similarity of election laws and procedures may or may not connote a similarity of political systems, according to the moral and social context within which those procedures operate. Democratic propaganda, then, is useless in a moral and social context that is indifferent or hostile to democracy. It remains again for policy to create the moral' and social conditions receptive to the ideals of democracy.

The same disregard for the actual aspirations of human beings and the same predilection for moral and philosophic abstractions has focused public attention upon piercing the Iron Curtain and bringing "the" truth to the peoples under Russian domination. Here again, we tend to overlook the fact that in the sphere of political action there is no such thing as one and the same truth for everybody. Even if information and ideas were allowed to move freely over the globe, the triumph of our ideas would by no means be assured. Those who believe that peace and good will among nations are the direct result of the free flow of news and of ideas fail to distinguish between the technical process of transmission and the thing to be transmitted: they deal only with the former and disregard the latter. The information and ideas transmitted reflect the experiences that have molded the philosophies, ethics, and political conceptions of different peoples. And since there are no identical experiences uniting mankind, above the elemental aspirations common to all men, the American and the Russian each will consider the same news item from his particular philosophic, moral, and political perspective, and each perspective will give the news a different color, and the interpretation of the news a different character.

IDEOLOGICAL WARFARE AND POLITICAL ACTION

The ability of Western democracy to speak effectively to the peoples of Europe and Asia is dependent upon its ability to establish two different relationships, one between the aspirations of those peoples and the political policies of the West, and the other between those policies and their verbal propagation. There are situations where concordance among these three factors can be brought about with relative ease. The waging of political warfare against Nazi Germany in occupied Europe during the Second World War was a relatively simple matter. Popular aspirations were clearly defined, and so were the policies pursued by the United Nations. Both sought the destruction of Nazi Germany, and it was easy to put that aim into words. Similarly, our political and military policies designed to maintain the territorial status quo in Europe against Russian expansion express the aspirations of the peoples of Western Europe and lend themselves to verbal formulation in terms of the Truman Doctrine, the Marshall Plan, and the North Atlantic Pact. Neither in Eastern Europe nor in Asia nor in the Soviet Union itself is the task of political warfare as simple. Two basic problems confront it, one the incompatibility of a certain political policy pursued in one region with the kind of ideological warfare waged in another, and the other the absolute impossibility of supporting a given political policy by means of ideological warfare.

The first problem is best illustrated by the relations between what is often considered to be the objective of American policy in Eastern Europe, and the objective of our ideological warfare with the Soviet Union. The objective of our policy in Eastern Europe may be defined as the liberation of the peoples from Russian domination. The objective of our ideological warfare with the Soviet Union is to appeal to the Russian people over the head of the Soviet government in terms of our real objectives and thus to force a revision of Soviet policies through the pressure of Russian public opinion. Yet the objective of the liberation of Eastern Europe, especially Poland and the Baltic States, runs counter to the centuries-old national aspirations of Russia, regarding which no cleavage between government and people has ever existed. A policy in Eastern Europe which seeks to thwart the aspirations of both the Russian government and the Russian people is bound to cancel out the chances, which otherwise might exist, of separating the Russian people from the Soviet government by means of ideological warfare. In situations such as these it is the task of over-all policy to establish a priority of objectives and either to subordinate the objectives of ideological warfare to those of political policy, or vice versa.

It may be noted parenthetically that the Soviet Union is faced with a similar problem in its policies with regard to Poland and Eastern Germany. The recognition of the permanency of the Oder-Neisse frontier is bound to condemn Russian ideological warfare in Eastern Germany to impotence. Willingness to revise it would have the same effect in Poland. Faced with this problem, Soviet policy has decided that, at least for the time being, it is more important to maintain and strengthen its political control over Poland by making the Soviet Union appear as the champion of Polish national aspirations, than to gain the allegiance of the inhabitants of Eastern Germany by satisfying in some measure their national aspirations.

A striking illustration of the other problem is provided by the ideological effect of the American intervention in the Korean War. However justified this intervention has been in terms of international law, political morality, and the long-term interests of the Korean people themselves, its immediate ideological effects have been unfavorable to the United States. Especially in South Korea, where the physical evidence of Russian intervention was not immediately perceptible to the common man, what the Indochinese peasant said to Mr. Sparks has found a widespread echo. Although in Pyongyang, the capital of North Korea, United Nations troops were enthusiastically received as liberators from the Russians, in devastated Seoul the welcome was rather restrained. It is important to this discussion that the United States was unable to counteract the ideological liability of that intervention with immediate ideological counter-measures. The appearances of white intervention in the affairs of Asia, in the traditional manner of Western imperialism, can be refuted at present not by means of political warfare, but only by subsequent political, military, and economic policies that will establish in the life experiences of the Korean people the anti-imperialistic, democratic objectives of American policy. In situations such as these the immediate answer to the ideological liability of a given political or military policy is not propaganda but policies that will establish the psychological pre-conditions for successful propaganda.

The struggle for the minds of men, then, is a task of infinite subtlety and complexity. Nothing is easier, more certain of popular support, and also more certain of failure than to approach so intricate a task in the spirit and with the techniques of a Fourth of July oration. The simple philosophy and techniques of the moral crusade are useful and even indispensable for the domestic task of marshaling public opinion behind a given policy; they are but blunt weapons in the struggle of nations for dominance over the minds of men. This is not a struggle between good and evil, truth and falsehood, but of power with power. In such a struggle virtue and truth do not prevail simply upon being communicated. They must be carried upon the steady stream of political policy which makes them both relevant and plausible. To conceive of the ideological task of democracy in the struggle with Bolshevism primarily in terms of the technological problem of piercing the Iron Curtain and communicating the eternal verities of democracy to all the world is in large measure to miss the point.

Ideological warfare is but the reflection, in the realm of ideas, of the political and military policies it seeks to support. It is the mere ideological expression of the objectives and methods of these policies. From the character of these policies it draws its strength. With them it wins or fails. The call for victory in the struggle for the minds of men, if it is to be effective in Asia as elsewhere, must be conceived primarily as a call for political and military policies that have the makings of victory. Here too, deeds speak louder than words.

VIII

The Failure of Will

It would be untrue and unjust to assert that nobody in Washington is aware of the fundamental intellectual weaknesses of American foreign policy which are described in the preceding pages. What surprises the close observer of the Washington scene is the great number of officials in the government who are aware of these weaknesses and who try to remedy them in the spirit of the great early achievements of American foreign policy. What surprises the observer still more and even shocks him is the contrast between the judgment and advice of these officials, on the one hand, and the policies actually pursued, on the other. Nor is it always one official who judges and advises and another official who in his actions disregards that judgment and advice. Judgment may be divorced from action in one and the same person. An official may reason one way and act in exactly the opposite way. Consider the case of Mr. Acheson, who in January 1950 developed a conception of our Asiatic policy [1] of which hardly a trace can be found in the policies he actually pursued only a few months later. And consider the case of the Joint Chiefs of Staff, who in December 1949 and January 1950 evaluated our interests and power with regard to Korea and Formosa and then sanctioned, hardly six months later, policies incompatible with such an evaluation.

[1] See Appendix III.

221

Here it is not judgment that failed us, but the will to act as our understanding counseled us to act. What are the reasons for this stultification of mind, this paralysis of will? They are twofold: the conduct of foreign policy under democratic conditions, especially as developed by the American constitutional system; and the weakness of our political leadership, especially since 1945.

1. *The Price of Democratic Government*

"Foreign politics," wrote Tocqueville with special reference to the United States,[2]

> demand scarcely any of those qualities which are peculiar to a democracy; they require, on the contrary, the perfect use of almost all those in which it is deficient. Democracy is favorable to the increase of the internal resources of a state; it diffuses wealth and comfort, promotes public spirit, and fortifies the respect for law in all classes of society: all these are advantages which have only an indirect influence over the relations which one people bears to another. But a democracy can only with great difficulty regulate the details of an important undertaking, persevere in a fixed design, and work out its execution in spite of serious obstacles. It cannot combine its measures with secrecy or await their consequences with patience. . . .
>
> The propensity that induces democracies to obey impulse rather than prudence, and to abandon mature design for the gratification of a momentary passion, was clearly seen in America on the breaking out of the French Revolution. It was then as evident to the

[2] *Democracy in America* (New York: Alfred A. Knopf; 1945), Vol. I, pp. 234, 235.

simplest capacity as it is at the present time that the interest of the Americans forbade them to take any part in the contest which was about to deluge Europe with blood, but which could not injure their own country. But the sympathies of the people declared themselves with so much violence in favor of France that nothing but the inflexible character of Washington and the immense popularity which he enjoyed could have prevented the Americans from declaring war against England. And even then, the exertions which the austere reason of that great man made to repress the generous but imprudent passions of his fellow citizens nearly deprived him of the sole recompense which he ever claimed, that of his country's love. The majority reprobated his policy, but it was afterwards approved by the whole nation.

The kind of thinking required for the successful conduct of foreign policy must at times be diametrically opposed to the kind of considerations by which the masses and their representatives are likely to be moved. The peculiar qualities of the statesman's mind are not always likely to find a favorable response in the popular mind. The statesman must think in terms of the national interest, conceived as power among other powers. The popular mind, unaware of the fine distinctions of the statesman's thinking, reasons more often than not in the simple moralistic and legalistic terms of absolute good and absolute evil. The statesman must take the long view, proceeding slowly and by detours, paying with small losses for great advantages; he must be able to temporize, to compromise, to bide his time. The popular mind wants quick results; it will sacrifice tomorrow's real benefit for today's apparent advantage.

By a psychological paradox, the most vociferous and uncompromising representatives of what is least conducive to the successful conduct of foreign policy are generally politicians who in their own constituencies would not dream of acting the way they expect the framers of foreign policy to act. To the contrary, in their constituencies they display the very qualities of moral discrimination, intellectual finesse, patience, live-and-let-live, culminating in the political "deal," that they detest and oppose in the conduct of foreign policy. The daily routine of their political lives is devoid of those moral and intellectual qualities which they really admire, which to the public they pretend to possess, and which they wish they were able to practice. In compensation for what they regard as their own shortcomings, they make foreign policy over into a sort of fairyland where virtue triumphs and vice is punished, where heroes fight for principle without thought of consequence, and where the knight in shining armor comes to the succor of the ravished nation, taking the villain's life even though he might in the process lose his own.

Thus the conditions under which popular support can be obtained for a foreign policy are not necessarily identical with the conditions under which a foreign policy can be successfully pursued. A tragic choice often confronts those responsible for the conduct of foreign affairs. They must either sacrifice what they consider good policy upon the altar of public opinion, or by devious means gain popular support for policies whose true nature they conceal from the public.

Countries with long experience and deep understanding of foreign affairs, such as Great Britain, have developed constitutional devices and political practices that tend to minimize the dangers to the vital interests of the nation which are inherent in the democratic conduct of foreign affairs. Parliamentary democracy, especially where the two-party system operates, provides in the parliamentary re-

sponsibility of the cabinet a mechanism that enables a
majority of the elected representatives of the people to control the foreign policies of the government. The cabinet's
collective responsibility for the policies pursued compels
the government to speak in foreign affairs with one voice,
so that there can be no doubt, either at home or abroad,
of what the government's foreign policy is at any given
moment.

THE CONDUCT OF FOREIGN POLICY
IN THE UNITED STATES

The peculiar quality of the conduct of foreign affairs in
the United States raises to a maximum the weaknesses inherent in a democracy, and aggravates these inherent weaknesses by unique constitutional devices and political practices.

The Constitution nowhere makes clear on whom the
ultimate responsibility for the conduct of foreign affairs
rests. It assigns to the President certain specific functions,
such as the reception of foreign diplomatic representatives;
it assigns other functions, such as the regulation of foreign
commerce and the declaration of war, to Congress; it provides that still other functions, such as the conclusion of
treaties, be discharged by the President in co-operation
with the Senate. Apart from making these specific grants,
the Constitution limits itself to an over-all distribution of
powers between the President and Congress by vesting in
the former the executive power and making him commander-in-chief of the armed forces and by vesting in Congress all legislative powers and the power of appropriations.

Thus the location of the seat of power for the conduct of
our foreign affairs remains an open question. Against
Jefferson's dictum that "The transaction of business with

foreign nations is executive altogether" there are many who claim for the Senate, if not for both Houses of Congress, at least an equal share in the conduct of foreign policy. Constitutional theologies have covered these two positions with legalistic cobwebs—and have left the issue where the Constitution has left it: undecided. For, in view of the affirmative powers granted by the Constitution to President and Congress, the issue cannot be decided through constitutional interpretation. By giving some powers to the President, some to the Congress, some to the Senate alone, and by remaining silent on the ultimate responsibility for the conduct of foreign policy, the Constitution, in the words of Professor E. S. Corwin, "is an invitation to struggle for the privilege of directing American foreign policy."

The President as Chief Executive and Commander-in-Chief has a natural eminence in the conduct of foreign affairs from which the constitutional arrangements and political practices can detract, but which they cannot obliterate. Although he operates under perpetual threat that a bipartisan majority of Congress will disavow his policies, the powers of the President in foreign affairs are, in the words of the Supreme Court, "delicate, plenary, and exclusive." Short of the expenditure of money, the binding conclusion of treaties, and the declaration of war, the President can well-nigh do as he pleases in formulating and executing foreign policies. He can independently make a public declaration of policy, such as the Monroe or Truman Doctrines. He can refuse to recognize a foreign government, or recognize it, as succeeding Presidents did with respect to the government of the Soviet Union. He can make promises and enter into informal commitments as he sees fit. He can send the armed forces of the United States anywhere in the world and can commit them to hostile acts short of war. In sum, he can narrow the freedom of choice which constitutionally lies with Congress to such an extent as almost to eliminate it.

While the President can originate a given foreign policy, it is also true that Congress can retard, deflect, and obstruct the policy's course. The Congressional power of appropriations has increased in potency with the expanding financial costs of our foreign affairs. Congress can withhold in part or in whole appropriations necessary to the execution of a certain policy, and thus weaken that policy or make its execution impossible. The Congressional changes in the appropriations for aid to Western Europe, for the Military Assistance Program, and for the Voice of America, illustrate the potentialities of this weapon. Congress can also attach a rider to an appropriation bill, providing expenditures for purposes not contemplated by the Chief Executive. In that case, the President must either reject the entire bill and give up the policy for which the original appropriation was to be used, or he must accept the bill *in toto,* and against his better judgment execute a policy imposed upon him by Congress. Thus Congress in 1948 supplemented the bill providing for aid to Western Europe with an appropriation for aid to China, a rider that the President had to accept, since he did not wish to jeopardize the whole European Recovery Program.

Another weapon at the disposal of Congress is the power of investigation. The threat of a Congressional investigation hangs constantly over the heads of all members of the executive department; at present it hangs particularly over those of the Department of State. This threat is formidable partly because an investigation is so time-consuming,[3] and partly because any investigation that is publicized

---

[3] The time that policy-making members of the executive branch must spend before Congressional committees, explaining policies, answering questions, and sometimes submitting patiently to abuse, by far exceeds the time required for the legitimate purposes of information. In 1949, for ex-

may well ruin the reputation of public officials and bring their public careers to a premature end.

The insistence by Congress upon the full use of its inquisitorial powers, especially on the part of its least responsible members, is the more jealous and bitter because the pre-eminence of the Chief Executive in foreign affairs is unassailable and Congressional frustration must find relief in harassment and delay. This is the crux of the relations today between the executive branch and Congress regarding the conduct of foreign affairs. In a period of international relations dominated by the psychology and technique of the cold war, the executive branch of our government is forced to make a greater effort to maintain friendly relations with its own Congress than to maintain them with the Soviet Union. The constitutional separation of powers and the political practices growing from it, together with the stalemate in Russo-American diplomatic relations, have brought about the paradox that the traditional diplomatic techniques of persuasion, pressure, and bargaining are applied by the executive branch of the American government to its dealings with Congress rather than with foreign powers.

Yet behind everything that the President and Congress do or do not do stands the force from which President and Congress derive their office and powers: public opinion. The Constitution makes public opinion the arbiter of American policy by calling periodically upon the American voter to pass judgment upon the President and his party. The American people live perpetually in a state of election or pre-election campaigns. Presidential and Con-

---

ample, Mr. Paul Hoffman, administrator of the Economic Cooperation Administration, and his principal aides spent for months the better part of their working time in giving identical testimony to four different Congressional committees. In the early months of 1950, the Secretary of State of the United States was principally occupied in proving to a Senate committee that he and his subordinates were loyal to their country.

gressional policies are always fashioned in anticipation of what the voter seems likely to approve. The President in particular, as the most exalted mouthpiece of the national will and the initiator of foreign policies, tests the state of public opinion by submitting to it new policies in the tentative form of public addresses and messages to Congress. These new policies are then openly or surreptitiously pursued or else shelved according to the reaction of public opinion. And ultimately, the degree to which the President is willing to execute the foreign policies his advisers suggest depends upon his estimate of the public support his policies will command.

2. *The Weakness of Political Leadership*

No President of the United States, handicapped as he is by constitutional and political conditions, is capable of translating his judgment and that of his advisers into action without overcoming great difficulties, running grave risks, and resorting at times to evasion, subterfuge, and manipulation. As Chief Executive, the President needs the active support of Congress for most of his foreign policies and, to ensure this, must disarm and persuade a legislative branch that is naturally hostile and suspicious. And, as head of his party, he must placate public opinion. A President who attempted to take the straight and short road from judgment to action, in disregard of the power of Congress and of public opinion, would generally either wreck his foreign policies or lose the popular support that elected and sustains him.

Yet in trying to avoid both Congressional hostility and popular disaffection, the President is apt to lose the substance of his foreign policy. In order to win Congress over and to placate public opinion, he may well be tempted to throw overboard the more controversial elements of that policy. In the end, he may win the support of Congress and of public opinion for policies that are hardly worth supporting. Considerations of domestic politics may ultimately corrupt foreign policy altogether, popular support may become an end in itself, and a foreign policy may be pursued regardless of its intrinsic merits simply because it is most likely to command popular support.

For the successful pursuit of foreign affairs between these extremes, three qualities, above all others, are required of the framers of American policy: one intellectual, one moral, one political. The framers of American foreign policy must possess a deep understanding of both our national interest and our national strength. They must be imbued with the moral determination to defend to the last what they know the national interest requires, and they must be prepared to face political defeat at home rather than gamble away the interests and perhaps the very existence of the nation for a fleeting triumph in the next elections. Finally, the framers of American foreign policy must be endowed with political prudence in gauging public opinion, in leading it forward as far as possible, and in retracting the policy as little as may be necessary. Public opinion and foreign policy must meet at a point compatible with the requirements of domestic and of foreign policies.

Tocqueville referred to these indispensable qualities when he spoke of "the inflexible character of Washington" and "the austere reason of that great man." These qualities, in order to be effective, must be present in combination, supplementing and strengthening each other. This combination of qualities does not appear to exist in the Capitol today. Where moral determination and political prudence are displayed, political understanding is not. Those who possess political understanding and moral determination are deficient in political prudence. Where po-

litical understanding and prudence are joined, moral determination is lacking. And at the very top we look in vain
for either understanding or prudence or determination. Or
should we take the perpetuation of popular prejudice
for understanding, small-town political manipulation for
prudence, stubbornness in little matters for moral determination?

Of these defects, the lack of moral determination is the
most fatal, for it corrupts both understanding and prudence. It debases understanding into a mere reflection of
what the public opinion "experts" think the crowd wants;
it relegates political prudence to the lowest level of political manipulation. This fatal lack arises from a profound
misunderstanding of the nature of public opinion and of
the intelligence and moral character of the American
people.

The picture that our leaders have formed of the intellectual and moral qualities of the American people is a
composite of intuitive impressions derived from press,
radio, public opinion polls, Congress, and private communications. A succession of Presidential elections has
given evidence of the distorted picture the mass media of
public opinion paint of the actual state of the American
mind. While these media may roughly indicate the American mind's lack of information, they give only a dim inkling of its native intelligence and moral reserves. Yet President and State Department seem to be taking at its face
value the discouraging picture that the mouthpieces of
public opinion convey of the moral and intellectual qualities of the American people. In particular, the fear of Congress has become a veritable obsession of many members of
the executive departments.

This fear derives from a misjudgment of Congress as
the representative of public opinion. That the temper of
Congress and especially of the Senate is not of necessity

truly representative of public opinion is evident from a consideration of the factors that limit the representative function of Congress: the disproportionate representation of rural compared with urban districts; the disproportionate influence of the less populous states by virtue of the representation of every state, regardless of population, by two Senators; the disproportionate influence exerted upon members of Congress by the spokesmen of special interest groups, of which in foreign affairs the China lobby and certain ethnic and religious minorities have been the most potent; and finally, the limited representative character of members of Congress from a number of Southern states where only a small fraction of the population votes.

DISTORTIONS OF WILL

The mistaken identification of press, radio, polls, and Congress with public opinion has had a distorting as well as paralyzing influence upon American foreign policy. It has induced the government to pursue mistaken policies, which might not have been pursued but for a mistaken notion of what public opinion demanded. It has also induced the government to misrepresent its policies.

There are two outstanding examples of the misdirection of our foreign policy due to a mistaken conception of public opinion: one is the over-all policy of the present Administration toward the Soviet Union, and the other is the Administration's policy in Asia.

There could never have been much doubt in the minds of the President's main advisers on foreign policy that strength and accommodation are the two pillars of peace, and that in order to do its share in maintaining peace with the Soviet Union the United States must make itself as strong as possible—that is, rearm with all possible speed and determination, and at the same time be ever ready to grasp opportunities for negotiations on a realistic basis. The rearmament of the United States became a political necessity virtually at the moment when disarmament, itself a concession to public opinion, was completed in 1945. As the years went by, that necessity became obvious to more and more observers. When in the fall of 1949 the Soviet Union produced an atomic explosion, rearmament became a matter not of political necessity but of national survival. Yet in all those years up to the beginning of 1951, the Administration equated what it thought Congress might approve with what it thought the American people might be willing to support. The Administration thus was apt to demand less of the American people than it could have obtained. In these and other respects, the foreign policy—and the domestic policies destined to support it—that the Administration presented to public opinion for approval often stopped short of what the Administration itself deemed necessary in the national interest.

It seems fair to assume that similar reasons have prompted the Administration to shy away from realistic negotiations with the Soviet Union. It has—in words—appeared convinced of their necessity, and has expressed its willingness to consider them seriously. Yet at the same time it has continually postponed them because of an alleged lack of strength. Frightened by a public opinion that is in good measure but a figment of a politician's imagination, the Administration has suspended diplomacy altogether rather than face with courage and determination the accusation of appeasement, or of worse, by demagogues who represent only a small minority of the American people.

The Asiatic policies of the Administration provide the other salient example of a foreign policy conceived in fear of public opinion, born in the certain knowledge of its inevitable failure, and nursed along half-heartedly and in embarrassment. Virtually none of the Far Eastern experts of the government—and that goes for the overwhelming majority of the academic experts as well—ever had any doubt that the policies the government was pursuing in the Far East were doomed to fail. Here again, a vociferous, passionate, well-financed, and well-organized minority was able first to impose its will upon a minority of Congress and then to frighten the Administration into pursuing, against its better judgment, policies that failed.

Failure, the inevitable result of unsound policies half-heartedly and inconsistently pursued, called forth renewed and ever stronger pressure, which in turn frightened the Administration into new and more costly blunders. Having accepted as their own the standards of the opposition, the fearful politicians, counting and miscounting votes, find no escape from this vicious circle. Prisoners of their critics, they obligingly commit every blunder that the opposition suggests—but is itself spared from making. Thus, by the very logic of its course, the Administration is never able to satisfy its critics or do for the country what needs to be done. And while the Administration involves itself ever more deeply in contradictions and confusions of its own making, the interests and the very safety of the country are imperiled.

Unfounded fear of public opinion has forced the Administration to embrace policies its judgment would not dictate. That same fear has also forced the Administration to misrepresent its policies in order to obtain popular support that it thought it could not otherwise command. Only future historians will be able to determine the extent to which the Administration has not only subordinated foreign policy to considerations of domestic politics, but has also deliberately distorted the nature and purposes of its foreign policies.

Two examples of such distortion are a matter of record.

When in 1947 the British government announced its inability to continue to meet its traditional commitments in the eastern Mediterranean, the government of the United States took them over. An appropriation from Congress was needed. There was nothing particularly sensational about this policy; it was simply one instance of the replacement all over the world of British interests and power by American interests and power. Nor was there anything sensational in the request for an appropriation—a relatively modest one, as appropriations go nowadays—to do what it was obviously in the interest of the United States to do. Yet the initiation of that policy and the request for an appropriation in support of it were made the occasion for a sensational, world-shaking declaration, delivered by the President in person, which announced a new American foreign policy of worldwide application.

The striking contrast between the modest occasion and the grandiose declaration, reminiscent of the message voicing the Monroe Doctrine or the messages of 1917 and 1941 asking for a declaration of war, was primarily, if not exclusively, a matter of domestic politics. The President had been advised, probably wrongly, that he had no chance of obtaining from Congress the appropriation for aid to Greece and Turkey without scaring the reluctant members of Congress into approval. Thus a crisis had to be created, imminent disaster had to be conjured up, and the American people had to be cajoled into believing that they had the mission and the ability to contain Communism all over the world by sending money, goods, and soldiers to all the danger spots. In consequence, the President got his appropriation, and the country got a permanent commitment to a worldwide policy that was—as we have tried to show—unsound in conception and unworkable in practice.

The other notable example of misrepresentation of the character and ends of our foreign policy is supplied by our

European policies. The misrepresentation here is typical not of the synthetic scare but of the spurious promise. From the Marshall Plan to the rearmament of Western Europe and Western Germany, the Administration has hailed every step as the last step, the one that not only would solve the problems of Europe's economic, political, and military recovery, but also would meet the challenges of Communism and Russian expansion. The Administration has tried to sell its European policies to Congress and the public by advertising them as schemes by which the United States could combine its world leadership with normalcy. Thus the Administration has erected one imaginary Maginot line after another, each described to the American people as a shield behind which the American way of life could flourish in safety. The Administration has continually and almost by instinct held out the hope that there is some way out, that there is an escape somewhere, and that the American people will somehow manage to have their cake of world leadership and eat it too.

In view of the requirements of political prudence of which we have spoken before, there would be no valid argument against the government's endeavor to marshal public opinion behind its foreign policy by presenting it in a favorable light. It is, however, quite another matter to misrepresent consistently the very nature and purpose of the foreign policy pursued; for this kind of habitual and imprudent misrepresentation, far from furthering the purposes of foreign policy, creates serious obstacles to the intelligent and successful conduct of any foreign policy that must enjoy popular support. First of all, tactics of shock and overselling, when indiscriminately resorted to, in the long run defeat their purpose. Bewildered, the people come to ask themselves whether they are faced with overwhelming danger all over the world or are safe behind some impenetrable wall; whether they must exert themselves to the utmost or need only furnish the money so that others may exert themselves. The doubt and confusion thus engendered soon lead to a real crisis of confidence. The word of the Administration is no longer believed, whether it scares or promises. The Administration must then resort to ever stronger doses of deception; and the people inevitably react with ever deeper doubt, bewilderment, and cynicism.

The Administration has succeeded in making illusory hope, fear, and hysteria the prime movers of popular support. In consequence, it has in large measure deprived itself of the ability to educate public opinion, to guide it toward an understanding of the new conditions of American existence, to engender the spontaneous support of policies that are approved because they are understood. Instead, the Administration must resort to ever grosser misrepresentations in order to be able to stimulate ever more exaggerated hopes and fears, and it must also pursue policies that seem to justify the hopes and fears it has itself created. In a word, the Administration has become the prisoner of its own propaganda.

THE ABDICATION OF LEADERSHIP

That failure of will which is the concern of this chapter begins by misdirecting policies and then misrepresenting them. It can only end in the dissipation of will, in the abdication of leadership itself. Its manifestations in the field of policy are thrift, muddling, improvidence, and fear of the new and unknown.

Any departure in foreign policy, especially in a period of cold war, means conflict—conflict with a half-informed and at times hysterical public opinion, conflict with a suspicious and reluctant Congress, conflict between and within executive departments. Such a situation makes expedients, if not virtues, of routine and inertia. If one wants to win the next election, if one wants to advance in the bureaucracy, if one wants to retain and increase the powers of one's office, it is well to avoid conflict and swim with the prevailing current. Thus the foreign policy of the cold war, with its emphasis on military preparations and its neglect of the traditional methods of diplomacy, has become the policy that the present Administration is best fitted to conduct.

Paralysis of will and abdication of leadership are nowhere more obvious than in our Asiatic policies. In the case of General MacArthur, the issue is not whether the policies advocated and partly pursued by the General were sound compared with those advocated and sometimes pursued by the Administration. Nor is it at all the issue whether or not General MacArthur has remained within the limits of his instructions; the record is clearly in favor of the General. The real issue is the deep cleavage that has obviously existed between the policies of General MacArthur and those of the Administration. General MacArthur's very conception of the nature of the conflict between East and West is incompatible with the concepts that the framers of American foreign policy, such as Mr. Acheson, have expressed in words and sometimes tried to translate into action. What is disquieting and indicative of a profound crisis in the American government is not primarily that General MacArthur, within the limits of his orders, has acted according to his convictions, but that the Administration has not dared to send him instructions in accordance with its own convictions—instructions that would restrict his discretion. Regardless of the merits of the case, for a country to have two different foreign policies, one propounded and timidly executed in Washington, the other energetically pressed in Tokyo, is to invite disaster.

The subordination of military to civil authority is one of the mainstays of the American constitutional and political system. Here one general in the field has opposed the highest military and civil authorities combined. Why in this instance did the President, the National Security Council, the Joint Chiefs of Staff—in short, the government of the United States—negotiate, temporize, compromise with and finally capitulate to one general's determined opposition?

In truth, it was not General MacArthur who imposed his will upon the government of the United States, but a segment of American public opinion identified with the General's views. The Administration yielded to the same minority that had deflected and paralyzed our Asiatic policies before the outbreak of the Korean War. In the face of so evidently potent a combination as that of a popular general and a vociferous minority, the Administration chose to drop the reins of government altogether and to execute, again half-heartedly and inconsistently, the measures that the policies of General MacArthur had made almost inevitable.

This is the disheartening tale of a noble people ignobly led. The Administration is both author and protagonist of that tale, and to the Administration must be read this indictment and this prophesy:

> *You have deceived once: now you must deceive again, for to tell the truth would be to admit having deceived. If your better judgment leads you near the road of rational policy, your critics will raise the ghost of your own deception, convict you out of your own mouth as appeaser and traitor, and stop you in your tracks.*
>
> *You have falsified the real issue between the United States and the Soviet Union into a holy crusade to*

stamp out Bolshevism everywhere on earth, for this seemed a good way of arousing the public: now you must act as though you meant it.

You have presented the Chinese Communists as the enemies of mankind, in order to appease the China lobby: now you must act as though you meant it.

You have told the people that American power has no limits, for flattery of the people is "good politics": now you must act as though you meant it.

Your own shouts, mingled with the outcries of the opposition, have befuddled your mind: now you wonder whether you are fighting Russian imperialism or trying to obliterate Communism; whether you want to defend Europe by sending troops or by creating the deterrent of a strong United States; whether you want to stay in Korea or get out; whether Formosa is vital for our security or might become a liability.

Instead of leading public opinion on the steady course that reason dictates, you will trail behind it on the zigzag path of passion and prejudice. You will meet public opinion not at a point still compatible with the national interest, but rather where, regardless of the national interest, a deceived populace will support policies fashioned in the image of its own prejudices.

Where a knowing, prudent, and determined government would endeavor to raise the people to the level of its own understanding and purpose, an ignorant, improvident, and weak government will follow its own propaganda to that low level where uninformed passion dwells. You will become, in spite of your own better self, the voice not of what is noble, wise, and strong in the nation, but of what is vulgar, blind, and weak.

*The leader will then have become the demagogue;
as the mouthpiece of popular passion, you will at last
have forsaken leadership altogether.*

Such is the tragedy of well-intentioned folly. Yet it is a
tragedy that does not need to happen. The great presidents
of the United States have been the leaders and educators
of the American people. Their greatness—which is the
greatness of the American people personified—has sustained the United States, from Washington through Lincoln and Wilson to Franklin D. Roosevelt. By their own
strength and wisdom they have awakened the strength and
wisdom dormant in that slumbering giant, the American
people. Today, the American people must take their fate
in their own hands. Who can doubt that their voices will
be heeded by their leaders, who as Americans partake of
the same great heritage? Let those voices cry out:

Forget and Remember!

Forget *the illusions of the recent past and remember the great and simple truths that the thoughts and
actions of the early statesmen of the Republic have left
you.*

Forget *the sentimental notion that foreign policy is
a struggle between virtue and vice, with virtue bound
to win.*

Forget *the utopian notion that a brave new world
without power politics will follow the unconditional
surrender of wicked nations.*

Forget *the crusading notion that any nation, however virtuous and powerful, can have the mission to
make the world over in its own image.*

Remember *that the golden age of isolated normalcy
is gone forever and that no effort, however great, and
no action, however radical, will bring it back.*

241

REMEMBER *that diplomacy without power is feeble, and power without diplomacy is destructive and blind.*

REMEMBER *that no nation's power is without limits, and hence that its policies must respect the power and interests of others.*

REMEMBER *that the American people have shown throughout their history that they are able to face the truth and act upon it with courage and resourcefulness in war, with common sense and moral determination in peace.*

And, above all, remember always that it is not only a political necessity but also a moral duty for a nation to follow in its dealings with other nations but one guiding star, one standard for thought, one rule for action:

THE NATIONAL INTEREST.

"*Is War Inevitable?*" *Editorial in* Osservatore Romano (*official Vatican newspaper*), *June 14, 1947*

The heavy clouds of these last days of spring do not tell us yet whether a short summer storm is brewing or a cyclone is on its way.

This very sinister portent is constantly insinuating itself among us under the name of the "final war" or the "war to end wars," whether it is talked about in the liberal or the Marxist world, whether war is feared as a new threat to democracy or as an extreme reaction to the conquests of communism.

Neither one side nor the other, however, should be deceived in this matter. Two wars have raised the banner promising an "end to war." But the first was a delusion; the second—so far as the fear which it engendered continues to exist—is becoming a delusion even now. Both sides therefore should ask themselves if the risk is reasonable: if a third war would not be the forerunner of still a fourth, a new link in the chain which makes of men slaves of their preoccupation with force, when by using force they claim to be following a vision of justice and peace.

But more important than such obvious remarks is the actual state of affairs.

I wrote about them in *Vita e Pensiero* last February. Today they touch us even more closely and with a greater threat. It is even more timely therefore to return to them again, in a daily paper rather than in the pages of a quarterly; not merely to

comment on the subject but argue about it; above all to re-
iterate these solemn words of the Pope: "In the face of the
present sad state of affairs, of the many distressing conflicts
which so grievously afflict the world today and bar the road to
peace, it would be equally culpable to close our eyes in order
not to see or to fold our arms in order not to act, offering as
an excuse that there is nothing more for us to do. Is there
nothing more to do?"

The origin of the present state of affairs is this: two programs, two diverse groupings of interests, two differing and
opposite conceptions of political and economic life—some even
say, two civilizations—are pitted against each other.

That there are two things underlying these differences—differences more complex now than in the past—we may infer
from that synthetic definition and catch-word which people use
in speaking of them: East and West—if not two worlds, two
hemispheres. This is significant. Every time when this phrase
was called to the attention of the nations of the world, was a
moment of great crisis: the end of the Roman Empire, the rise
of Charlemagne, the age-long struggle against Islam. There
were always ideologies, ambitions, armed imperialisms; there
were always wars. What is debatable is whether battles themselves ever decided which side would prevail. Today this is
even more debatable when civilization has advanced further
along the road beyond the obstacles and barriers to its progress.

However this may be, here we are at such a point in history.
And yet there are optimists who still think of this as an exaggeration. But even exaggeration is an actuality; for it indicates
a state of mind. And from what else are facts determined if
not from states of mind? When, in short, the states of mind are
not merely those of the anonymous crowd, but especially those
of politicians, governments, parties, the press, what emerges is
indeed a state of fact.

We start then from the principle, the supposition that there
are two fundamental and decisive ideologies for the future, in
irreconcilable opposition with each other: on the one hand,
communism with its philosophy, habits, methods; on the other,
democracy with its ideas, its systems, its techniques. The incompatibility of the two appears all the more absolute as communism and democracy have faith each in its own brand of
righteousness. This seems to be established all the more be-

cause neither the one nor the other confines itself to the field of theory, but each opposes the other in the field of practical application. The Western Powers are experiments in democracy and its concrete examples; the USSR is the same for communism. From the classroom the two ideologies and systems have passed out into life; they are established and organized in political and social realities. The desire and will to defend an ideal existence and make it secure is now transformed into the need to defend and secure an existence that is, as it were, material. The problems of philosophers have thus become economic and political facts. The incompatibility of theories in the classroom, lecture hall, and press remains in the infinite space of thought where the most hostile ideas can exist without suffocating or destroying each other; but in geographical space states and especially ideological states either agree or say: *mors tua vita mea* (your death is my life).

The reasoning based on such premises continues. We must therefore come to the conclusion that a conflict between the two hemispheres is inevitable, as was the plague for Don Ferrante; and for men there is nothing to do but blame it on the stars, for them as for the heroes of Metastasio—and even the more so now, since it is really from above, from the stars that in modern war the greatest misfortunes descend—whether buzz bombs or atomic bombs.

But Don Ferrante was a logician with erroneous premises.

Is there an erroneous premise in the present argument? It would seem so.

The argument takes its start from the irreconcilability of two sets of ideas, of two conceptions of civilization and of life. Well and good. But the matter assumes a quite different aspect from mere philosophical intransigency when—and this is the case in question—the idea takes on a body, descends from the spiritual sphere to that of this poor earth, and is obliged to travel with other ideas enclosed with it in a vessel—whether of clay or iron—which we have called the state, "the political power," as it is in fact.

And here we cannot avoid measuring the argument against practical necessity, against that actuality from which there is no need or possibility of separation. The Church, spotless proponent of an ideology, teaches that practical necessity nourishes it, makes it a matter of living belief, directly part of the Creed, a truly spiritual force. It has passed through twenty centuries of its immortal existence, living and working on the way, fulfilling its mission, inimitable in the wisdom with which it takes consideration of its fellow-wayfarers, both men and states. If this then is a fact for him who, like the Church itself, must be concerned with not getting lost along the way and at the same time not losing sight of the goal to be attained for the sake of everyman's salvation then it cannot indeed be otherwise for anyone else who, according to reason and political exigency, aims especially to make his own life secure in order to be worthier and better able to join it with that of others.

It is true, in fact, that even the ideological state must ask itself whether for the triumph of its ideology it ought to risk its very existence as a state: to risk being trampled down and destroyed. For that would mean also the defeat and end of the ideology itself in the same way that a perfume is wafted away if the vessel which contains it is shattered.

If then—for there is indeed another hypothesis in the political actuality we are considering—if then the question is not limited to that of an ideological state which gives force to the ideology, preserves and champions it, but if the question deals also with a state which builds up its powers and merely uses an ideology in order to promote its own political aspirations then the entire subject assumes a more persuasive aspect and indicates to us an erroneous premise—namely, that from an incompatibility in ideals there must necessarily arise a practical and political irreconcilability and inevitable war, instead of the possibility of agreement.

This statement is not based simply on logical abstractions. We can cite actual examples. The centuries have given us certain types of ideological states from the pre-Christian, the Christian, and the non-Christian worlds: the Hebrews, France and Spain, the Turks. There have been ideologies which gave special power to states, and there have been states which, in the face of the vicissitudes of history (in which it is clear that the foresight, will and plans of men did not always prevail over time and circumstance), ended by being absorbed and balanced in an international commonweal, as the immediate interests of the life of their people demanded. To make use of an example closer to our times, we recall the France of the Revolution. The ideological state of 1793, led by the First Consul, and the Emperor, saw its ideology come to terms with the interest of the state and ended by losing its own genuine features. The Russia of the Revolution, which has not been political alone or even chiefly political but social, has already, from Lenin to Stalin, traveled such a set course as to lead men to think that its evolutionary development, worthy even of being considered an historical law, is not to be gainsaid.

It suffices to consider that Bolshevism, having started at the beginning of the war from a position of Russian neutrality in the name of its ideology, was found in the course of three years successively allied to the two parties in conflict with each other, considering each one equally as an adversary; going to the point first of fighting on the side of the Germans and then on the side of the Anglo-Saxons, not for the principles which it might have had in common with one side or the other, but only to secure better boundaries for itself, to liberate its homeland, and to guarantee itself a place in a Europe which would be no longer at the mercy of aggressors. It acted not for the communistic ideology, not for the ideological state, but for its very life, for the nation, for the idea of a state which is free, independent, and secure.

And so we are back in the present. If this happened during the war, if during the war there was found nothing irreconcilable, nothing incompatible even in contradiction, even in an absurdity, so to speak; if the principle of *primum vivere deinde philosophari* (first live, and then philosophize) was not at that time absurd; why should it have to be excluded, after the war, for the peace and a peace so difficult as to make necessary and urgent for all peoples, victors and vanquished alike, this principle of "First live, and then philosophize"?

Those, in fact, who, in order to give a reason for the inevitability of war, whether near or remote, want states to be thought of as ideological in the East as in the West, themselves come today, as they did yesterday, from those very states that are seeking after their own interests, their own security. The problem remains certainly a great and difficult one, but it remains essentially a political one, and as such open to all solutions, without the prejudice of inevitability.

Here someone will say: but the point at issue has been shifted from the superiority of ideological motives to the superiority of practical motives.

True. But it is inevitability which must arise from ideological motives. To put these aside in order to consider practical ones is to set aside the conviction that neither the good will of men nor, if this seems too naive, the eventual profit to each side can provide a common meeting-ground.

And conviction is, in truth, a state of mind. A state of mind which is no longer that of inevitability, of destiny, of inaction, carries with it another atmosphere, another qualification, another state of facts. It creates above all a sense of responsibility with respect to the ability of man not only to will but also to determine. This is true for men in positions of authority and men who as leaders have the right and duty to declare their own ideas, their intentions, and to set the course for others.

War is not inevitable. It never was. What is inevitable is only that peace becomes impossible if people think that war is a matter of destiny. What for Christianity is an error is for all human kind barbarity. War is not inevitable especially if we add to the irrefutable counsels of experience, reality, and reason our faith and the sense of God without which these very counsels were in the past too often rejected.

"For those who see things in the light of the divine order," Pius XII reiterates, "there is no doubt that even in the gravest conflicts of human and national interests there is always place for a peaceful settlement."

APPENDIX II

Speech of Winston Churchill in the House of Commons, January 23, 1948

I am often asked, "Will there be war?", and this is a question I have often asked myself. Can you wonder, Sir, that this question obtrudes itself upon us when the Lord President of the Council speaks, as he did ten days ago, of the "risk of war" with Russia—twice, I think, he used that phrase—and speaks of:

> The availability and, if necessary, the readiness of armed force to prevent the outbreak of violence—

and when the Prime Minister says—and I agree with him when he says:

> Soviet Communism pursues a policy of Imperialism in a new form—ideological, economic, and strategic—which threatens the welfare and way of life of the other nations of Europe.

These are statements from men whose whole lives have been spent in denouncing the dangers of militarism, when they have not been actively engaged in fighting for their lives against tyranny. These are the speeches of Socialists. It is not a question of Jingoism. These are the speeches of Socialists and the Ministers responsible.

Can you doubt that times are grave when the word "sabotage" is used in accusation of one of the greatest Powers of the world, both by Mr. Marshall in the United States and by the Foreign Secretary in this House? Such language in any previous period would have been incompatible with the maintenance of any form of diplomatic relations between the countries affected. I think it quite right to say the things said, but when they are said it is certainly not odd that we should have to ask ourselves this grim and hateful question, "Will there be war?" When I last spoke on these questions in the House in October, 1946, fifteen months ago—I venture, by the way, to refer to what I have said in the past, because I do not speak on these matters on the spur of the moment, but from a steady stream of thought which I have followed and pursued with a study and experience of these matters over many years—I said:

I am not going to attempt to examine this afternoon whether war, which would, of course, be total war, is imminent or not. I cannot tell at all what the men at the head of the different Governments will do. There are too many of what Bismarck called, "Imponderabilia." It was easier in Hitler's day to feel and forecast the general movement of events. But now we have not to deal with Hitler and his crude Nazi-gang. We are in the presence of something very much more difficult to measure. We are in the presence of a collective mind whose springs of action we cannot judge. Thirteen men in the Kremlin hold all Russia and more than a third of Europe in their grip. Many stresses and pressures are working on them. These stresses and pressures are internal as well as external. I cannot presume to forecast what decisions they will take. Even less can I attempt to foresee the time-factor in their affairs. Still, it is certain that these thirteen, or it may be fourteen, men have it in their power to loose on the world horrors and devastations, compared with which all we have gone through would be but a prelude. We are told that they would never do such a thing, and I earnestly hope this may be true. They are certainly calculating, ruthless men, officially divorced from Christian ethics in any form, and with Asiatic views of the value of human life and liberty. On the other hand, they have a vast expanse of the land surface of the globe and all its populations to guide and develop as they choose, with arbitrary power and with all that science—if not perverted—can bestow upon future generations of mankind.

I beg the House to permit me to remind them of this, because I do not wish to say the same thing again, but I would use very much the same language now.

Appendix II

Eight months ago—speaking on this subject fifteen months ago—

I made a speech at Fulton in the United States. It had a mixed reception and quite a number of Members of this House put their names to a Motion condemning me for having made it; but as events have moved what I said at Fulton in the presence of the President of the United States has been outpaced and overpassed by the movements of events and of American opinion. At that time, I said that I did not believe that the Soviet Government wanted war. I said that what they wanted were the fruits of war, and I pointed to the heavy impact of Soviet Russia upon Eastern and Central Europe—the Iron Curtain and so forth—their demands in the Dardanelles and Persia, and their aspirations in the Far East. I fervently hope and pray that this view, which I then expressed, is still correct. But now, I cannot tell. I should not blame His Majesty's Government if, even with all the information at their disposal, they also were not able to come to a definite conclusion. For all these reasons there, I expressed no opinion tonight upon the future, upon what the Soviet Government intend, or upon whether war is imminent or not.

Certainly, in the interval that has passed, the Soviet Government have not used their overwhelming military power in Europe to march westward to the North Sea, the Channel and the Atlantic Ocean. Nevertheless, it is common ground between all parties that the situation has deteriorated, especially in the last six months. No, indeed, it is not odd that this ugly question should still be put, and force itself upon us: "Will there be war?" I will only venture now to say that there seems to me to be very real danger in going on drifting too long. I believe that the best chance of preventing a war is to bring matters to a head and come to a settlement with the Soviet Government before it is too late. This would imply that the Western democracies, who should, of course, seek unity among themselves at the earliest moment, would take the initiative in asking the Soviet for a settlement.

It is idle to reason or argue with the Communists. It is, however, possible to deal with them on a fair, realistic basis, and, in my experience, they will keep their bargains as long as it is in their interest to do so, which might, in this grave matter, be a long time, once things were settled. When this Parliament first assembled, I said that the possession of the atomic bomb would give three or four years' breathing space. Perhaps it may be more than that. But more than two of those years have already gone. I cannot think that any serious discussion which it may be necessary to have with the Soviet Government would be more likely to reach a favourable conclusion if we wait till they have got it too.

We may be absolutely sure that the present situation cannot last. The Foreign Secretary spoke yesterday of the Russian frontier line which runs from Stettin to Trieste. This was exactly the line which I mentioned in my speech at Fulton—Stettin to Trieste. He also mentioned the Elbe, and who can ever believe that there will be a permanent peace in Europe, or in the world, while the frontiers of Asia rest upon the Elbe? But now this line runs farther south along the Adriatic shore, and there is actual fighting now going on in Greece to decide whether it shall not curl round Athens, and so to the Dardanelles and Turkey. Surely, there can be doubt in our minds that this is highly dangerous, and cannot endure. It is not only here in Europe that there are these iron curtains, and points of actual collision. In China and in Korea there are all kinds of dangers which we here in England find it baffling to measure. There is also much to be considered in the Middle East. There are very grave dangers—that is all I am going to say today—in letting everything run on and pile up until something happens, and it passes, all of a sudden, out of your control.

With all consideration of the facts, I believe it right to say today that the best chance of avoiding war is, in accord with the other Western democracies, to bring matters to a head with the Soviet Government, and, by formal diplomatic processes, with all their privacy and gravity, to arrive at a lasting settlement. There is certainly enough for the interests of all if such a settlement could be reached. Even this method, I must say, however, would not guarantee that war would not come. But I believe it would give the best chance of preventing it, and that, if it came, we should have the best chance of coming out of it alive.

APPENDIX III

Speech of Dean Acheson before the National Press Club, January 12, 1950

Crisis in Asia—an Examination of United States Foreign Policy

FOUNDATIONS OF POLICY

This afternoon I should like to discuss with you the relations between the peoples of the United States and the peoples of Asia, and I used the words "relations of the peoples of the United States and the peoples of Asia" advisedly. I am not talking about governments or nations because it seems to me what I want to discuss with you is this feeling of mine that the relations depend upon the attitudes of the people; that there are fundamental attitudes, fundamental interests, fundamental purposes of the people of the United States, one hundred and fifty million of them, and of the peoples of Asia, unnumbered millions, which determine and out of which grow the relations of our countries and the policies of our governments. Out of these attitudes and interests and purposes grow what we do from day to day.

Now, let's dispose of one idea right at the start and not bother with it any more. That is that the policies of the United States are determined out of abstract principles in the Department of State or in the White House or in the Congress. That is not the case. If these policies are going to be good, they must grow out of the fundamental attitudes of our people on both sides. If they are to be effective, they must become articulate through all the institutions of our national life, of which this is one of the greatest—through the press, through the radio, through the churches, through the labor unions, through the business organizations, through all the groupings of our national life, there must become articulate the attitudes of our people and the policies which we propose to follow. It seems to me that understanding is the beginning of wisdom and therefore, we shall begin by trying to understand before we announce what we are going to do, and that is a proposition so heretical in this town that I advance it with some hesitation.

Now, let's consider some of the basic factors which go into the making of the attitudes of the peoples on both sides. I am frequently asked: Has the State Department got an Asian policy? And it seems to me that that discloses such a depth of ignorance that it is very hard to begin to deal with it. The peoples of Asia are so incredibly diverse and their problems are so incredibly diverse that how could anyone, even the most utter charlatan, believe that he had a uniform policy which would deal with all of them. On the other hand, there are very important similarities in ideas and in problems among the peoples of Asia and so what we come to, after we understand these diversities and these common attitudes of mind, is the fact that there must be certain similarities of approach, and there must be very great dissimilarities in action.

To illustrate this only a moment: If you will consider as an example of the differences in Asia the sub-continent of India and Pakistan, you will find there an area which is roughly comparable in size and population to Europe. You will find that the different states and provinces of that sub-continent are roughly comparable in size to the nations of Europe and yet you will find such differences in race, in ideas, in languages, and religion, and culture, that compared to that sub-continent, Europe is almost one homogeneous people.

Or take the difference, for instance, between the people and problems of Japan and Indonesia, both in the same Asian area. In Japan, you have a people far advanced in the complexities of industrial civilization, a people whose problems grow out of overpopulation on small islands and the necessity of finding raw materials to bring in and finding markets for the finished goods which they produce. In Indonesia, you find something wholly different—a people on the very threshold of their experience with these complexities and a people who live in an area which possesses vast resources which are awaiting development. Now, those are illustrations of complexities.

EMERGING INDEPENDENCE

Let's come now to the matters which Asia has in common. There is in this vast area what we might call a developing Asian consciousness, and a developing pattern, and this, I think, is based upon two factors which are pretty nearly common to the entire experiences of all these Asian people.

One of these factors is a revulsion against the acceptance of misery and poverty as the normal condition of life. Throughout all of this vast area, you have that fundamental revolutionary aspect in mind and belief. The other common aspect that they have is the revulsion against foreign domination. Whether that foreign domination takes the form of colonialism or whether it takes the form of imperialism, they are through with it. They have had enough of it, and they want no more.

These two basic ideas which are held so broadly and commonly in Asia tend to fuse in the minds of many Asian peoples and many of them tend to believe that if you could get rid of foreign domination, if you could gain independence, then the relief from poverty and misery would follow almost in course. It is easy to point out that that is not true, and of course, they are discovering that it is not true. But underneath that belief, there was a very profound understanding of a basic truth and it is the basic truth which underlies all our democratic belief and all our democratic concept. That truth is that just as no man and no government is wise enough or disinterested enough to direct the thinking and the action of another individual, so no nation and no people are wise enough and disinterested enough very long to assume the responsibility for another people or to control another people's opportunities.

That great truth they have sensed, and on that great truth they are acting. They say and they believe that from now on they are on their own. They will make their own decisions. They will attempt to better their own lot, and on occasion they will make their own mistakes. But it will be their mistakes, and they are not going to have their mistakes dictated to them by anybody else.

The symbol of these concepts has become nationalism. National independence has become the symbol both of freedom from foreign domination and freedom from the tyranny of poverty and misery.

Since the end of the war in Asia, we have seen over five hundred million people gain their independence and over seven new nations come into existence in this area.

We have the Philippines with twenty million citizens. We have Pakistan, India, Ceylon, and Burma with four hundred million citizens, southern Korea with twenty million, and within the last few weeks, the United States of Indonesia with seventy-five million.

This is the outward and visible sign of the internal ferment of Asia. But this ferment and change is not restricted to these countries which are just gaining their independence. It is the common idea and the common pattern of Asia, and as I tried to suggest a moment ago, it is not based on purely political conceptions. It is not based purely on ideological conceptions. It is based on a fundamental and an earthy and a deeply individual realization of the problems of their own daily lives. This new sense of nationalism means that they are going to deal with those daily problems—the problems of the relation of man to the soil, the problem of how much can be exacted from them by the tax collectors of the state. It is rooted in those ideas. With those ideas they are going forward. Resignation is no longer the typical emotion of Asia. It has given way to hope, to a sense of effort, and in many cases, to a real sense of anger.

RECENT DEVELOPMENTS IN CHINA

Now, may I suggest to you that much of the bewilderment which has seized the minds of many of us about recent developments in China comes from a failure to understand this basic revolutionary force which is loose in Asia. The reasons for the fall of the Nationalist Government in China are preoccupying many people. All sorts of reasons have been attributed to it. Most commonly, it is said in various speeches and publications that it is the result of American bungling, that we are incompetent, that we did not understand, that American aid was too little, that we did the wrong things at the wrong time. Other people go on and say: "No, it is not quite that, but that an American general did not like Chiang Kai-shek and out of all that relationship grows the real trouble." And they say: "Well, you have to add to that there are a lot of women fooling around in politics in China."

Nobody, I think, says that the Nationalist Government fell because it was confronted by overwhelming military force which it could not resist. Certainly no one in his right mind suggests that. Now, what I ask you to do is to stop looking for a moment under the bed and under the chair and under the rug to find out these reasons, but rather to look at the broad picture and see whether something doesn't suggest itself.

The broad picture is that after the war, Chiang Kai-shek emerged as the undisputed leader of the Chinese people. Only one faction, the Communists, up in the hills, ill-equipped, ragged, a very small military force, was determinedly opposed to his position. He had overwhelming military power, greater military power than any ruler had ever had in the entire history of China. He had tremendous economic and military support and backing from the United States. He had the acceptance of all other foreign countries, whether sincerely or insincerely in the case of the Soviet Union is not really material to this matter. Here he was in this position, and four years later what do we find? We find that his armies have melted away. His support in the country has melted away. His support largely outside the country has melted away, and he is a refugee on a small island off the coast of China with the remnants of his forces.

As I said, no one says that vast armies moved out of the hills and defeated him. To attribute this to the inadequacy of American aid is only to point out the depth and power of the forces which were miscalculated or ignored. What has happened in my judgment is that the almost inexhaustible patience of the Chinese people in their misery ended. They did not bother to overthrow this government. There was really nothing to overthrow. They simply ignored it throughout the country. They took the solution of their immediate village problems into their own hands. If there was any trouble or interference with the representatives of the government, they simply brushed them aside. They completely withdrew their support from this government, and when that support was withdrawn, the whole military establishment disintegrated. Added to the grossest incompetence ever experienced by any military command was this total lack of support both in the armies and in the country, and so the whole matter just simply disintegrated.

The Communists did not create this. The Communists did not create this condition. They did not create this revolutionary spirit. They did not create a great force which moved out from under Chiang Kai-shek. But they were shrewd and cunning to mount it, to ride this thing into victory and into power.

That, I suggest to you, is an explanation which has certain roots in realism and which does not require all this examination of intricate and perhaps irrelevant details. So much for the attitudes of the peoples of Asia.

U.S. ATTITUDE TOWARD ASIA

Let's consider for a moment another important factor in this relationship. That is the attitude of our own people to Asia. What is that fundamental attitude out of which our policy has grown? What is the history of it? Because history is very important, and history furnishes the belief on the one side in the reality and truth of the attitude.

What has our attitude been toward the peoples of Asia? It has been, I submit to you, that we are interested—that Americans as individuals are interested in the peoples of Asia. We are not interested in them as pawns or as subjects for exploitation but just as people.

For one hundred years some Americans have gone to Asia to bring in what they thought was the most valuable thing they had—their faith. They wanted to tell them what they thought about the nature and relationship of man to God. Others went to them to bring to them what they knew of learning. Others went to them to bring them healing for their bodies. Others and perhaps fewer went to them to learn the depth and beauty of their own cultures, and some went to them to trade and they traded with them. But this trade was a very small part of American interest in the Far East, and it was a very small part of American interest in trade. It was a valid interest; it was a good interest. There was nothing wrong about it, but out of the total sum of the interests of the American people in Asia, it was a comparatively small part.

Through all this period of time also, we had, and still have great interests in Asia. But let me point out to you one very important factor about our interests in Asia. That is that our interests have been parallel to the interests of the people of Asia. For fifty years, it has been the fundamental belief of the American people—and I am not talking about announcements of government but I mean a belief of people in little towns and villages and churches and missionary forces and labor unions throughout the United States—it has been their profound belief that the control of China by a foreign power was contrary to American interests. The interesting part about that is it was not contrary to the interests of the people of China. There was not conflict but parallelism in that interest. And so from the time of the announcement of the open door policy through the nine-power treaty to the very latest resolution of the General Assembly of the United Nations, we have stated that principle and we believe it. And similarly in all the rest of Asia—in the Philippines, in India, in Pakistan and Indonesia, and in Korea—for years and years and years, the interests of Americans throughout this country have been in favor of their independence. This is where their independent societies, and their patriotic groups have come for funds and sympathy. The whole policy of our government insofar as we have responsibility in the Philippines was to bring about the accomplishment of this independence and our sympathy and help. The very real help which we have given other nations in Asia has been in that direction, and it is still in that direction.

THE FACTOR OF COMMUNISM

Now, I stress this, which you may think is a platitude, because of a very important fact: I hear almost every day someone say that the real interest of the United States is to stop the spread of communism. Nothing seems to me to put the cart before the horse more completely than that. Of course we are interested in stopping the spread of communism. But we are interested for a far deeper reason than any conflict between the Soviet Union and the United States. We are interested in stopping the spread of communism because communism is a doctrine that we don't happen to like. Communism is the most subtle instrument of Soviet foreign policy that has ever been devised, and it is really the spearhead of Russian imperialism which would, if it could, take from these people what they have won, what we want them to keep and develop, which is their own national independence, their own individual independence, their own development of their own resources for their own good and not as mere tributary states to this great Soviet Union.

Now, it is fortunate that this point that I made does not represent any real conflict. It is an important point because people will do more damage and create more misrepresentation in the Far East by saying our interest is merely to stop the spread of communism than any other way. Our real interest is in those people as people. It is because communism is hostile to that interest that we want to stop it. But it happens that the best way of doing both things is to do just exactly what the peoples of Asia want to do and what we want to help them to do, which is to develop a soundness of administration of these new governments and to develop their resources and their technical skills so that they are not subject to penetration either through ignorance, or because they believe these false promises, or because there is real distress in their areas. If we can help that development, if we can go forward with it, then we have brought about the best way that anyone knows of stopping this spread of communism.

It is important to take this attitude not as a mere negative reaction to communism but as the most positive affirmation of the most affirmative truth that we hold, which is in the dignity and right of every nation, of every people, and of every individual to develop in their own way, making their own mistakes, reaching their own triumphs but acting under their own responsibility. That is what we are pressing for in the Far

East, and that is what we must affirm and not get mixed up with purely negative and inconsequential statements.

SOVIET ATTITUDE

Now, let me come to another underlying and important factor which determines our relations and, in turn, our policy with the peoples of Asia. That is the attitude of the Soviet Union toward Asia, and particularly towards those parts of Asia which are contiguous to the Soviet Union, and with great particularity this afternoon, to north China.

The attitude and interest of the Russians in north China, and in these other areas as well, long antedates communism. This is not something that has come out of communism at all. It long antedates it. But the Communist regime has added new methods, new skills, and new concepts to the thrust of Russian imperialism. This Communistic concept and techniques have armed Russian imperialism with a new and most insidious weapon of penetration. Armed with these new powers, what is happening in China is that the Soviet Union is detaching the northern provinces [areas] of China from China and is attaching them to the Soviet Union. This process is complete in outer Mongolia. It is nearly complete in Manchuria, and I am sure that in inner Mongolia and in Sinkiang there are very happy reports coming from Soviet agents to Moscow. This is what is going on. It is the detachment of these whole areas, vast areas—populated by Chinese—the detachment of these areas from China and their attachment to the Soviet Union.

I wish to state this and perhaps sin against my doctrine of nondogmatism, but I should like to suggest at any rate that this fact that the Soviet Union is taking the four northern provinces of China is the single most significant, most important fact, in the relation of any foreign power with Asia.

TWO RULES OF U.S. POLICY

What does that mean for us? It means something very, very significant. It means that nothing that we do and nothing that we say must be allowed to obscure the reality of this fact. All the efforts of propaganda will not be able to obscure it. The only thing that can obscure it is the folly of ill-conceived adventures on our part which easily could do so, and I urge all who are thinking about these foolish adventures to remember that we must not seize the unenviable position which the Russians have carved out for themselves. We must not undertake to deflect from the Russians to ourselves the righteous anger, and the wrath, and the hatred of the Chinese people which must develop. It would be folly to deflect it to ourselves. We must take the position we have always taken—that anyone who violates the integrity of China is the enemy of China and is acting contrary to our own interest. That, I suggest to you this afternoon, is the first and the greatest rule in regard to the formulation of American policy toward Asia.

I suggest that the second rule is very like the first. That is to keep our own purposes perfectly straight, perfectly pure, and perfectly aboveboard and do not get them mixed-up with legal quibbles or the attempt to do one thing and really achieve another.

The consequences of this Russian attitude and this Russian action in China are perfectly enormous. They are saddling all those in China who are proclaiming their loyalty to Moscow, and who are allowing themselves to be used as puppets of Moscow, with the most awful responsibility which they must pay for. Furthermore, these actions of the Russians are making plainer than any speech, or any utterance, or any legislation can make throughout all of Asia, what the true purposes of the Soviet Union are and what the true function of communism as an agent of Russian imperialism is. These I suggest to you are the fundamental factors, fundamental realities of attitude out of which our relations and policies must grow.

MILITARY SECURITY IN THE PACIFIC

Now, let's in the light of that consider some of these policies. First of all, let's deal with the question of military security. I deal with it first because it is important and because, having stated our policy in that regard, we must clearly understand that the military menace is not the most immediate.

Appendix III

What is the situation in regard to the military security of the Pacific area, and what is our policy in regard to it?

In the first place, the defeat and the disarmament of Japan has placed upon the United States the necessity of assuming the military defense of Japan so long as that is required, both in the interest of our security and in the interests of the security of the entire Pacific area and, in all honor, in the interest of Japanese security. We have American—and there are Australian—troops in Japan. I am not in a position to speak for the Australians, but I can assure you that there is no intention of any sort of abandoning or weakening the defenses of Japan and that whatever arrangements are to be made either through permanent settlement or otherwise, that defense must and shall be maintained.

This defensive perimeter runs along the Aleutians to Japan and then goes to the Ryukyus. We hold important defense positions in the Ryukyu Islands, and those we will continue to hold. In the interest of the population of the Ryukyu Islands, we will at an appropriate time offer to hold these islands under trusteeship of the United Nations. But they are essential parts of the defensive perimeter of the Pacific, and they must and will be held.

The defensive perimeter runs from the Ryukyus to the Philippine Islands. Our relations, our defensive relations with the Philippines are contained in agreements between us. Those agreements are being loyally carried out and will be loyally carried out. Both peoples have learned by bitter experience the vital connections between our mutual defense requirements. We are in no doubt about that, and it is hardly necessary for me to say an attack on the Philippines could not and would not be tolerated by the United States. But I hasten to add that no one perceives the imminence of any such attack.

So far as the military security of other areas in the Pacific is concerned, it must be clear that no person can guarantee these areas against military attack. But it must also be clear that such a guarantee is hardly sensible or necessary within the realm of practical relationship.

Should such an attack occur—one hesitates to say where such an armed attack could come from—the initial reliance must be on the people attacked to resist it and then upon the commitments of the entire civilized world under the Charter of the

United Nations which so far has not proved a weak reed to lean on by any people who are determined to protect their independence against outside aggression. But it is a mistake, I think, in considering Pacific and Far Eastern problems to become obsessed with military considerations. Important as they are, there are other problems that press, and these other problems are not capable of solution through military means. These other problems arise out of the susceptibility of many areas, and many countries in the Pacific area, to subversion and penetration. That cannot be stopped by military means.

SUSCEPTIBILITY TO PENETRATION

The susceptibility to penetration arises because in many areas there are new governments which have little experience in governmental administration and have not become firmly established or perhaps firmly accepted in their countries. They grow, in part, from very serious economic problems, some of them growing out directly from the last war, others growing indirectly out of the last war because of the disruptions of trade with other parts of the world, with the disruption of arrangements which furnished credit and management to these areas for many years. That has resulted in dislocation of economic effort and in a good deal of suffering among the peoples concerned. In part this susceptibility to penetration comes from the great social upheaval about which I have been speaking, an upheaval which was carried on and confused a great deal by the Japanese occupation and by the propaganda which has gone on from Soviet sources since the war.

Here, then, are the problems in these other areas which require some policy on our part, and I should like to point out two facts to you and then discuss in more detail some of these areas.

The first fact is the great difference between our responsibility and our opportunities in the northern part of the Pacific area and in the southern part of the Pacific area. In the north, we have direct responsibility in Japan and we have direct opportunity to act. The same thing to a lesser degree is true in Korea. There we had direct responsibility, and there we did act, and there we have a greater opportunity to be effective than we have in the more southerly part.

In the southerly part of the area, we are one of many nations who can do no more than help. The direct responsibility lies with the peoples concerned. They are proud of their new national responsibility. You can not sit around in Washington, or London, or Paris, or The Hague and determine what the policies are going to be in those areas. You can be willing to help, and you can help only when the conditions are right for help to be effective.

LIMITATIONS OF U.S. ASSISTANCE

That leads me to the other thing that I wanted to point out, and that is the limitation of effective American assistance. American assistance can be effective when it is the missing component in a situation which might otherwise be solved. The United States cannot furnish all these components to solve the question. It can not furnish determination, it can not furnish the will, and it can not furnish the loyalty of a people to its government. But if the will and if the determination exists and if the people are behind their government, then, and not always then, is there a very good chance. In that situation, American help can be effective and it can lead to an accomplishment which could not otherwise be achieved.

Japan: Now, with that statement, let's deal very briefly—because the time is going on and I am almost equaling my performance in the Senate and House—let's deal very briefly with some of the problems. Let's take the situation in Japan for a moment. There are three great factors to be faced. The security matter I have dealt with. Aside from that, there are the economic questions and the political questions. In the political field, General MacArthur has been very successful and the Japanese are hammering out with some effort, and with some backsliding, and regaining and backsliding again of progress, a political system which is based on nonmilitaristic institutions.

In the economic field, we have not been so successful. That is in very large part due to the inherent difficulty of the problem. The problem arises with the necessity of Japan being able to buy raw materials and sell goods. The former connections of Japan with the mainland and with some of the islands have been disrupted. That has produced difficulties. The willingness of other countries to receive Japanese goods has very much contracted since the war.

Difficulties of currency have added to those problems. But those matters have got to be faced and have got to be solved. Whether they are solved under a treaty or if the procedural difficulties of that are too great under some other mechanism, they must be solved along lines which permit the Japanese greater freedom—complete freedom if possible—to buy what they need in the world and to sell what they have to offer on the mainland of Asia, in southeast Asia, and in other parts of the world. That is the nature of the problem and it is a very tough one. It is one on which the occupation authorities, the Japanese government, ourselves, and others are working. There can be no magic solution to it.

Korea: In Korea, we have taken great steps which have ended our military occupation, and in cooperation with the United Nations, have established an independent and sovereign country recognized by nearly all the rest of the world. We have given that nation great help in getting itself established. We are asking the Congress to continue that help until it is firmly established, and that legislation is now pending before the Congress. The idea that we should scrap all of that, that we should stop half way through the achievement of the establishment of this country, seems to me to be the most utter defeatism and utter madness in our interests in Asia. But there our responsibilities are more direct and our opportunities more clear. When you move to the south, you find that our opportunity is much slighter and that our responsibilities, except in the Philippines and there indirectly, are very small. Those problems are very confusing.

Philippines: In the Philippines, we acted with vigor and speed to set up an independent sovereign nation which we have done. We have given the Philippines a billion dollars of direct economic aid since the war. We have spent another billion dollars in such matters as veterans' benefits and other payments in the Philippines. Much of that money has not been used as wisely as we wish it had been used, but here again, we come up against the matter of responsibility. It is the Philippine Government which is responsible. It is the Philippine Government which must make its own mistakes. What we can do is advise and urge, and if help continues to be misused, to stop giving the help. We cannot direct, we should not direct, we have not the slightest desire to direct. I believe that there are indications that the Philippines may be facing serious economic difficulties. With energetic, determined action, they can perhaps be avoided or certainly minimized. Whether that will be true or not, I can not say, but it does not rest within the power of the American Government to determine that. We are always ready to help and to advise. That is all we can and all we should do.

Asia: Elsewhere in southeast Asia, the limits of what we can do are to help where we are wanted. We are organizing the machinery through which we can make effective help possible. The western powers are all interested. We all know the techniques. We have all had experiences which can be useful to those governments which are newly starting out if they want it. It cannot be useful if they don't want it. We know techniques of administration. We know techniques of organizing school districts, and road districts, and taxation districts. We know agricultural and industrial techniques, all of which can be helpful, and those we are preparing to make available if they are wanted, where they are wanted, and under circumstances where they have a fighting chance to be successful. We will not do these things for the mere purpose of being active. They will not be done for the mere purpose of running around and doing good, but for the purpose of moving in where we are wanted to a situation where we have the missing component which, if put into the rest of the picture, will spell success.

The situation in the different countries of southeast Asia is difficult. It is highly confused in Burma where five different factions have utterly disrupted the immediate government of the country. Progress is being made in Indochina where the French, although moving slowly, are moving. There are noticeable signs of progress in transferring responsibility to a local administration and getting the adherence of the population to this local administration. We hope that the situation will be such that the French can make further progress and make it quickly, but I know full well the difficulties which are faced by the Foreign Minister of France and my admiration and respect for him are so great that I would not want one word I say to add a feather to the burden that he carries.

In Malaya, the British have and are discharging their responsibility harmoniously with the people of Malaya and are making progress.

Indonesia: In Indonesia, a great success has been achieved within the last few weeks and over a period of months. The round table conferences at The Hague in which great statesmanship and restraint were displayed, both on the Dutch and the Indonesian side, have resulted in this new government being formed. Relations of this government with the Dutch will be very good, and the Dutch can furnish them great help and advice, and we will be willing to stand by to give whatever help we can rightly and profitably give. That situation is one which is full of encouragement although it is full of difficulty also.

India and Pakistan: As one goes to the end of this semicircle and comes to India and Pakistan, we find really grave troubles facing the world and facing these two countries there, both with respect to Kashmir, and to the utter difficulties—economic difficulties growing out of the differences in devaluation, settlement of monetary plans back and forth, et cetera. We know that they have assured one another, and they have assured the world, that as stubborn as these difficulties may be and difficult as they may be of solution, they are not going to resort to war to solve them. We are glad to hear those assurances and the whole world is glad to hear it, but we know also that the problems are in such a situation and in such an area that they are most inflammable, and we believe that in addition to these most desirable assurances there should be some accommodation of wills to bring about a result as soon as possible.

In India and in Pakistan we are willing to be of such help as we can be. Again, the responsibility is not ours. Again we can only be helpful friends. Again the responsibility lies with people who have won their freedom and who are very proud of it.

THE NEW DAY FOR ASIA

So after this survey, what we conclude, I believe, is that there is a new day which has dawned in Asia. It is a day in which the

Appendix III

Asian peoples are on their own, and know it, and intend to continue on their own. It is a day in which the old relationships between east and west are gone, relationships which at their worst were exploitation, and which at their best were paternalism. That relationship is over, and the relationship of east and west must now be in the Far East one of mutual respect and mutual helpfulness. We are their friends. Others are their friends. We and those others are willing to help, but we can help only where we are wanted and only where the conditions of help are really sensible and possible. So what we can see is that this new day in Asia, this new day which is dawning, may go on to a glorious noon or it may darken and it may drizzle out. But that decision lies within the countries of Asia and within the power of the Asian people. It is not a decision which a friend or even an enemy from the outside can decide for them.

APPENDIX IV

Speech of Dean Acheson at Freedom House, October 8, 1950

. . . The direction in which we wish to go is plain and clear to all of us. We wish to move toward peace and security, toward a life of freedom and dignity for man, the individual, toward a better life for people everywhere.

The course we take, in order to move in this direction, has two markers on it.

One marker indicates what we must do in order to have peace and security. The other points toward the advancement of human well-being. Both are essential to our course. Both are vital aspects of the work of the United Nations.

In the world in which we live, the best hope of peace and security can be found in the strength and unity of free nations.

There are still some among us to whom it seems a paradox that free nations must arm themselves, with the utmost energy, in order to have peace.

But surely one clear lesson of the thirties, and now again of the fifties, is that the will to peace is no guaranty of peace, unless those who hold it are both willing and able to stop aggression.

It is with the world as it is—not as we might wish it to be—that we must begin.

In the year of our Lord one thousand nine hundred and fifty, we find ourselves in a world of peril. The values we cherish and our right to fulfill them in peace are in grave jeopardy.

The small group of men who hold the Russian people in an iron grip is not content to entrench the power of its regime. These men seek to expand their control over other peoples.

Wherever there is prospect of success, they have reached out for more territory, more people. They have mobilized arms and armies for this purpose.

It takes more than bare hands and a desire for peace to turn back this threat.

It takes very considerable military strength, organization, and a strong will to insure that aggression does not have further prospect of success and may therefore be discouraged.

Great progress has been made in the forging of instruments of collective security.

Korea is a milestone on the way to a collective security system.

The delegates to the United Nations General Assembly will, tomorrow, consider a proposal for the maintenance of elements in their armed forces trained so as to be available for prompt service with the United Nations.

The North Atlantic Treaty countries are now at work upon the creation of an integrated defense force under a unified command.

But a vast amount still remains to be done, and there is not much time in which to do it. This period of gathering and organizing strength is a period of great peril. The job has to be done despite the danger. The alternative is not merely greater danger; it is certain disaster.

Now, it seems to me a waste of time to debate—as some do—whether the decision to meet this imperative necessity is a positive or a negative policy. The point is that it is an essential course of conduct, without which the rest of what we do may be of no consequence.

What is important, however is never to lose sight of why we are embarked on this course. We are embarked on it because it is our best—indeed, our only way of preserving peace and freedom.

Building the strength of free nations is not by itself a method of settling differences with the Soviet leaders. It is a way—and again, the only way—to prevent those differences from being settled by default.

As the great military inequality is reduced negotiation becomes possible.

The common objectives which make broad compromise possible between the Soviet leaders and the rest of the world are now lacking. A compromise which moves one just a little closer to his own elimination is not a compromise.

But as the strength and durability of the free nations bite into the consciousness of the Soviet leaders, some modification of their determination to achieve world domination could follow. This would open a door on many possibilities for the peaceful adjustment of differences.

This process of adjustment is the purpose of our efforts.

The problems we are dealing with are complex and difficult. They do not have neat and tidy answers. They are not problems that can be disposed of once and for all.

Diplomacy in our world is like a housewife's job; it is never finished. It is a process of life—of growth—and we must be prepared to work away, seeking improvements and adjustments where we can.

We can anticipate that our efforts may lead toward a long series of negotiations, deeply molded by time and by the recognition of realities.

This task we are set upon is a difficult one—to build military strength with the hope that we shall never have to use it.

We do not have ambitions or designs that threaten any other people. We desire only a world in which we can live in peace.

We must find ways of making this absolutely clear to the world. The word "peace" has been so much abused, propaganda has so perverted its meaning, that when we speak of our desire for peace, to some it seems the undeniable cloak of ulterior purposes.

This is one of our constant preoccupations—how to break through this barrier of tangled words and make it unmistakably clear to all people everywhere that the purpose of our efforts is a peaceful world.

The other marker on our course indicates the creative job before us. We must go forward with the creation of the life which we are defending at the very time that we are building the defense.

In the early days of our history, the clearing and tilling of fields went on while the militia drilled and guards kept a lookout from the blockhouses.

There will come a time when we can devote more of our energies and resources to the constructive work of building a better life for people, but we cannot postpone these efforts until that time. For millions of people, the immediate, urgent preoccupation is with the simple elements of survival—food, land, and human dignity.

These wants can best be satisfied by democratic societies. Democracy as we know it is still a revolutionary idea in many large parts of the world. It is a young idea, a growing idea. It is a wellspring of hope.

Behind the shields of our defenses, free societies must demonstrate their vitality, their responsibility, their superior ability to respond to man's true needs and wishes.

One of the tasks of the older democracies is to make their purposes meaningful in the lives of the peoples of the younger democracies. This means translating democracy into loaves of bread, as well as into the Bill of Rights.

We must go about this task with a vigor and determination and keep it before us as a symbol of our basic purposes.

We have found it true in our national life that when, in times of peril, the values by which we live are challenged, we have become more keenly conscious of their preeminent importance and have spurred ourselves to great efforts in realizing some of their promise.

It was during the days of revolutionary dangers that many of the great statements of American purposes were made and some of the great advances in our political life were brought about. In the midst of the fearful trials of the Civil War, Lincoln enacted the Homestead Laws.

Just as we have found, in our national experience, that our great energies and resources have been equal to both of these tasks, so can the free nations of the world, even as they take measures to insure their security, move ahead to unfold the creative possibilities which lie within their power.

The combined efforts of the United Nations to rebuild Korea is an important step forward. It is not only as an earnest of our intentions but shall also be a practical example of what can now be done on a cooperative basis to help people raise themselves up from poverty, disease, and hunger.

In this one place, ravaged by the consequences of a ruthless aggression, the United Nations can demonstrate all that it has learned about helping people to build better lives for themselves, to educate their children and keep them well, to grow more food, to prosper, and enjoy the fruits of their efforts.

What the United Nations will be able to do in helping the people of Korea to rebuild their country will be watched with keen interest by the people of many other countries, whose need is for development aid.

The Korea recovery effort can be an inspiring example. Others may see what can be done and draw from this project the courage and the knowledge to make their own lives better.

Now this course we are on, which seeks to maintain peace and security at the same time that it moves ahead toward a better life for people, takes maturity, steadiness, and restraint on our part.

This is not a job which can be handled by a few public officials. Our entire people are called upon to participate in the leadership which our nation must exercise in the world in which we live. The press, public leaders, the Congress, individuals share the responsibility of the role our country must perform.

Restraint and self-discipline can help us to avoid some of the dangers which lie along our course.

One of the dangers, in particular, is avoidable. If we keep always before us that our purpose in building military power is to enable us to settle our differences by peaceful means, then we shall avoid the terrible error of talking and acting as though the end of our effort is war.

The purpose of our effort is the exact opposite. But foolish talk about preventive war, or the inevitability of war, will help to make war inevitable. It does not need to be so at all.

There is a very common tendency for people who are putting their whole hearts and soul into a great task to think in terms of logical absolutes. This leads some few people to forget why we are making this great effort and to proclaim that our object should be to bring about the very thing which we are trying so desperately to avoid—that is, war.

Our friends can foresee, very well indeed, the terrible results to them—and to us—of another general war. They do not shrink from these dangers in doing what must be done to preserve their freedom. They are ready to join with us—indeed to accord us leadership—in the hard task of building the military power essential to deter war.

But they expect, and they have a right to expect, a serious

and responsible associate, and serious and responsible leadership.

The dangers about us are deadly dangers. Here, in all somber truth, is a situation where the consequences of error may be death. It is with these thoughts that our friends hear the irresponsible statements I have mentioned and ponder the consequences of our mutual association.

And upon those who are not friendly to us these statements have their effect also. To them, partly deceived by the excesses of their own propaganda, we seem to confirm their picture of us as the warmongers.

No one can tell the errors which such irresponsible talk among us may bring into their calculations. No one can believe that any good can come of it. It is not hard to imagine the vast evil which may result.

Another danger, which restraint and self-discipline can help us to avoid, is division among us and our friends. There is no lack of eager hands to help this forward.

The price of unity is to cling to the essentials and to find accommodations for all lesser problems. It is not to insist upon an American attitude upon every matter and to insist that our friends must adjust themselves to this.

On foreign affairs, it is easy to become clearer than truth itself—in the press, on the radio, in our literature, in Congress. No one is ever so sure about domestic problems.

Let us apply some of the genius for accommodation which has made our nation, to making the larger association with the free nations. For here, we are all seeking the same end in the light of the same values.

If we do this, we can be as firm as the Rock of Gibraltar in insisting that all who wish to remain free do their full part in the organization of strength to defend that freedom. We can also find ways of reaching common views on lesser problems.

The demands upon us are very great. To escape the avoidable dangers requires restraint of a high order. And self-discipline does not come easily to us.

To escape the dangers which we cannot control will take coolness, steady nerves, and, above all, the greatest possible speed in the creation of our common military strength.

Foreign policy is not a disembodied thing. The outward

strength of a democracy can be no greater than its inward strength. As we at home make progress in achieving the promise of our society—as we encourage the individual's opportunities —as we strengthen the foundations of justice and freedom—so shall we demonstrate that democracy is a vital, a progressive, a hopeful way of life.

The vitality of our free institutions at home, of our individual and community life, will determine the influence we can exert abroad in support of freedom.

This, too, is part of the responsibility of each individual among us. The fulfillment of this responsibility through such an organization as Freedom House is one of the bedrocks of our foreign policy.

The road to freedom and to peace which I have pictured is a hard one.

The times in which we live must be painted in the somber values of Rembrandt. The background is dark, the shadows deep. Outlines are obscure. The central point, however, glows with light; and, though it often brings out the glint of steel, it touches colors of unimaginable beauty.

For us, that central point is the growing unity of free men the world over. This is our shaft of light, our hope, and our promise.

Speech of Winston Churchill in the House of Commons, November 30, 1950

I hope that the level calm of yesterday's debate will be regarded as an example of our composure in times of danger and not as an instance of any failure on our part to realise its gravity. Perhaps the calm in all its aspects represents various characteristics in our national character. Certainly we are in danger, but the danger is not new. It was visible in all its terrible potential from the moment when the armies of democracy dispersed and melted away in the hour of victory while the armies of the Soviet oligarchy were maintained at an enormous strength and were re-equipped to a very high degree and when, on top of this, Russian imperialism, clothed in a new garb, advanced to carry the creed of Communism and the authority of the Kremlin forth in every direction until some solid obstacle was reached.

This danger became apparent to some of us before the war ended and was recognised widely throughout our confidential circles. It began to be realised by much larger numbers of people in Britain and the United States when the first conference of the Council of the United Nations took place at the beginning of 1946. Up till then for the great masses of the people all had been softened and shrouded in the Western democracies by the comradeship of the great struggle, by their relief in hard-won victory and by their admiration of the valour and sacrifices of the Russian armies.

However, I must remind the House that already at the beginning of 1946 the Foreign Secretary felt himself forced to describe, to his face and in public, Mr. Vishinsky's statements as lies. I am not blaming the Foreign Secretary, but it showed how rapidly, in the course of a year, we had been disillusioned, or the outer world had been disillusioned. Since then, the increasing realisation by the Western democracies of the danger in which they stood and stand has been continuous.

There were two major differences between the state of the world after the First and after the Second World Wars. The sour aftermath of triumph in arms, however complete, brought with it in both cases many troubles, but here are the two differences. After the First War, when the victors had disarmed the Germans and their allies, no powerful organised army remained upon the scene except the French Army. After this war the armed might of Russia has emerged steadily year by year, almost month by month, as a rock shows more and more above an ebbing tide.

The second difference, which arose out of the realisation of the first, was that the United States, instead of retiring into isolation, instead of demanding full and prompt repayment of debts and disinteresting herself in Europe and even in the League of Nations, of which she had been one of the founders, has come forward step by step as the knowledge of the situation has dawned upon her and has made the great counterpoise upon which the freedom and the future of our civilisation depends. This fundamental change in the policy of the United States constitutes, in my view, the best hope for the salvation of Christian civilisation and democracy from Communist and Russian conquest and control. I hope, therefore, that we shall regard it as our first objective not to separate ourselves in action or in understanding or in sympathy in any degree, however slight, that can be avoided from the United States.

But the favourable policy of the United States after this last war, which has been so helpful to us in so many ways, did not affect the military disparity caused by the maintenance of immense Russian armies year after year and the development of their armoured forces, their air power and their submarines. We did not come to terms with them at the moment of German surrender while we, too, had the weapons in our hands. The Western Allies abandoned the whole of Eastern Germany, including an immense area of which they stood in occupation, to Soviet control, and Russia remained the overwhelming armed power, towering up in Europe and in Asia, avid for the expansion of their creed and their rule.

The war had liberated Russia from her two pre-occupations —Germany and Japan. Both these warlike nations have inflicted terrible defeats and injuries upon Russia in this present twentieth century. Now both have ceased to be military factors and the years that have followed our victory have brought enormous increases of power and territory to Soviet Russia. In one form or another they have gained control of half Europe and all China without losing a single Russian soldier. They have every right to be encouraged by the progress they have made, but they show no signs of being in any way satiated or satisfied or even contented with it, and we can perceive no limits at present to their aims.

So much for the past. Let me now, in the very few minutes I shall detain the House, look to the present and the future. I hoped myself—and my view was shared by my colleagues at that time—that a lasting settlement might be reached with Russia before we evacuated our portion of central and eastern Germany, and before the United States' armies were demobilised and dispersed. Later, in 1948, I hoped that we might come to terms with them before they gained the secret of the atomic bomb. Now I hope that we may come to terms with them before they have so large a stockpile of these fearful agencies, in addition to vast superiority in other weapons, as to be able to terrorise the free world, if not, indeed, to destroy it.

Let us look at the time factor. In some aspects it is in our favour; in some it is adverse. The Soviets, under the restraint of the immense United States' superiority in the atomic sphere, and also by the consolation of the rapid and immense gains which they have made and are still making in many directions without incurring any direct risk—under these two opposite forces—have hitherto been under restraint and control.

They have repeatedly been assured that the United States would not fight what is called a "preventive" war. The United States have expressed the general opinion of the civilised world upon that aspect. On this basis the war, if ever it comes—which God forbid—will come at the moment of their choice. It, however, should be noted that the two restraining or consoling arguments which I have mentioned are both diminishing. The Soviet stockpile of atomic bombs is growing. How fast, I have no idea. I do not know whether the Government have knowledge. At any rate, we have none. And the Soviets must expect, while this stockpile is growing in their favour behind them, more resistance to their further expansion, and they will not find their progress so easy as it has been in the past.

It is impossible to prophesy what they will do, or when, or how they will do it. One can only judge these matters by estimating what is their interest. The great Duke of Marlborough quoted a saying in his day: "Interest never lies"; and there is no doubt that trying to put oneself in the position of the other party to see how things look to him is one way, and perhaps the best way, of being able to feel and peer dimly into the unknowable future. It is, at any rate, the only guide—and it does not include accident, passion, folly or madness, madness which may arise from some error, some blunder, or from the results of some internal convulsion. All that can be said is that it certainly does not seem to be in the Russian interest to begin a major struggle now.

We are told that it is provocative to organise an Atlantic army, with, as I see it, a European army inside of it and a German contingent, on honourable terms, inside that. We are told that that is provocative. It does not seem likely, however, that anything that we can do in the next two years in Europe will reverse the balance of military power. We may be stronger, but not strong enough in that time to deter, still less to prevail. There is plenty of room for us to get much stronger without altering the situation in Europe decisively.

Therefore, while it is right to build up our forces as fast as we can, nothing in this process, in the period I have mentioned, will deprive Russia of effective superiority in what are called now the conventional arms. All that it will do is to give us increasing unity in Europe and magnify the deterrents against aggression, and, perhaps, give us the means of gradually approaching the situation when relations between world Powers may express themselves in normal terms and not only be measured in the strange and novel methods of the atomic age.

Dangerous as it may be to make such a prediction—I make it in all good faith, and without official knowledge—I would venture to express the opinion that a major attack by Russia in Europe is unlikely in the near future, and that it will not be provoked or produced by the modest measures of defence now being so slowly, so tardily and ineffectively developed up to the present by the Atlantic and Western Powers. Even if our preparations developed more rapidly, a long period must elapse before they could offset the Russian superiority, even if the Russian strength itself were not increased meanwhile.

It is upon this that I found my hope that we still have time, that there is still a breathing space for us to pursue the policy of seeking an understanding, and for us to also pursue the essential counterpart and foundation of any such hope, namely, the building up of a more reasonable measure of defensive strength. This may be a vain hope. I may live, perhaps, to be mocked at if proved wrong by events. It is, at any rate, the working hypothesis of my thought in these anxious and agonising times.

Therefore I am in favour of efforts to reach a settlement with Soviet Russia as soon as a suitable opportunity presents itself, and of making those efforts while the immense and measureless superiority of the United States atomic bomb organisation offsets the Soviet predominance in every other military respect and gives us the means to talk together in a friendly and dignified manner and, at least as equals. . . .

I hope, however, that at the right and best time, especially after matters are stabilised in the Far East, a conference will arise which will not merely be like those of which we have had too many in the past, of two sides arguing against each other in the glare of publicity, but that the decisive conversations will take place in confidence, in privacy and even in secrecy, and will be conducted at the highest levels. It is what I asked for at Edinburgh six months ago.

I agree that much has happened since then, particularly these great developments in the Far East and also the immense and active leadership now assumed by the United States, with whom we must march, or walk, hand in hand and to whom we must give all the help and good will which our power and experience allow. Much has happened since then but I do not think we should exclude from any of the discussions which may take place, perhaps after the present unhelpful crisis has passed away, the personal touch between those who have the right and the power to speak for the great States involved. That is only what I said at Edinburgh. I fully agree that time and the new circumstances which have come into view must influence, and even perhaps govern, our action.

This brings me to the crisis in Korea and China. We all find much that is disquieting in it, but I do not see that what is happening in the Far East should make the Soviets in a hurry to depart from their present policy of expansion by means of the cold war and of using others to advance their aims. The Foreign Secretary asked yesterday: Is this move of the Chinese into Korea part of a grand strategy for a definite purpose?

"Is there a Russo-Chinese conspiracy on a world-wide scale?"—[*Official Report,* 29th November, 1950; Vol. 481, c. 1172.]

They were very proper questions for the right hon. Gentleman to ask, and to ask himself out loud. He said that he did not know the answers. I do not know who does. If it were true, that certainly would not suggest that the Russians contemplated an immediate violent action in Europe. We can only use the facts as they are known to us and endeavour to deduce conclusions from them.

On the contrary, the plan would evidently be to get the United States and the United Nations, so far as they contribute, involved as deeply as possible in China, and thus prevent the reinforcement of Europe and the building up of our defensive strength there to a point where it would be an effectual deterrent. It is one of the most well-known—almost hackneyed—strategical and tactical methods, to draw your opponent's resources to one part of the field and then, at the right moment, to strike in another. Military history shows countless examples of this and of variants of it. Surely, however, the United Nations should avoid by every means in their power becoming entangled inextricably in a war with China.

For this reason I had hoped that General MacArthur's advance in Korea—and I paid my tribute to him the other day, and to the extraordinary skill with which the operations had been handled, up to the point which we had then reached—would stop at the neck or wasp waist of the peninsula and would leave the country between the neck and the Yalu River and the Chinese frontier as a kind of No-man's-land which Allied air power would dominate. Under this cover there might have been constructed an ever-stronger fortified line across the neck, wherever it might be found suitable. Of course, to hold such a line it is essential that the approaches to it should also be commanded, and therefore such a line cannot be exactly along the imaginary lines which are drawn on the maps to indicate the parallels. To take a practical guide, the shortest space might be chosen and the strongest defence made there, with a hinterland or neutral space before it—or if not neutral, a No-man's-land, a disputed No-man's-land—which would give the necessary facilities to the defence.

Whether this will be possible now depends upon the result of the great battle which is at this moment raging. I suppose we shall know in a few days what the results are. I am sure, however, that the whole House feels that the sooner the Far Eastern diversion—because, vast as it is, it is but a diversion—can be brought into something like a static condition and stabilised, the better it will be for all those hopes which the United Nations have in hand. For it is in Europe that the world cause will be decided. As my right hon. Friend the Member for Warwick and Leamington said yesterday, it is there that the mortal danger lies. I am sure that we all agree with that. Perhaps we are biased by the fact that we live there or thereabouts. But none the less, one cannot conceive that our natural bias has in any way distorted the actual facts.

Index

Acheson, Dean: on American policy toward Asia, 221; on American policy toward Soviet Union, 121, 147, 190, 214; on atomic bomb explosion in Soviet Union, 168, 169; on breach of treaties, 147; on communism, 121; Freedom House speech, 77; National Press Club speech, 77, 120; on Russian imperialism, 77, 121; and Truman Doctrine, 120, 121

Adams, John Quincy, foreign policy of, 19, 20

Alexander the Great, and world conquest, 59

America, *see* United States

Appeasement, 137, 138. *See also* negotiated settlement

Asia: American foreign policy in, 6, 202, 208; balance of power in, 6, 67, 127, 161, 201, 206; ideological struggle for, 208 ff.; political power of, 66, 67; as prize in East-West conflict, 208, 209; revolutions in, 79, 80, 201, 208. *See also individual countries*, Soviet Union, United States

Atlantic Alliance, *see* North Atlantic Pact

Atlantic Charter, 97, 99

Atomic bomb: American and Russian strength in, 173, 176, 177; American monopoly of, 95, 163, 168 ff., 180, 195; defense against, 172, 173; effects on warfare, 57, 58; fear of, as deterrent to war, 156, 163, 183; monopoly of, 192; Russian and American strength in, 173, 176, 177; Russian possession of, 140, 168 ff. *See also* balance of power, Soviet Union, United States, war

Atomic war, *see* atomic bomb

Atomic weapons, *see* atomic bomb

Balance of power, 33, 41, 42; Asiatic, 6, 67, 127, 161, 201, 206; bipolar

Balance of power (*continued*) between United States and Soviet Union, 45; disappearance of, 50, 51; disappearance of balancer, 44, 45; European, 5, 6, 25 ff., 108, 161, 162, 178, 179, 201; flexibility of, 47, 48, 51; and Russian atomic power, 174; United Nations as substitute for, 100; after World War II, 43, 66; before World War II, 43, 46, 47. *See also* bipolarity, major powers, United Nations

Baldwin, Hanson, 169

Baruch, Bernard, 181

Berlin: blockade, 104, 190, 191; status of West, 183

Berlin, Congress of (1878), 146, 150

Bipolarity, in international politics, 43 ff., 50 ff., 66, 67; effect on diplomatic relations, 52; effect on small countries, 58; and ideological differences, 62; and morality, 93. *See also* balance of power

Bolshevism, *see* communism, ideological warfare, political religions, Soviet Union

Bradley, General Omar, 170

Bright, John, 10

British Empire, *see* Great Britain

Brussels Treaty, 179

Burke, Edmund, 73

Byrnes, James F.: on atomic bomb, 168; on Paris Peace conference (1946), 133, 134; *Speaking Frankly*, 133, 168

Calhoun, John C., 10

Castlereagh, Viscount Robert, 82, 83, 86

Cavour, Camillo B., 143

Chiang Kai-shek, 203, 206

China: American policy toward, 6, 119, 120, 213; civil war in, 203, 206; communism in, 205, 207; Communist party in, 203, 208; domestic history of, 202, 203; im-

Index